The Creative Curriculum®
for Family Child Care

Diane Trister Dodge
Laura J. Colker

Illustrated by
Julie Headland

Design and Layout by
Elisabeth Hudgins

TEACHING
STRATEGIES
INC.

Washington, DC

Developed with funds received under an Innovative Head Start Grant from the
U.S. Department of Health and Human Services to the National Child Day Care
Association, Washington, DC.

Teaching Strategies, Inc.
P.O. Box 42243
Washington, DC 20015
ISBN 978-0-9602892-7-1
LCCN 90-071845

Printed and bound in the United States of America.
Revised edition: 1998
Seventh Printing: December 2006

Acknowledgments

This effort was made possible through an Innovative Head Start Grant from the Administration for Children, Youth and Families, U.S. Department of Health and Human Services, to the National Child Day Care Association, Inc. (NCDCA). We are deeply indebted to Helen Taylor, who was the Executive Director, and Mattie Jackson, who was the Education Coordinator. They believed in the importance of high-quality programs in both center and home environments and saw the value of having a curriculum for their family child care program.

We initially proposed the idea of adapting our center-based curriculum, *The Creative Curriculum,* for use by Head Start grantees that were operating family child care programs. Several of these grantees had expressed a need for practical curriculum materials that would be appropriate for infants, toddlers, preschoolers, and school-age children. In designing our approach, we have tried to preserve the special characteristics of a home environment, not turn family child care homes into mini-centers. We wanted to show how children's growth and development can be nurtured through developmentally appropriate activities and caring relationships.

We were assisted in this effort by numerous individuals and agencies, each of whom we would like to acknowledge and thank. Dr. Trellis Waxler, then Government Project Officer, was an enthusiastic participant in all our meetings and meticulously reviewed and commented on all products. We are especially grateful for the support we received from E. Dollie Wolverton, Chief of the Education Services Branch of the Head Start Bureau, and Dr. Mary Lewis, former Program Specialist, who attended design team meetings and reviewed many of the materials under development.

Two colleagues with extensive experience in the family child care field deserve special mention, as they assisted in the writing of the curriculum. Marilyn Goldhammer was part of our initial team and worked closely with us in designing the format and approach. She also prepared original drafts of several chapters in the curriculum. Later in the project, we were fortunate to meet Leanne Sponsel, a family child care trainer in St. Paul, Minnesota, who reviewed the curriculum, used it in her work, and gave us invaluable feedback and suggestions for improving the content. She also wrote the vignettes for each of the activities in Part Two that portray the challenge of involving children of all ages in activities.

An effort of this magnitude benefits from the input of experts who bring a range of perspectives. We are particularly indebted to the following people who piloted the materials with their providers and evaluated their effectiveness:

- Helen Taylor, Executive Director
  Mattie Jackson, Education Coordinator
  National Child Day Care Association, Inc.
  Washington, DC

- Beverly Langford Thomas, Executive Director
  Linda McKay, Director of Home-Based Programs
  District of Columbia Public Schools Head Start Program
  Washington, DC

- Cynthia Davenport, Family Child Care Coordinator
  Catholic Charities Model Cities Center
  Washington, DC
- Renee Riblet, Director
  Cindy Perez, Family Child Care Coordinator
  Northwestern Ohio Community Action Committee Head Start Program
  Defiance, Ohio

- Nels Andersen, Director
  Rhonda Robson and Rhonda Schroeder, Family Child Care Supervisors
  Saginaw County Child Development Center
  Saginaw, Michigan

Over forty family child care providers reviewed and tried out many of the ideas in the curriculum. They generously gave their time to share their experiences in using the curriculum and to validate its usefulness.

Several other people made contributions that were invaluable to us in producing *The Creative Curriculum for Family Child Care*. Dr. Joan Lombardi, an infant/toddler and Head Start specialist, ensured that we consistently addressed the needs of all age groups and that our materials conformed with the Head Start Program Performance Standards. Linda Smith, Deputy Director, Office of Family Policy and Support for Child Development Programs, United States Department of Defense, shared the perspective of the military, which operates the largest child care system in the world. Ruth Uhlmann and Barbara Andrews, who at different times served as the family child care coordinator for the National Child Day Care Association, reviewed all drafts and also assisted us in preparing the videotape *Caring and Learning* that accompanies the curriculum.

Finally, we would like to thank several people who assisted us in completing the final document: our colleague, Derry Gosselin Koralek, who reviewed and critiqued the close-to-final draft; and Martha Cooley, our editor.

In 1998, we revised many of the examples of activities for infants and toddlers in order to make this approach more consistent with our work on curriculum for infants and toddlers. We gratefully acknowledge the assistance we received from Hazel Osborne and Donna Bloomer in this effort. In 2001, we updated the list of recommended children's books.

The Creative Curriculum
for Family Child Care

Introduction

Family child care is a growing and important profession. Today, more than half of all children under six years of age have mothers who work outside the home, and most of these children go to family child care homes, not day care centers.

Many parents choose home settings for their children because they recognize that such settings have several important benefits. They are often conveniently located; they can accommodate siblings of different ages; and they generally consist of small groups of children that allow for individual attention and a calmer atmosphere. Perhaps the most important reason why parents like family child care, however, is that they can depend on reliable and consistent care from one provider.

As a child care provider, you offer children and families an important service. You provide a secure environment where children can learn to trust other adults and children. You plan activities each day that help children solve problems, express their ideas, and learn about the real world—all crucial skills in preparing for school and for life. You and the parents of the children in your program form a partnership that promotes the healthy development of each child. You also support parents by allowing them to attend to their jobs without having to worry about their children's care.

It is a challenging task to provide a high-quality program for children of different ages in your home. Many family child care providers are seeking help in meeting this challenge. *The Creative Curriculum for Family Child Care* is designed to provide practical and comprehensive assistance to family child care providers in a range of settings.

How a Curriculum Can Help

What is a "curriculum" and what can it offer you? A curriculum is a **plan for your program**. It helps you understand how children grow and provides practical ideas for organizing your home and planning activities for children that will help them develop. It is a framework for what actually happens in a planned environment when children interact with materials, with other children, and with adults. An appropriate curriculum will make your job as a family child care provider easier and more rewarding.

This curriculum begins with goals for children's learning. Curriculum goals tell you where you are heading. Someone once said, "If you don't know where you are going, how will you know when you get there?" Stating goals for children helps you know where you are going and whether you are accomplishing your objectives. The underlying goals of this curriculum are to help children:

• learn about themselves and the world around them; and
• feel good about themselves and capable as learners.

Specific goals are identified for each area of development:

- *Socially:* to feel secure and comfortable, trust their environment, make friends, and feel part of the group.

- *Emotionally:* to experience pride and self-confidence, develop independence and self-control, and have a positive attitude toward life.

- *Cognitively:* to become confident learners by trying out their own ideas and experiencing success and by acquiring thinking skills such as the ability to solve problems, ask questions, and use words to describe their ideas, observations, and feelings.

- *Physically:* to increase their large and small muscle control and feel confident about what their bodies can do.

The Creative Curriculum for Family Child Care gives you a plan for achieving these goals. It provides you with the information you need to run a high-quality program. Each of the chapters in the curriculum will help you do the following:

- Understand how children develop and how their family, culture, and community impact development.
- Organize your home as a setting for learning.
- Plan and carry out activities to help children develop.
- Build a partnership with parents that respects their values and culture.

Teaching young children (which is what you do while caring for them in your home) requires spontaneity—the ability to see and use everyday opportunities to help children solve problems, explore new materials, and find answers to questions. It also requires continuous thinking and decision making on your part:

- Should I intervene or should I step back and let the child try to solve the problem?

- What questions can I ask to help a child think creatively?

- Is the child ready for these materials, or will they prove frustrating? Are they appropriate to the child's background and family expenses? What else could I offer?

- Is my space arrangement working or do I need to modify it?

A good curriculum for children must be "developmentally appropriate."[1] This means that the quality of the care will be related to how well the provider understands the different developmental stages of childhood—what is generally appropriate for a particular age group and how individual children may differ within each stage. What you plan for the children in your care and how you respond to a given situation or unanticipated problem will depend on your knowledge of each child's interests, abilities, needs, and background.

To plan appropriately, you will need to find answers to questions such as these:

- What can I expect of a child at each stage of development?
- How does a child learn at each stage of development?
- What do I know about each child that will help me individualize my care?
- What activities and learning materials are appropriate for each child?
- How can I adapt my home and materials for children with special needs?
- What is my role in children's play?
- How can I involve familes and include their perspective?

---

[1]See Sue Bredekamp and Carol Copple (ed.), *Developmentally Appropriate Practice in Early Childhood Programs* Revised Edition, (Washington, DC: NAEYC, 1997.)

The Creative Curriculum for Family Child Care will help you answer these questions. It will serve as a framework for making appropriate decisions by giving you the following:

- *A statement of philosophy*—the beliefs and theories that guide your planning, including an understanding of how children develop socially, emotionally, cognitively, and physically.

- *Goals and objectives*—the skills, attitudes, and understandings targeted for mastery; in other words, what the children will gain through involvement in your program.

- *The physical environment*—how room arrangements and selection and display of materials support the development of trust, independence, initiative, and industry in children.

- *Your role*—the activities you plan each day and how you talk with children and guide their learning and growth.

- *The parents' role*—how the involvement of parents can promote each child's growth and development.

A lot of the information in this curriculum will be familiar. This is because you are already using your home as a learning environment to help children gain an understanding of themselves and the world around them. *The Creative Curriculum for Family Child Care* builds on what you already know and offers you new ideas and strategies to help you in providing children and families the best program possible.

How This Curriculum Is Organized

The Creative Curriculum for Family Child Care is divided into two parts. The first, **Setting the Stage**, helps you formulate a philosophy of child care, understand child development, prepare your home, and plan your program. You will find many ideas for making your home safe and inviting, selecting the right kinds of materials, managing your day, guiding children's learning and behavior, and building a partnership with parents.

Part Two of *The Creative Curriculum* is called **Activities.** Here you will find ideas on how to select materials and plan experiences that help children of all ages—infants, toddlers, preschoolers, and school-age children—to grow and develop. Nine different types of activities are described in Part Two:

Dramatic Play	Sand and Water
Blocks	Cooking
Toys	Music and Movement
Art	Outdoor Play
Books	

You might begin by selecting the activities you like best and trying out some of the ideas to see how they work for you. When you plan appropriate activities for the children you care for and offer them more choices, you will find that the day goes more smoothly and that you have more fun. At the end of each activity section, there is a letter for parents to help them understand what you are doing and why.

Finally, it should be noted that we call this *The **CREATIVE** Curriculum for Family Child Care* to emphasize that learning is a creative process for both children and adults. The curriculum supports children's creativity by encouraging them to learn through their active explorations in an interesting and safe environment. It supports your creativity by encouraging you to build on what you already know about children, try out new ideas, and be responsive to each child in your program. We hope that this curriculum will help you achieve a high-quality program and have more fun in the process.

Part One
Setting the Stage

Understanding Child Development

A high-quality program for young children is based on a knowledge of child development. Because children's abilities and needs change rapidly, each stage of children's development is different. Knowing what these stages of development are will help you to care for children and guide their growth.

In planning a program based on child development, we rely a great deal on the research findings of two psychologists who studied children: Jean Piaget and Erik Erikson. Piaget has shown us how children learn. By using all of their senses, children come to understand what the world is like. As they grasp, roll, pound, smell, suck, and crawl around and over everything they come into contact with, children discover how things work. As they run, jump, knock things over, lift things, watch, and listen, they are gaining information and learning. As they use their bodies—their entire bodies—to imitate the actions of others or to try out their own ideas, they learn how people act and react and what they are capable of doing themselves. These active explorations lead to knowledge. For young children, learning comes from doing.

Piaget also taught us that children do not think like adults. For example, a baby doesn't realize that a toy hidden under a blanket still exists; to the infant, that toy has suddenly disappeared. Toddlers and young preschoolers are likely to think that one cracker broken into many pieces represents more food than one whole, unbroken cracker, or that friendships should be based on the fact that both people have the same color socks. Children change the way they think when they have many opportunities, over time and on their own, to observe conflicting and agreeing information. As children grow and develop, they begin to realize that things exist even when hidden, that one cracker is the same amount whether broken or not, and that there are lots of reasons to be friends with different people.

By understanding that children learn—and change their ways of thinking about things—by being actively involved with materials and other people, you can create many opportunities for them. When children are spontaneously involved in activities such as kicking toward a mobile, crawling, or building a structure with blocks, they are adding pieces of information to what they already know and generating new information and ideas. Piaget terms these processes "assimilation" (soaking up knowledge) and "accommodation" (adjusting thinking to include the new knowledge).

You can encourage children of all ages to think by helping them label and organize their world. For young babies you can do this by talking to them, pointing out what is happening around them, and responding to their efforts to communicate with you. For older children you can do this by making statements and asking children to describe what they are doing or remembering about their activities:

- "Oh, look. I see the older children making big piles of sand in the sand box."

- "You're using the spoon to stir the batter. How does the batter feel?"

- "How could you get that big rock to move even though it is too heavy for one person to lift alone?"

- "What did you see on our neighborhood walk this morning?"
- "What did you like best about the book you just read?"

We have learned from Piaget, then, that we cannot tell children what we want them to know—they must learn it for themselves by being actively involved.

Erikson outlined the stages of social and emotional development that people go through from birth through old age. According to Erikson, each person has special needs that must be met at each stage of development in order for that individual to grow and move successfully to the next stage.

The first four stages of development outlined by Erikson—Trust, Autonomy, Initiative, and Industry—are important for family child care providers to know about because they address the needs of infants, toddlers, preschoolers, and school-age children. In the remainder of this chapter, we will use Erikson's first four stages of development plus the theories of Jean Piaget to explain what children are like and how *The Creative Curriculum* can help you meet their needs.

Infants

Erikson calls the first stage of development **Trust**. During this stage (from birth through 18 months), infants are introduced to the world. At first they can do very little for themselves; they are totally dependent on adults to feed them, care for them, make them comfortable, and hold them. Although they are very dependent, young infants are still interested in what they can see, hear, taste, and smell in their environment. They are good observers and respond to everything around them. Before long they develop the ability to crawl and move around to explore their environment on their own. If you meet the basic needs of infants and give them interesting things to look at and safe spaces in which to explore, they will learn that the world is a place they can trust.

Understanding the developmental needs of infants, as explained by Piaget and Erikson, allows us to plan a program that meets their needs and helps each infant grow and develop. In the following chart we have outlined what infants are like and how the curriculum helps you meet their needs.

What Infants Are Like:	The Curriculum Helps You:
Emotionally, they . . .	
Depend on adults to meet their basic needs—to be fed, kept dry and comfortable, picked up, and held.	Respond consistently to each infant's needs and schedule and use routines to help infants grow and feel bonded to you and your program.
Are born with individual and unique personalities: some are quiet, some active; some like to be cuddled and held; others don't like to be touched.	Observe each child's unique characteristics and use that information to build a relationship and meet each child's basic needs.

Socially, they . . .

Develop attachments to their primary care-givers.

Provide consistent responsive care and build a positive relationship with each infant's parents.

Like to watch other children and join in the ac-tion.

Find ways to include infants in activities without allow-ing them to disrupt what older children are doing.

Cognitively, they . . .

Use all their senses—tasting, touching, smell-ing, hearing, and seeing—to learn about the world.

Check all materials to be sure that infants can safely suck, squeeze, throw and push them to learn about them.

Experiment with objects and sounds and enjoy discovering what effect their actions have.

Select materials that will be responsive to infant's explo-rations and actions.

Communicate with others through actions and sounds.

Respond to infant's early sounds and words and encour-age their language development.

Physically, they . . .

Explore and move by creeping, crawling, pulling themselves up, and walking.

Organize the environment so that there are large stretches of floor space on which infants can move around safely.

Practice new skills such as grasping, touching, hitting, rolling, and grabbing.

Plan activities that enable infants to learn and practice de-veloping physical skills.

Toddlers

The second stage of development, the toddler years (18-36 months), is one that Erikson called **Autonomy.** Autonomy means independence, learning to do things for oneself and to make decisions. They love to repeat actions and words over and over, to solidify their learn-ing and sense of self-control. They also love to elicit the same response, over and over, from you — to learn they can trust you and begin to predict your reactions. One of their favorite words is "no." They don't say this to make you or parents angry; they say it to try out their independence and to let you know that they can make decisions for themselves.

Toddlers are also constantly on the move, busily exploring the world around them and getting into everything. It takes a lot of energy to address the needs of toddlers success-fully which is where the curriculum can help.

What Toddlers Are Like:

The Curriculum Helps You:

Emotionally, they . . .

Establish their independene by trying to do things for themselves.

Plan and organize an environment where toddlers can find what they need and do things on their own.

Are easily frustrated because they want to do more than they can do or more than adults will let them do.

Plan activities that toddlers can do successfully and that will hold their interest; avoid overstimulating toddlers with too many props or more choices than they can handle.

Have strong attachments to family members and their caregivers.

Build a partnership with parents and with each child through daily contact.

Socially, they . . .

Enjoy being with other children but are not always able to play with others cooperatively.

Include toddlers in routines and activities involving other children.

Like to imitate what others do.

Provide activities through cooking and dramatic play experiences that give children an opportunity to "do the things grown-ups do."

Cognitively, they . . .

Like to practice new skills by doing them over and over.

Plan activities that allow toddlers to practice familiar skills and apply them to new tasks.

Learn to use language to express feelings and ideas.

Talk with toddlers to help them understand new words and to encourage them to use language to communicate with others.

Get excited by new things and may turn quickly from one activity to another.

Collect a variety of materials and ideas for activities that will interest toddlers and keep them busy and happy.

Physically, they . . .

Are very active and want to explore everything: climbing, jumping and running with increasing skill (gross motor development).

Set up safe indoor and outdoor environments that allow toddlers to explore safely and use their large muscles.

Develop increasing skills in eye-hand coordination and use of small muscles (fine motor control).

Select materials that will challenge toddlers' developing coordination and balance abilities without frustrating them.

Preschool Children

Initiative is the term Erikson used to describe the preschool years (three to five years of age). It's a good word for preschoolers because they are active, talkative, and creative: they "initiate" a lot. Preschool children seem to have endless energy. They are eager for new experiences and have gained many skills that help them learn. They can build, draw, mold, paint, put things together, climb, and swing with increasing skill. They are curious and ask questions about everything to find out more about the world around them. Preschoolers are very social and often have best friends. They are learning to cooperate and play with others, and they want to be liked.

What Preschoolers Are Like:	The Curriculum Helps You:
Emotionally, they . . .	
Are aware of how others respond to them and use these experiences to develop their own self-concepts.	Plan a program and learn ways of talking to preschoolers that help them feel accepted and special.
Express their feelings and display a wide range of emotions—fears, anger, happiness, embarrassment.	Recognize what children are feeling and help them express and cope with fears and emotions.
Socially, they. . .	
Play cooperatively with other children and often have best friends.	Help children get along with others and feel part of the group.
Enjoy role-playing and make-believe play.	Plan dramatic play experiences and take an active role in helping children use make-believe to further their growth.
Respond well to praise and encouragement.	Give children opportunities to talk about their own work and develop pride in their accomplishments.
Cognitively, they . . .	
Love to talk, ask questions, and share what they know.	Talk with preschoolers and ask questions that encourage them to think and put their ideas into words.
Are curious about how things work and why.	Select a variety of materials and activities that children can take apart and explore.
Take pride in mastering and completing tasks.	Plan activities that challenge preschoolers and allow time in the schedule for them to stay with a task as long as they wish.
Learn by active play with real materials and by making their own discoveries.	Select materials that will interest preschoolers and encourage them to try out their own ideas.
Physically, they . . .	
Develop increasing control over the small muscles in their hands.	Include a variety of art materials, writing and drawing tools, and toys that develop children's small muscles.
Develop increasing coordination and control over the large muscles in their legs and arms.	Plan music and movement activities indoors and a safe environment outdoors for children to run and climb and build.
Develop increasing coordination of eye and hand movements.	Select toys, art materials, and props that will challenge children to practice eye-hand coordination skills.

11

School-Age Children

When children enter school, Erikson says that they begin the stage of **Industry**. During this period (5 to 12 years of age), children focus on developing the skills they need for their work in school and in life. They enjoy working on real projects and making things. They are refining the physical skills they have learned and can become quite skillful at games and athletic activities. School life and friends are very important to school-age children. They feel less need for supervision, yet they are still dependent on adults. The family child care home environment can provide a safe and welcoming place for children before and after their day at school and during school vacations.

What School-Age Children Are Like:	The Curriculum Helps You:
Emotionally, they . . .	
Are eager to be independent of adults.	Give school-age children opportunities to make choices, play on their own, and be with their peers.
Act self-assured but can still have many doubts about themselves.	Plan activities that enable school-age children to succeed.
Socially, they . . .	
Are concerned about being accepted by peers and conforming to group expectations.	Create an environment where all children feel part of the group and are accepted for their unique abilities and interests.
Display strong likes and opinions.	Provide opportunities for children to talk about their feelings and express their ideas.
Enjoy assisting young children and being leaders.	Include school-age children in activities you have planned for the younger children and give them responsibilities that help them develop leadership skills.
Cognitively, they . . .	
Enjoy working on long-term projects and like to produce finished products.	Work with school-age children on designing projects that hold their interest over a period of time.
Can follow directions and think abstractly.	Plan cooking activities and science projects that require following directions.
Enjoy cooperative games and games with rules but may have difficulty accepting when they lose.	Select games and plan activities that school-age children can play together or on their own.
Are increasingly skilled and interested in reading and expressing themselves verbally and in writing.	Select appropriate books and provide writing and drawing tools and materials.

Physically, they . . .

Are increasingly able to coordinate their actions.	Plan activities that enable school-age children to develop their large and small muscle skills.
Are interested in developing specific physical skills.	Plan athletic or sports-related special activities that will enable school-age children to refine their skills.

An Overview of Development

As a summary to this chapter, we have prepared a series of charts that can be used for quick reference. As you review these Child Growth and Development Charts, keep in mind that no two children are exactly the same. Although all children go through the same developmental steps in the same order, they do so at their own pace. For each child, some skills are learned quickly while other skills may develop over time. We know, for example, that at 6 months most babies can sit, that at about 12 months they start to walk, and by 2 years they are talking in simple sentences. These steps in development tell us a lot about children in general, but they give us only a rough idea of what we can expect for each child. You have probably seen infants who are walking well at 12 months while others are still crawling. We know that some 2-year-olds are still repeating single words while others can speak in complex sentences. Parents will probably tell you that each of their children walked, drank out of a cup, were potty-trained, or learned to read at different ages. Everything depends on the child's individual developmental timetable.

If a particular child seems very far behind, however, you should pay attention because this may be a warning sign that the child needs special help. For example, if you care for an 18-month-old who is not yet walking or for a 2-1/2 year old who is not talking at all, you should discuss your observations with the parents and encourage them to discuss the situation with their child's doctor. Because you spend so much time with children, you are in a good position to identify problems that can then be addressed in their early stages.

CHILD GROWTH AND DEVELOPMENT

AGE	PHYSICAL	SOCIO-EMOTIONAL	COGNITIVE
0-3 MONTHS	Born with birth reflexes—sucking, grasping Lifts head when held at shoulder Moves arms and legs actively Able to follow objects and to focus	Concerned with satisfaction of needs Smiles spontaneously and responsively Likes movement—being held and rocked Expresses discomfort by crying or tensing body	Makes sounds (coos) Smiles and expresses pleasure when sees faces Looks at patterns (e.g., faces, shapes)
3-6 MONTHS	Rolls over Holds head up when held in sitting position Lifts up knees—crawling motions Reaches for objects Uses both hands to grasp objects	Makes sounds to get attention Smiles responsively Laughs aloud Socializes with anyone but knows mother or father and other primary caregivers Smiles at reflection in mirror	Recognizes primary caregiver Likes to watch objects and people Recognizes bottle
6-9 MONTHS	Able to sit in upright position Explores objects by mouthing them May be able to crawl May be able to climb stairs Develops eye-hand coordination Transfers objects from hand to hand Drops objects repeatedly	Prefers primary caregivers May cry when strangers approach Commonly exhibits anxiety when parent or caregiver leaves Pats own reflection in the mirror May push away things not wanted (e.g., bottle, toys) Begins to "play" with adults (e.g., peek-a-boo)	Babbles to himself or herself Solves simple problems (e.g., will move obstacles aside to reach object) Responds to changes in environment and is able to repeat actions that cause change (e.g., sound of rattle) Fascinated with small objects Begins to respond to words

NOTE: Children move through developmental stages at their own pace; within each age group, children acquire skills at different times. The ranges prescribed here are approximate rather than precise times when children acquire these skills.

CHILD GROWTH AND DEVELOPMENT (continued)

AGE	PHYSICAL	SOCIO-EMOTIONAL	COGNITIVE
9-14 MONTHS	Achieves mobility—strong urge to climb, crawl Stands and walks Learns to grasp with thumb and finger Feeds self	Extends attachment for primary caregivers to the world—in love with world and wants to explore everything Knows that objects exist even when they can't be seen (object permanence); thus knows that when parents or caregiver leave, they will return Typically friendly and affectionate with caregivers—less so with strangers Responds to his or her name	Demonstrates intentional behavior—initiates actions Eager for sensory experiences; explores everything, has to touch and mouth every object Curious about everything Realizes objects exist when out of sight and will look for them (object permanance) Stares for long periods to gain information Interested in and understands words Says words such as "mama" and "dada" Likes to look at books Combines gestures with words—waves hand and says "bye-bye"
14-24 MONTHS	Walks and runs Drinks from a cup alone Turns pages of books Scribbles spontaneously Walks backward Loves to practice new skill Likes gymnastics, climbing, going down slides Stacks two to three blocks Climbs into chairs	Tends to be opinionated—"no" stage—and/or very directive Aware of being an independent person; starts to assert independence Tests limits Develops concept of self, is fearful of injury (bandaid stage, "I wanna" stage, everything "mine," stage) Tends to stay near mother or father and make regular overtures—seeks approval, asks for help Plays beside other children but has difficulty sharing	Can follow simple directions Uses language to serve immediate needs ("mine," "cookie") and names familar objects Imitates words readily and understands a lot more than he or she can say Has improved memory Experiments to see what will happen and observes cause-and-effect relationships Learns to use new means to achieve end (i.e., can tilt objects to get them through bars in crib) Spends long periods of time exploring a single object Loves to play with objects Recognizes self in mirror Begins to be able to think about an action before doing it (e.g., reaching for a toy)

CHILD GROWTH AND DEVELOPMENT (continued)

AGE	PHYSICAL	SOCIO-EMOTIONAL	COGNITIVE
2-3 YEARS	Has sufficient muscle control for toilet training Highly mobile—skills are refined Uses spoon to feed self Throws and kicks a ball Takes apart simple objects and puts them back together Has increased eye-hand coordination—can do simple puzzles, string beads, stack blocks Likes to help dress and undress self Washes and dries hands	Has strong urges and desires but is developing ability to exert self-control; wants to please parents but sometimes has difficulty not acting impulsively Displays affection—especially for caregiver Imitates own play activity and occupies self Able to hold a conversation Developing interest in peers but may still have difficulty sharing Displays sense of humor May exhibit fears of the dark, "scary" faces, masks, or witches	Has a beginning awareness of time Capable of thinking before acting Becoming very verbal Enjoys talking to self and others Loves to pretend and to imitate others Enjoys creative activities such as block play, art Thinks through and solves problems in head before acting (has moved beyond action-bound stage) Can make simple choices Begins to use language to express ideas and feelings
3-4 YEARS	Jumps in place Walks down stairs Balances on one foot Uses toilet consistently Begins to dress self Builds with blocks and construction toys Has developed fine muscle control Has boundless energy	Knows name, sex, age, and sees self as part of family unit Plays alongside other children and begins to interact with them; is learning to share Helps with small household tasks Likes to be "big" and to achieve new skills Shows affection for friends Can express anger verbally	Believes there is a purpose for everything and asks "why?" Uses symbolic play—has strong fantasy life, loves to imitate and role-play Understands some number concepts, comparisons, colors Shows logical thinking Interested in letters Able to scribble and draw recognizable objects and circles Speaks in longer sentences and uses language to describe events and explain behavior Asks lots of questions

CHILD GROWTH AND DEVELOPMENT (continued)

AGE	PHYSICAL	SOCIO-EMOTIONAL	COGNITIVE
4-6 YEARS	Has improved coordination and is learning many new skills Has improved coordination in fingers—able to hold and use a pencil, cut with scissors, catch a ball, use a fork and spoon, brush his or her teeth Climbs, hops, skips, and likes to do stunts Able to ride a tricycle	Plays cooperatively with peers Can share and take turns Identifies with own gender and ethnic group Displays independence Protects self and stands up for rights Identifies with parents and likes to imitate them Often has "best friends" Likes to show off skills to adults Continually forms new images of self Enjoys being a leader	Shows increased attention span Expands dramatic play with attention to detail and reality Has increasingly more complex language skills Expresses ideas, asks questions, engages in discussions Speaks clearly Able to draw pictures that represent objects or things Likes to tell or act out stories
6-12 YEARS	Enjoys using new skills, both large and small muscle skills Likes to achieve in sports Energetic and may have large appetite Gaining in height and weight Has increased coordination and strength Developing body proportions similar to adult Practices self-care habits independently (e.g., brushing teeth, combing hair, dressing)	Developing a more defined personality Acts very independent and self-assured but at times can be childish and silly Enjoys working/playing with others and alone Defines self-image in part by success at school Has a strong group identity May play exclusively with same sex Begins to experience conflicts between parents' values and those of peers Has a strong sense of fairness and fair play Believes that rules are important and must be followed Likes affection from adults Increasingly independent but still emotionally dependent on adults—wants them to be there to help Able to assume responsibility for self and may help care for younger siblings	Enjoys projects that are task oriented (e.g., sewing, cooking, woodwork) Highly verbal—enjoys jokes and puns, uses language creatively Asks questions that are fact oriented—wants to know how, why, and when Likes to make up stories, plays, and puppet shows Understands cause-and-effect relationships Able to deal with abstract ideas Judges success on ability to learn to read, write, and do arithmetic Organizes collections and enjoys sorting objects by shape, size, color, etc.

Setting Up Your Home for Child Care

In many ways your home is a natural environment for learning. You have soft and safe places for children to explore, you may have plants growing in the living room that the children can help care for as well as books and magazines to look through. Your kitchen is filled with pots and pans that a child can bang to music or use in a cooking activity.

The way you arrange space for children can make it easier for them to learn, get along with others, and become independent. It can also make it easier for you to care for these children. This chapter will give you some suggestions on how to set up your home to promote children's learning and overall growth.

Good Environments Encourage Positive Behavior

We are all affected by our environments. Think about how you feel and act in a place that is overcrowded, too hot, poorly lit, and generally disorganized. You probably feel uncomfortable and frustrated and wish you were someplace else. The same feelings hold true for children. When their environment is overcrowded, physically uncomfortable, or hard to maneuver in, they get frustrated and upset and often act out.

Children respond best to an environment that makes them feel safe and secure. When they are given a special place to keep their belongings safe, children feel respected. When they know where to play, they are less likely to wander. When children know which things are clearly theirs and which are off-limits, they learn to respect the rights of others.

And children who have a wide variety of interesting and age-appropriate toys to play with are more likely to become involved in purposeful activities throughout the day.

One way to encourage positive behavior is to create specific areas in your home for different activities. Here are some suggestions:

- Identify which areas of your home are **"off limits"** to the children. For example, a tool shed or storage area can be locked or your bedroom door closed. Rooms that you do not wish to use for your program can be blocked off by a door, a gate, or a large piece of furniture. Breakable objects can be stored in these off-limits areas.

- Decide where you will allow **active play** such as musical games, block building, and dramatic play.

- Look for comfortable places for **quiet activities** such as looking at books, drawing with crayons, or listening to stories.

- Set aside a place for **older children** to keep their games and special materials such as paper, scissors, markers, or glue. A bedroom could be a quiet and private place for school-age children to play or do their homework.

- Decide if you are going to use **designated areas for child care** and leave them set up that way at all times. You can also convert the space back into a "normal" living area at the end of each day, storing equipment in closets and moving furniture around.

It should be clear to the children what activities are allowed where in your home. You can accomplish this by setting up "activity areas"—places that are designated for specific choices in play. For example, children need a protected space for playing with blocks, an easy-to-clean area for messy activities such as art or water play, and some cozy corners to slow down and relax in. A family child care home can provide these different activity areas without losing its homelike atmosphere.

To do this, some family child care providers set up special play areas where they can rotate activities. For example, a small table with chairs might be used to offer table toys during one part of the day and an art activity during another. The amount of space in your home will dictate how many areas you can set up at any given time. It is, preferable, however, to be able to offer the children several choices at once. Here are some tips on designing your space:

- Separate noisy areas from quiet ones.

- Clearly define each area by using shelves, tables, or tape so children have a physical indication of boundaries.

- Store materials and toys at a height accessible to the children, and keep adult materials out of their reach.

- Place activities near needed resources (for example, art activities near a water source, books in an area with enough light, etc.).

- Allow for traffic flow so that children are not constantly bumping into crawling infants or interrupting each other's play.

- Make your home welcoming and child-friendly by adding touches of what's familiar to them: pictures of their families and themselves, and items that they see at home that reflect their culture.

When the environment is working, children are busy and happily engaged in play; fights are few and the day proceeds well. In contrast, when the environment is not well-planned, children may be confused and generally unhappy. Of course, there are many possible reasons why such behavior occurs, but it's always a good idea to check the physical environment first, to see if it is contributing to the problems. Here are some things to consider.[2]

PROBLEM BEHAVIOR	POSSIBLE CAUSE	HOW TO CHANGE THE ENVIRONMENT
The children run around the house in circles.	All the rooms in the house are interconnected.	Restructure the space by (1) making one of the rooms "out-of-bounds," (2) moving a piece of furniture in front of a pass-through, or (3) boxing in a play area with furnishings.
Children run "wild" when outside.	The outdoor area has not been organized.	Organize outdoor areas into activity areas that promote learning—for example, a sand box, an old tree trunk for woodworking, a garden, etc.
Children run "wild" when inside.	There is no indoor area for noisy exercise or large muscle activity.	Plan a space where children can dance to music or roll on rugs or mattresses to release energy.
Children act as if they are in "school"; there is little interaction with the provider or each other.	The home has been structured into a mini-school.	While leaving areas for the children to work on activities, put back those elements of a home that make family child care special (e.g., sofas, pillows, stuffed chairs). Children want and need a warm, cozy atmosphere.
A child with a disability bumps into furniture, becomes frustrated at having to go so far for play materials, and acts generally unhappy.	The home environment is not structured for children who are disabled.	Change the arrangement to make it easier for a child with a disability to function independently. This may mean moving furniture, making props more accessible, widening pass-throughs, or installing pull-away ramps.
Children don't take care of materials or put them away.	Toys and materials are not organized in containers and placed where children can find them and return them.	Use a low shelf to store materials you want children to use freely. Place toys with small pieces in dishpans or other containers and label them.

[2]This chart is adapted from *A Handbook for Education Specialists* (Washington, DC: Creative Associates, 1989).

Making Your Home Safe for Children

"Childproofing" your home to eliminate dangers and potential injuries is a vital step in preparing your home for children. Creating and maintaining a safe environment enables children to explore, satisfy their curiosity, and learn through play. Your choice of materials and equipment and the way you orgranize space can prevent injuries. In a safe environment, you can then focus on what the children are doing rather than worrying about possible injuries.

Your first step is to do some childproofing. Use the following charts to check the health and safety of your indoor and outdoor areas.

INDOOR HEALTH AND SAFETY CHECK LIST

THINGS TO CHECK	SATISFACTORY	NEEDS ATTENTION
Environment		
Electrical outlets are capped with safety covers.		
Cleaning materials, detergents, medicines, and plastic bags are stored only in locked cabinets and out of the children's reach.		
Furniture has no sharp edges or corners at children's eye level.		
Steps and platforms have enough padding to keep toddlers safe.		
Pillows, mattresses, or mats are placed where children might climb.		
Adult scissors, knives, and other sharp or pointed objects are out of children's reach.		
There are no highly flammable furnishings or decorations. Gasoline is not stored in either the house or garage.		
Walls and furnishings are painted with lead-free paint.		
Matches are in containers out of children's reach, as are cigarettes and lighters.		
Electric garage door openers have an auto-reverse feature.		
Telephone cords are out of reach, and table phones are placed so that young children cannot pull them down on themselves.		
Drapery cords are out of reach of all children, whether drapes are open or closed.		

INDOOR HEALTH AND SAFETY CHECK LIST

THINGS TO CHECK	SATISFACTORY	NEEDS ATTENTION
Decorative decals are placed on glass doors at the children's eye level to prevent injuries.		
Floors are kept dry, and there are no slippery throw rugs.		
Hinges, screws, and bolts in furniture and equipment are securely fastened; there are latches on doors to places that are off limits to children.		
Electrical wires on stereo equipment, tape recorders, and other appliances are not frayed and are out of the children's reach.		
Radiator and hot water pipes are covered or insulated; fireplaces and hot air registers are secured.		
The TV set is in a cabinet or pushed against a wall so that children can't get at the back of the set. If the TV is on a rolling cart, the cart is secure and not movable by children.		
Fireplaces or space heaters are protected by unmovable screens and separated from all objects by three feet of space.		
Step ladders or stools with rubber slats are available for use at sinks.		
There are no indoor poisonous plants such as diffenbachia or poinsettias.		
Halogen lamps (which get very hot) are away from curtains or drapes.		
Cribs		
Cribs are not placed within reach of venetian blind cords.		
Pillows are not used in cribs for infants.		
Mattresses fit snugly into corners and sides so that an infant's head cannot become wedged.		
Breakable or hard objects such as framed pictures are not hung on walls over cribs.		
Crib slats have no more than 2-3/8 inch spacing between them to prevent a baby's head from slipping between the slats.		
Crib latches are not easily released.		

INDOOR HEALTH AND SAFETY CHECK LIST (Continued)

THINGS TO CHECK	SATISFACTORY	NEEDS ATTENTION
Emergency Measures		
Smoke detectors and fire extinguishers are working properly and exist in sufficient numbers.		
Telephone numbers for police, ambulance and fire emergencies are posted by the phone; 911 is posted if applicable, as well as a poison control number.		
There is a plan for escape in case of fire, and practice drills are held each month.		
A permission form for emergency care is signed by each parent.		
An operating flashlight is available.		
A first-aid kit is stocked.		
Health		
Parent's names, addresses, and phone numbers at home and work are accessible.		
Information on any child's health problems is available.		
Written permission to administer medication is on file.		
There is a system for keeping track of the times and amount of medication administered.		
The refrigerator is kept clean, and thermometers are available to monitor the temperature of the refrigerator and freezer.		
Dishcloths are clean; those used for art, food, and floor cleanups are kept separately and not interchanged.		
Soap and single-use towels are available for washing hands after toileting, diapering, and messy activities and before meals.		
Animal cages are cleaned regularly.		
Kitty litter boxes are cleaned regularly and kept in an area inaccessible to children.		

Completing this checklist is only the first step in making sure your environment is safe and healthy for children. Any items you have checked as needing attention should be addressed immediately. Keep this checklist in a convenient place and review it regularly to see if the items you said were satisfactory are still in order. You must continually ensure that the environment is safe for children.

Using this checklist will also protect you. If a child is injured because of something you failed to do, there can be serious consequences. The first step in maintaining a safe environment is to eliminate any hazards in your indoor and outdoor environments. The Outdoor Safety Checklist begins below.

OUTDOOR SAFETY CHECK LIST

THINGS TO CHECK	SATISFACTORY	NEEDS ATTENTION
There are no poisonous plants such as oleanders, elephant ears, and lilies of the valley. (Contact your local poison control center for a listing of poisonous plants.)		
The yard is fenced (unless you are prohibited from doing so by housing regulations). The fence should be free of protruding wires or nails.		
All play equipment surfaces are smooth and splinter free.		
There is cushioning material under climbers, slides, and swings.		
No objects or obstructions are under or around equipment where children might fall.		
There are no frayed cables or worn ropes and no chains that could pinch.		
No broken glass or debris are present.		
Screws, nuts, and bolts on climbing and other equipment are securely fastened and recessed.		
Riding toys and carriages are in good repair (screws tightened, etc.).		
The ground surface is free of drains or culverts.		
Trash cans are placed outside the yard or behind barriers.		
Animals are kept separate from the play area and no animal wastes are present.		
Swings and slides are firmly anchored to the ground and have plenty of space around them.		

OUTDOOR SAFETY CHECK LIST (Continued)

THINGS TO CHECK	SATISFACTORY	NEEDS ATTENTION
Lawn mowers and yard tools are stored out of the children's reach.		
Children have been taught safety rules, such as how to cross the street, the meaning of stoplights and signs, and to not run into the street after balls.		

Selecting Furnishings and Materials

To operate a family child care program successfully in your home, you will need to obtain some furniture and equipment. The following furnishings are considered essentials for working with young children:

- A child-size table and chairs.

- Low shelves to store toys and materials so children can reach and return the items they need.

- A place for each child to nap.

If you care for infants, you will also need a crib for each child, a stroller that accommodates two to three children, a backpack carrier, and high chairs.

Selecting children's toys and materials represents an investment of time and money, so you'll want to be sure you get the best value. Here are three questions to keep in mind as you consider making a purchase:

1. Is the toy well made and sturdy so it will last a long time?

2. Can children of different ages use the toy in different ways? For example, babies and four-year-olds can both enjoy nesting cubes, baby dolls, and plastic measuring cups.

3. Can the toy be used creatively, or does it have only one function? Children tire of "gimmicky" toys such as mechanical dolls or wind-up cars but enjoy toys that can be used in many ways and challenge their imagination such as fit-together toys.

Purchased toys and games can be supplemented by common household objects such as wooden spoons, lightweight pots, and measuring spoons. A coffee can with a secured plastic lid can be used as a drum or for storage. If you are good at carpentry or know someone who is, you might build a doll house or attach an old car steering wheel to a wooden box to use for make-believe play. Vocational schools with woodworking classes

may be willing to make things for child care programs (such as hollow blocks or storage shelves) if you give them the specifications. Parents who like to sew could make bean bags, stuffed animals, or dress-up clothes. Wallpaper stores, lumber yards, grocery stores, newspapers, and hospitals are good places to tap for donations, and parents can help look for needed items at yard sales.

In selecting materials, keep in mind safety issues. Check any items children will use to ensure that the following hold true:

- There are no sharp edges, points, and splinters.

- There are no small pieces (such as buttons) that could be swallowed.

- The toy isn't too heavy for the children.

- Riding toys are stable and well balanced.

- Cloth toys are marked "flame resistant," "flame retardant," or "nonflammable."

- Stuffed toys do not contain loose pellets that will fall out if the seams tear open.

- Plastics toys are sufficiently strong or flexibel that they won't break and leave sharp or jagged edges.

- Toys are not made with straight pins, easily removable nails, or wires that could easily become exposed.

- Electrical toys are labeled "UL" (for Underwriters Laboratories, which means that the electrical parts have been safety tested).

- All painted toys and paints are labeled "nontoxic."

- Mechanical toys with driving springs are adequately encased.

- Metal toys are not rusted.

To help you select toys and materials for your program, we have developed a master list for each age group. The suggested items are organized into threee categories: items to purchase, items to collect, and items to make.

Toys and Materials for Infants

To Purchase or Borrow:

Crib mobile or "busy box"
Washable, cuddly toys and stuffed animals
Sturdy wooden or durable plastic rattles
Plastic key rings
Nonbreakable plastic mirror
Teething rings and other toys to chew on
Grasping toys
Chime balls
Toy telephones
Balls of different sizes
"Fill and dump" toys
Large plastic or wooden animals
Soft cloth blocks

Cloth and vinyl dolls
Stacking and nesting toys
Cloth, heavy cardboard, or nontoxic plastic books

To Collect:

Household items such as pots, pans, rubber spatulas, wooden spoons, empty cardboard boxes, plastic food containers, large plastic napkin rings, coffee cans with plastic lids, and measuring cups and spoons

To Make:

Textured balls
Cloth animals from old towels or material scraps stuffed with old socks
Bell rattles by securely sewing bells onto ribbon
Picture books made from cardboard covered with clear contact paper

Infants may also enjoy and learn from some of the toys and materials listed for the older children, such as music recordings, trucks and cars, and household items.

Toys and Materials for Toddlers

Any of the above materials that the children still enjoy using, plus the following:

To Purchase or Borrow:

Records, tapes, or compact discs of children's music or stories
Push-and-pull toys
Peg boards and large pegs
Large wooden stringing beads
Wooden or rubber puzzles with large pieces (3 to 8)
Simple matching games such as Lotto
Wooden or plastic animal and people figures for dramatic play
Balls
Trucks, cars, and wagons
Large crayons
Pails and shovels for sand play
Wagons, tricycles, and riding toys
Large cardboard blocks and interlocking blocks
Climbing equipment

To Collect:

Picture books from the local library

Cardboard boxes of all sizes

Donated paper for art projects, such as used computer paper or newsprint from your local newspaper

Household items for sand and water play, such as sieves, funnels, sifters, strainers, measuring cups and spoons, basters, sponges, and food coloring

Dress up clothes, hats, suitcases, and shoes for dramatic play

To Make:

Playdough, modeling clay, finger paint (see the chapter on Art in Part Two)

Musical instruments: coffee cans with secured plastic lids for drums; wooden dowels for rhythm sticks; bells sewn on ribbon; shakers made by filling yogurt containers with beans and securing with duct tape

Bean bags

Books about the children in the program

Toys and Materials for Preschoolers

Any of the above materials that the children still enjoy, plus the following:

To Purchase or Borrow:

Small play house, zoo, garage, farm sets
Family sets and animal figures
Plastic snapping blocks
Games (see the list in the chapter on Toys)
Pegboards and pegs
Interlocking toys
Parquetry or pattern blocks
Magnetic boards with shapes
Felt boards with shapes and felt animals, and people
Wooden, sturdy cardboard, or rubber puzzles with 8-20 pieces
Writing materials such as pencils, colored pencils, washable pens
Crayons and washable markers, chalk, glue, scissors, and hole punches
Balls and hula hoops for outdoor play
Wagons, baby carriages, and tricycles
Water-based paints and brushes
Props for block play, such as small animals, buses, airplanes, cars, doll furniture, traffic signs, and trains

To Collect:

Additional props for sand and water play, such as squirt bottles, shells, combs, and rakes

Additional props for dramatic play, such as brooms, mops, full-length mirrors, plastic dishes, male and female dress-up clothes, hats of all types, costume jewelry, and accessories related to specific themes such as grocery stores, offices, or hospitals

Materials to sort or play with, including buttons, keys, seashells, fabric squares, coffee scoops, and plastic bottle tops

Collage materials for art, such as feathers, glitter, Styrofoam, scraps of wrapping paper, toilet paper tubes, egg cartons, and macrame

Library books, tapes, and records

Household plants to care for

To Make:

Puppets

"Self-help" frames (a wooden frame to which two pieces of material with a zipper, buttons, or snaps in the middle are attached)

Homemade puzzles (a cut-out magazine picture covered with clear Contact paper, glued onto sturdy cardboard, and cut into pieces)

Bubbles and frames (see the recipes in the chapter on Sand and Water)

Toys and Materials for School-Age Children

Any of the materials suggested for preschoolers that would still be of interest to the children, plus the following:

To Purchase or Borrow:

Board and card games and manipulatives (see the list in the chapter on Toys)

Decks of cards

Jigsaw puzzles

Materials for art projects and science projects

Writing materials such as pens, pencils, colored pencils, markers, and crayons

Jump ropes, balls, and various sports equipment

Construction materials for wood working

To Collect:

Library books, tapes, and records

Sewing materials such as burlap, felt, large tapestry needles, and yarn

Additional props for dramatic play, such as puppets, masks, and doctor's kit materials donated by a hospital (e.g., a real stethoscope, old uniforms, masks)

Wallpaper sample books

Large cardboard boxes for outdoor play

Flashlights, measuring tapes, and rulers

To Make:

Playdough that hardens (see the chapter on Art in Part Two)
Masks and puppets

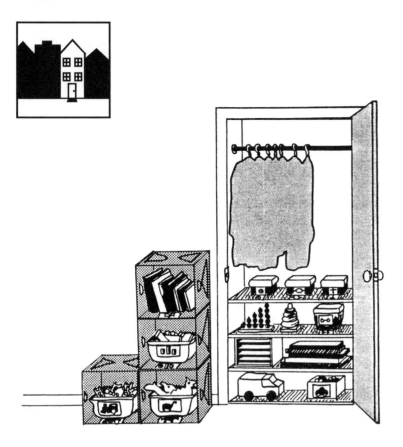

Storing Materials

How you store materials determines how effectively they will be used. If the materials are accessible to the children, they can be readily used for learning. Children learn:

- to be independent because they can select for themselves what they want to play with;

- that there is order in their environment because every object has its place;

- responsibility because they help take care of their environment; and

- that materials are valued because you provide a special place for everything.

Low bookcases or plastic milk crates make excellent storage places. You can turn a closet into a storage space by installing shelves. Materials can be further organized in cans, shoe boxes, and dishpans. Placing a picture of the item being stored on the container and above the spot where it is kept helps children find and return the materials on their own.

Here are some additional ideas for storing materials in your home:

- Ice cream barrels are perfect for storing the children's personal belongings. (You can get these at your local ice cream store.) Add hooks on the wall over these containers for hanging coats.

- Stack wooden or plastic food crates and glue or bolt them together. Paint them and use them for storage shelves—a safe place for books or maybe for the stereo equipment, records, tapes, and CDs if the crates are sturdy.

- Add casters to an empty crate and you have a moveable trunk for dress-up clothes.

- Collect shoe boxes to store scissors, crayons, paper scraps, puzzles—anything! Be sure to label each box.

- Keep toys such as table blocks with small pieces in plastic dishpans.

- Store sensory materials such as sand, rice, or beans in covered containers.

Good storage of materials maximizes their use by children and thus encourages learning. In the next chapter we'll discuss how you can schedule your day so children can effectively use the materials in your home to further their growth and development.

Managing the Day

Caring for young children in your home means managing both time and space. Having a schedule helps structure the day's activities and events. Attention to daily routines and preparing for the hectic times can make your day go a lot more smoothly.

The Daily Schedule

A daily schedule helps children learn the order of their day. Young children like to know that they can depend on certain daily routines. This helps them feel secure. When you say things like "after nap we will go play outside," children learn what to expect. The daily schedule also helps you organize your day and plan a good balance of activities and experiences for the children.

Although almost everyone recognizes the importance of a schedule, the reality is that schedules are often ignored in family child care. Why does this happen? Basically, it's because children have their own internal schedules. Babies need to be fed, changed, and put to rest on demand. Children of differing ages have differing needs, interests, and attention spans. School-age children have to deal with school and teachers as well. When you put this all together, it's sometimes a wonder that any of the day proceeds as planned. Yet for all the reasons mentioned earlier, planning is vitally important. It's what ensures that everyone—including you—has a productive day.

A good schedule for young children:

•   offers a **balance** between these kinds of experiences:

> indoor and outdoor times;
> quiet and active times;
> time to play alone and time to play with others; and
> time to select activities and a time to join one that you have planned.

•   pays special attention to **transition times** during the day, such as:

> greeting children when they arrive and are separating from parents;
> cleaning up after breakfast, lunch, and snacks;
> getting ready to go outside;
> cleaning up after one activity so that another can be started;
> getting ready for nap after lunch;
> arrival and departure of school-age or part-time children; and
> preparing to go home.

•   reflects your **unique** situation:

> when each child arrives and leaves;
> when babies need to nap and be fed; and
> when the children have breakfast, lunch, and snacks.

The following schedule is an example of how the daily program might be organized in a family child care home to meet the needs of children of many ages.

SAMPLE SCHEDULE

Early Morning

6:30-8:30 am   Children arrive. Your own children may be getting ready for school or to begin the day with you. Some children need breakfast. Following breakfast, infants are changed and put down to nap.[3] (Infants and young toddlers should be allowed to nap on their own schedules, and even older children may need to nap unexpectedly at times.) Older children help with clean-up and play with table toys, read books, or listen to story tapes until everyone finishes breakfast and cleans up.

Morning Activities

8:30-9:45   Toddlers and preschool children select an activity of their choice or join in a noisy group activity such as finger painting, water play, cooking, or puppet making. As babies wake up, they are brought in to join the group activity. Children help clean up after the play time.

9:45-10:15   Snack

10:15-11:00   Get ready to go outside: use the toilet, wash hands, change diapers, and so on. Outdoor play and/or walks. Perhaps a science project such as gardening.

11:00-11:30   Free play again—perhaps a special planned activity such as making and using playdough at the kitchen table.

11:30-11:45   Clean-up and story time; get ready for lunch.

Lunch and Rest

11:45-12:45 pm   Family-style lunch and conversation. After lunch, older children help put food away and clean up. Hands are washed, diapers changed, and teeth brushed.

12:45-2:45   Everyone (except, perhaps, for a baby who has just woken up), has a rest period. Preschool children who can't sleep rest quietly on their cots or beds, looking at a book. It is reasonable to expect children to rest or play in bed quietly for 30 to 40 minutes before they are allowed to get up and begin a quiet activity. As children wake up, diapers are changed, hands are washed, and hair is combed. Cots are put away.

---

[3]Infants will nap two and sometimes three times a day on their own schedules, which will change as they grow. Toddlers may take one or two naps each day, often around 10 a.m. and 2 p.m. Like infants, their sleep demands will change over time and may even increase and decrease at different times. It's helpful to learn the sleep schedule for each infant and then plan active and messy activities that most need your supervision when the infants are sleeping.

Afternoon Activities

2:45-3:15   Children have a snack together. School-age children arrive and help themselves to a snack of their choice. This does not mean they can eat anything they want but rather that they should choose from a provider-approved selection. Children discuss choices for afternoon activities. Clean-up follows.

3:15-4:00   Active indoor or outdoor play for all children. School-age children are invited to join in. A special project may be planned.

Late Afternoon/Evening

4:00-4:45   Free play: children play with table toys, blocks, crayons, read books, or build with blocks.

4:45-5:00   Group story time or singing (nondisruptive play for those who do not wish to participate in the group); quiet group activity.

5:00-6:00   Children go home at staggered times. Projects are assembled, diapers changed, and parent information made ready. Children color, look at books, play with table toys until their parents arrive. Events of the day and plans for the next day are discussed with children and parents as they leave.

Allowing for Flexibility

Although your daily schedule can help organize the day, you don't want it to limit your ability to be spontaneous and flexible. For example, if it is a particularly beautiful day, you may want to spend most of the day outdoors. Or if a child starts dancing to a record you have put on during free play, you might lead a group movement activity.

Throughout the day, unplanned events often occur that offer **"teachable moments,"** unexpected learning opportunities. A sudden thunderstorm, the discovery of a cocoon, or a new litter of puppies in the neighborhood may arouse the children's curiosity. When the mail or a delivery arrives, you can talk about different jobs people have in the community or discuss the idea that letters go in and out of the mailbox. Watch the children's activities and listen to their conversations and questions. In this way, you'll discover many such teachable moments.

Routines

Daily routines such as diapering, mealtimes, and rest times are as much a part of your program as the activities you plan for children. Giving some thought to how you want to handle routines will help make these daily activities more enjoyable for you and the children, as well as opportunities for learning.

Making Mealtimes Enjoyable

Mealtimes are exceptionally good learning times. Children begin to serve themselves, try new foods, and develop attitudes about food and nutrition.

There are many things providers can do to make mealtimes enjoyable and to foster positive attitudes about food and nutrition. First, it is important to remember that children have individual eating patterns and preferences that must be respected. Find out about any allergies or health constraints. Talk with parents about how and what they feed their children and offer the same, comfortingly familiar foods in your home. Take advantage of the diverse food choices in the children's families and introduce foods from each child's background and culture to all the other children. Ask the parents to help you plan meals and show you how to prepare food you may be unfamiliar with. Encourage, but don't force, children to try new foods, and focus on the pleasure of a shared meal rather than the finer points of table manners. Let them practice with utensils such as forks, chopsticks, or straws, and allow the older children to teach the younger ones how to use them. Listed below are some suggestions for making mealtimes enjoyable.

Make Mealtime a Social Time

- Try to establish a calm and pleasant atmosphere. A quiet activity, such as a story before lunch, helps set a quiet tone.

- Encourage children to talk about what they are eating, how the food is prepared, or something of a solely social nature. Pleasant conversation will create a comfortable atmosphere.

- Organize mealtimes so that you don't have to keep jumping up from the table. This is disruptive and causes children to do the same. Keep extra food on or near the table and have extra napkins, sponges, and paper cups nearby.

- Allow children enough time to eat. Some children are slow eaters. Ample time should be allowed for setting up, eating, and cleaning up.

Encourage Children to Help

- From an early age, even as young as toddlers, children can learn to set the table, sponge the table after eating, and put their napkins in the trash can.

- Serve food in family-style serving bowls and small pitchers so that children can learn to pour their own milk or juice and serve their own food. Give children time to practice with pitchers during water play, and be tolerant of spills and accidents.

- Allow infants and toddlers to feed themselves when possible.

Don't Use Food as a Reward or Punishment

- Avoid promises or threats involving food. It is especially important that children not be threatened with having a snack taken away.

- If a child acts out during a meal, the best response is to deal with the inappropriate behavior and sit near the child or separate the child from the group but allow the child to finish eating.

Rest Time

Because young children often associate sleep with their parents and being at home, rest time can be difficult for them. This is normal and to be expected.

It helps to remember that each child has a different sleep pattern and a different way of falling asleep: some drop off right away, some need to suck their thumbs or pacifiers to relax, and others keep their eyes open until the very last minute, reluctant to miss a single thing that may be going on. Young children also need different amounts of sleep: you may have two toddlers who are the same age but require different amounts of sleep, a four-year-old who sleeps routinely for one hour, or a child who needs to rest only once a day.

Here are some suggestions for making rest time a relaxing period of the day:

- Have each child sleep in the same place and in the same bed, cot, or crib every day.

- Encourage children to bring sleep toys or special blankets from home to use at rest time. These objects can be kept on the child's bed/crib. Children should not be teased about needing these things; they will give them up when they are ready.

- Plan a quiet activity for the children right before rest time, such as reading a story or playing soft music.

- Give children time to settle down at their own pace. Children should not be forced to sleep but encouraged to relax. Sleep usually follows. This is a good time to spend a few minutes alone with each child.

- For children who can't sleep, offer a "quiet time." Children can read books or listen to a story for a pre-determined time, following which they could choose a quiet activity.

Dealing with Hectic Times

Some times of the day tend to be more challenging than others. With some advanced planning, though, these hectic times can go more smoothly. Here are some tips.

Early Morning

Children will arrive at different times, and you may have your own school-age children to get off to school. It helps to have something interesting planned that children can do independently. Books, story tapes, and table toys are a good choice for this time of day, and children can use them right on the kitchen floor or table. Some family child care providers offer special "hello" toys, making them available only at this time of day, and the children look forward to this morning play time.

Mid-Afternoon

If you care for school-age children or have older children of your own, the time at which they return from school can be very hectic. School-age children, like all children, have different needs. Some may want to do something very active, to "let off steam" after sitting in school all day. Others may want to relax with a book or listen to music. Some children will want to talk to you about their day.

Children waking up from their naps may also want you to sit with them and may demand your attention. This is often a time when your own children become jealous of sharing you with others. Advance planning can help. For example, have a snack ready for the older children when they arrive, or have on hand snacks they can prepare for themselves. Also, plan some individual time with your own children each day so they know they won't have to share you all the time.

End of the Day

Children are picked up at different times, and some will become anxious when they see other children leaving with their parents. It helps to plan some quiet activities for this time of day. Select toys and materials that can be put away easily, such as puzzles, table blocks, crayons and paper, books, story tapes and records. Some providers offer special end-of-day toys the same way that they offer morning toys. If you can spend a little time alone with each child, this usually keeps things calm. Many providers find that an additional outdoor time also works well at this time of the day. Urge parents to try to keep to a regular schedule so that their children and you can anticipate their arrivals. At the same time, try to keep yourself and the children calm if parents are unavoidably late because of heavy traffic or an emergency.

This chapter has presented ideas on how to plan a daily schedule to accommodate children of differing ages. A well-planned day gives you a framework for the day's activities. In the next chapter we'll show how you can use these activities to guide children's learning and behavior.

Working with Children

This chapter examines two aspects of working with children: promoting their learning and guiding their behavior. If you do these two things successfully, the chances are good that you will have an effective program.

Promoting Children's Learning

The goals that are outlined in the Introduction to *The Creative Curriculum for Family Child Care* can actually help you guide children's learning. Keep in mind that you want to help children become capable and enthusiastic learners. This means helping them become independent, self-confident, and active explorers of their environment. You do this every day when you:

- encourage them to try new things on their own;

- praise their efforts and their successes;

- allow them to make their own mistakes and learn from them;

- allow them the time they need to practice and try out new skills and build on interests;

- treat each child as an individual with his or her own interests, abilities, and needs; and

- listen to what children have to say and explain things simply in words children can understand.

One of the best ways to guide children's learning is to observe regularly what children do. This enables you to see if the activities you have planned are appropriate for their level and if they are ready for more challenges. You can use your observations to plan for addressing each child's individual needs, interests, and abilities.

Observing Children

Observing what a child does allows you to determine a child's level of development so you know what materials and experiences the child is ready to tackle. For example, you wouldn't hand a ten-piece puzzle to a child who has never played with puzzles and expect the child to know how to put it together. Before getting to this point, the child needs experience and success in putting together simple puzzles in order to learn how they work. Once the child has become competent in putting together three- and five-piece puzzles, the child can then take on the challenge of a ten-piece puzzle. Some children may need months or even years to get to this point; other children may pass through these steps in less time. The only way to know what a child is ready for is to observe the child in action. Here are some questions you might ask:

- Has the child had previous experience playing with puzzles?

- What does the child do with a five-piece puzzle? Does the child put it together with ease? Is the child frustrated? Does the puzzle bore the child? Does the child require your assistance?

- Does the child seek out puzzles on his or her own?

- What type (and complexity) of puzzles does the child choose?

- How long does the puzzle hold the child's attention?

- Does the child use words such as "next to" and "inside" to describe what he or she does with the puzzle pieces?

In general, focus on three areas: the materials children use; how they use the materials; and what they are learning.

In observing what **materials children select,** consider whether they:

- have special favorite toys;

- play with a variety of materials or use the same materials all the time;

- select materials that hold their interest for a period of time or go from one thing to another; and

- select materials with reference to their culture and/or gender.

In observing how **children use materials,** consider whether they:

- do the same thing with the materials each time they play with them, or try new things;
- play with materials in expected ways or also try out innovative uses;
- get frustrated or bored easily;
- try out newly learned skills in their play;
- use the materials for dramatic play;

- invite other children to join in their play;
- prefer you to play with them;
- are able to share with others; and
- have favorite play partners.

In observing children to determine **what learning experiences** are taking place, try to assess their abilities to:

- use the materials to express their feelings;
- compare how materials are alike and different;
- tell you what they are doing with the materials;
- describe the materials (e.g., size, color, shape, texture, etc.);
- initiate new projects and activities;
- use the materials to solve problems; and
- predict what will happen before they try out their ideas.

There are two principal ways of observing. The first way is to observe all the children in your care doing a group activity such as painting a mural or working with playdough to see how each child approaches this same activity. Let's say you care for a nine-month-old, a preschooler, and a toddler. All three children are sitting at a table with their own fistfuls of playdough. How does each child play with the dough? Does the toddler put the playdough in his mouth without regard to what is going on? Does the preschooler concentrate on rolling the dough over and over to form a long rope? Does the school-age child form her playdough into a dinosaur and use it to make-believe? Each of these children will approach the playdough experience in a different way. By observing each child's play, you can provide appropriate experiences at each child's level.

A second way of observing children is to follow a particular child at play for a period of time and make brief notes on what that child does. Does the child play with a variety of toys? Which toys hold the child's attention? Does the child appear content, frustrated, or bored by any of the play experiences? Does the child interact with other children? By observing the child's behavior carefully you can determine what developmental skills this child now possesses and how to plan the next steps in learning.

Talking With Children

Your daily observations of the children provide you with the information you need to plan activities and respond to what children do in ways that will promote each child's growth and development. Each of the activities described in Part Two of *The Creative Curriculum for Family Child Care* provides ideas for selecting materials and planning activities that address children's developing needs and abilities. In this material you will find suggestions of what you can say to help children learn through their play. Here we summarize four recommended strategies:

- ***Describe what you see the child doing.*** This helps even preverbal children organize their thoughts. "You're shaking the rattle. Listen to the nice shaking sound!" Or, "Look at all the bubbles you made by adding soap flakes to the water!"

- ***Ask children what they're doing.*** Once you've described for children what they're doing, try getting them to do this for you. "You've been playing with this doll for a long time. Tell me about what you're doing." Or, "That looks like fun. What are you doing with the soap flakes?"

- *Ask children questions that will make them think about what they're doing.* Through thoughtful questioning, you can help children learn to compare, solve problems, apply what they are learning in new situations, and predict what will happen. "What other toys do we have that make a ringing sound when we shake them?" (comparisons) "What could you do to the block tower to keep it from falling over?" Or, "The finger paint seems awfully runny. What could we do to make it thicker?" (problem-solving) "Can you think of any other place we could use this measuring cup besides the kitchen?" (applying what they have learned) "What will happen to this picture frame if we don't nail it together?" (predicting)

- *Ask questions that encourage children to explore their feelings and emotions.* "I think you're happy with the mobile you made. Tell me what you like best about it." Or, "How do you think Ira feels about sleeping overnight at a friend's house?"

Open-ended questions such as these, which do not demand one correct answer, show children you are interested in what children have to say. They are thus encouraged to be creative and take risks in both what they say and do.

Extending and Enriching Children's Play

Because learning is a dynamic process, your role is to be responsive to the children's changing needs and interests. Periodically, you will need to enhance and alter the environment to provide new experiences, challenge the children's abilities, and respond to their growing interests. Additionally, you will probably be working with several different age groups and will need to plan for a variety of levels of play. You can accomplish this by doing these things:

- *Adding new materials, equipment, and props* to the various activity areas. For example, add plastic dinosaurs and sticks to the sand box and large bottle caps to drop in a cardboard box.

- *Asking questions, offering suggestions, and answering questions* to expand children's play experiences. "This airport looks like a busy place. Where do you suppose all of those people are going?"

- *Bringing in outside resources,* such as visitors and people with special talents, to generate new ideas that children can use in play. Invite a storyteller from your local library, or an artist who will paint or sculpt with the children.

- *Taking children places such as on neighborhood walks* that expand their areas of interest. Visit a construction site if they are playing with toy trucks and equipment or go to a music store when they seem particularly interested in musical instruments.

Planning for Each Child

Planning for each child's individual needs and interests is called **individualizing learning**. Family child care, with its small group size, provides an ideal setting for such individualization. By observing children as described earlier, you can collect information to use as you design activities and experiences that address each child's individual needs and interests. If you see that during a music activity a child is fascinated by different sounds, you can provide homemade musical instruments so that the child can experiment with making musical sounds. (See the chapter on Music and Movement in Part Two.) Similarly, to help a child practice fine motor skills, you can plan activities such as cutting paper, sifting sand, or playing with self-help boards. By knowing where each child is developmentally at any given time, you can build on and extend each child's skills.

Individualization is important for all children, and is especially important for a child with special needs. You may be the first to identify a developmental delay in a child that should be brought to the parents' attention, or a child may come to you with a special need that is already identified. In either case, use all the resources available from the family, health care provider, and community to provide the same learning experiences you give to the other children, while also attending to the special need.

Through individualizing, you promote children's growth in all areas: social, emotional, thinking (cognitive), and physical. In each of the activity chapters of Part Two in *The Creative Curriculum for Family Child Care,* you'll find suggestions for planning activities that address a wide range of needs and interests. When children are involved in meaningful activities they feel good about themselves and you experience the joy of helping children grow. Yet anyone who cares for young children knows that children's behavior is not always ideal. Guiding behavior, another important aspect of your role, is a subject covered in the following section.

Guiding Children's Behavior[4]

One of the important tasks in growing up is learning which behaviors are appropriate and which are not permissible. For children to gain this understanding and develop self-discipline, they need adults to guide them. How you provide this guidance depends on your goals for children: Do you want them to behave out of fear of punishment or because they understand the reasons for rules and want to live cooperatively with others?

An important part of caring for young children is providing an environment that helps children feel good about themselves and their growing abilities. Developing a positive self-concept is one of the most important goals of early childhood. Children are learning who they are, what they can do, and how they relate to others. How you care for children each day, what expectations you set, and how you guide children's behavior can help children develop self-discipline and also feel good about themselves.

Guiding children's behavior to promote self-discipline is not as difficult as it may seem. The caring relationship you build with each child goes a long way in promoting children's self-discipline. Children who like and trust you will naturally want to please you. The age-appropriate activities you provide, along with the opportunities for children to learn by doing, keep them active and involved. Children who are engaged in activities that are meaningful to them and who know that their needs will be met by a caring provider are more likely to behave in appropriate ways.

A Child Development Approach to Guiding Behavior

As in all aspects of a child-development-based curriculum, knowing what children are like at each stage and what they are capable of understanding and learning is the basis for guiding children's behavior. The methods you use will vary according to the children's developmental ages, but the underlying goal is the same for all children: to help them develop self-discipline and the ability to live cooperatively with others.

[4] This section is based on D.T. Dodge, D.G. Koralek, and P.J. Pizzolongo, *Caring for Preschool Children,* 2nd Ed.,(Washington, DC: Teaching Strategies, Inc. 1996), Volume II, Module 10, and D.T. Dodge, A.L. Dombro, and D.G. Koralek, *Caring for Infants and Toddlers* (Washington, D.C.: Teaching Strategies, Inc. 1991).

Infants

The most effective way to guide infants' behavior is to love them and be responsive to their needs. Until they are about six to eight months old, infants cannot control their own behavior. Adults need to step in to make sure that infants do not hurt themselves. Creating a safe environment and preventing problems from occurring are two of the ways you can guide infants' behavior. For example, you should remove a mobile from a crib when an infant is strong enough to pull it down and possibly get hurt himself or stop an infant who is about to poke another child in the eye. Show children how to play with each other gently.

Here are some suggestions for keeping infants safe:

- Keep infants away from potential problems. If an infant is trying to climb up on the table, redirect the infant to climb on some pillows on the floor or a soft mattress.

- Remove temptations or dangerous objects. For example, keep the bathroom door closed, and put pencils and other sharp objects and breakables out of reach.

- Offer an infant something interesting to play with if another child is playing with something the infant wants. Infants are very receptive to "trades."

- Separate infants who are hurting each other and show them other ways to relate—for example, how to stroke hair instead of pulling it.

Between 10 and 12 months, infants begin to realize that adults don't always approve of everything they do. A firm "no" can be quite effective in stopping an infant's behavior. Here are additional ideas for setting limits with mobile infants:

- Vary your facial expressions and tone of voice to convey your feelings rather than using a lot of words.

- If no one will be hurt, give infants a chance to work things out for themselves. Intervene only when you have to.

- Resist the temptation to say "no!" habitually. Save this word for dangerous situations so that when you do use it, the effect will be more immediate. The word "stop" is very effective—it tells the child exactly what to do. Then you can offer a positive suggestion for another play option.

- Always respond in ways that meet the needs of infants and help them to feel good about themselves. "Such a tired boy. That's why you're cranky. You'll feel better after you nap. I'll rub your back until you fall asleep."

- Try to show an infant why something is dangerous and then give her another interesting thing to do rather than distracting her or just focusing on what you don't want her to do.

Toddlers

Toddlers, who are striving to be independent and want to do everything for themselves, can sometimes try the patience of even the most caring and patient provider. Their push for independence must be balanced by the need to learn limits. Although toddlers are very likely to forget what you tell them from one minute to the next, they are beginning to learn what is acceptable behavior and what is not.

By this stage of development, toddlers are starting to use words to express their feelings. They can listen and usually understand what you say to them. The words you use and your tone of voice are very powerful tools in guiding a toddler's behavior. A calm but firm tone conveys that you care and that you mean what you say. Angry and loud words may startle toddlers so they don't hear what you are saying.

To encourage self-discipline for toddlers, try these strategies:

- Stop the behavior in ways that show respect and help toddlers feel good about themselves. "It's hard for you to stop pulling Laura's hair. We'll find something else for you to do."

- Try to understand why a toddler is misbehaving. Perhaps the child is overtired or worried about something. "You miss Mommy and you're afraid she won't be back. But she'll come soon and she loves you even when she is at work."

- Acknowledge the toddler's feeling but protect the child and others. "I know you are angry, but I can't let you hurt Sam."

- Anticipate dangerous situations and set up a safe environment to prevent problems. "You like to climb but this table is too high. Let's try climbing over here on these big pillows."

- Explain what children can do. "You can drive the truck on the rug, not in the bathroom." Or, "Use the crayons on the paper, not on the table."

- Offer as many choices as they can handle, to help them gain a sense of control/mastery of their experiences, while at the same time not offering a choice when they really can't make one. (For example, don't say "Would you like to have your lunch now?" when there really isn't a choice about lunchtime.

Preschool Children

Children between the ages of three and five are able to understand the differences between acceptable and unacceptable behavior, although sometimes their judgment is clouded by their desires. Explanations from an adult of what behavior is expected and why have more meaning for preschool children; they are developmentally capable of learning self-discipline. They can use words to express their feelings and to work out problems. Even so, preschoolers sometimes lose control and hit out. It is easy for them to become overwhelmed and behave in unacceptable ways. They need caring providers who can help them gain control over their behavior and learn more acceptable ways of expressing their feelings.

When you care for preschool children, you do a lot of talking and explaining to guide their behavior. Sometimes you can give children choices and help them to make decisions based on an understanding of the consequences. For example, if a child knocks down a tower built by another child, you might say, "Jessie, if you keep knocking down Carla's blocks, you'll have to find another place to play. You can build with the blocks, or I can help you find something else to do." This approach gives the child a choice but lets him know what is not acceptable. It helps the child develop self-discipline without losing self-esteem.

To encourage self-discipline for preschool children, try these ideas:

- Help children use their problem-solving skills to come up with a solution they can accept. "I can see it's hard for you to share your doll, Billy. Where shall we keep it until you go home?"

- Avoid problems by anticipating them and having children help problem solve. "If you keep the bubble solution on the floor, the little ones might knock it down. What can we do with the bucket so this won't happen?"

- Try to understand what is behind a child's misbehavior; talk with parents if you can't figure out the problem. "Jeremy didn't seem to be himself today. Is there anything you can think of that might be bothering him?"

- Focus on the child's behavior; don't make general statements that judge the child. For example, say "I like the way you folded up your blanket" rather than "what a good girl you are!"

- Help children understand how their actions cause a problem. "Anne, John hit you because you took his playdough. John, I can't let you hurt anyone. Tell Anne you don't want her to take your playdough. Anne, if you want some playdough, just ask me. I can find some for you, too."

- Stop behavior that is dangerous immediately and firmly so children learn to obey automatically when they hear your tone of voice. "Don't move, Matthew! A car is coming." "No biting is allowed here! I can't let you hurt anyone and I won't let anyone hurt you."

- Notice when children are getting restless and give them a way to release their energy constructively. "It looks like you both need to have some time to run. Let's get the stroller and we can all go to the park for a while."

School-Age Children

School-age children know the differences between appropriate and inappropriate behavior. However, they are still children, and they will act irresponsibly simply because of their young age. At about age eight or nine, they gain an understanding of right and wrong. They are interested in rules and are very concerned that problems be handled fairly. Problem solving can be used with younger children, but the school-age years are perhaps the time when children are most interested in working with adults to solve their own problems.

School-age children are more able than younger children to tell an adult what is bothering them, and they will even offer solutions. For example, an eight-year-old may say, "Tom cheats at Monopoly! I don't think he knows the rules at all." With a little prompting from the adult, the eight-year-old may offer a suggestion of going over the rules again so that everyone is sure Tom knows how to play. Your job is to be a good listener and to help children come up with solutions to their own problems.

Here are some strategies for helping school-age children solve problems:

- When a problem develops, help children stop, calm down, and consider what the problem is. If children are physically fighting, it will be necessary for you to separate them and let them know the rules: "I will not let you hurt each other. Let's talk about the problem."

- When the children are calm and have identified the problem, ask them to suggest some solutions. "What are some other ways we can solve this problem?"

- After you have a list of several ideas, remind the children what those choices are and ask them to choose one they want to try. "You've given a number of good ideas. Here's what I heard you say. Which one do you want to try?"

- Later, you and the children can decide if the solution worked. If not, they can try the process again and find a new solution for the next time the problem arises.

Problem solving with children takes time, but there are long-term benefits for both the child and you. When children can solve their own problems, they will be more independent and need less help from you.

As always, it is important to observe children to see if their behavior is telling you something about what is going on in their lives. School-age children have so many things to deal with, ranging from sharing you to winning their teacher's approval and being accepted by their peers. Sometimes their behavior reflects what is going on inside them or troubles they may be dealing with at school. Learn to "read" school-age children for these signs. If you simply react to the behavior, you're not really getting at what is bothering the child.

If you notice a school-age child acting differently than normal—bossing the younger children, sulking, or craving your constant attention—then chances are the child is "acting out" a problem. Gently talk with the child to determine what is going on and how you can work together to resolve the problem. Once the actual problem is addressed, the problem behavior will probably disappear.

Helping Children Learn to Share

One of the biggest challenges that you will undoubtedly face is helping children learn how to share. It is important to have developmentally appropriate expectations for learning this social skill. Young children are unable to take on another person's perspective. Therefore, sharing is foreign to them. With children younger than school-age, it often works very well to have a simple rule: The toy is yours until you are finished with it. This rule accomplishes two things. First, it gives children the security of knowing that they will be able to complete their play and feel satisfied. Without this sense of security, children will begin to hoard toys and spend their energy protecting their selections instead of playing and learning. Second, it places the burden of sharing on the child who wants to take away the toy. That child must share by waiting for a turn. Because most young children do not play with any one thing for long periods of time, usually the wait is of a tolerable length.

Of course, there will be times when a particular toy or material is so enjoyable that the play time does become too long for other children to wait. In that case, you can say to the child, "Other children are waiting to use this toy. Please finish your turn and then give Robby a turn." This approach leaves the child still in control of the exact moment of surrendering the turn, but you have still moved things along.

Note: It is important to remember that good care involves having some duplicate toys available so that children are not required to share all the time. Two or more pegboards, doll buggies, sets of crayons or markers, and so on are a must in a child care setting.

As children get older (later preschool years and early school-age), they become more capable of sharing. One of the best ways to encourage this is to help them see for themselves the rewards of sharing. When children play together successfully and work cooperatively on a joint project, they naturally learn to share. Encouraging children to play together is one way of promoting sharing.

Part of learning to share is learning to wait for a turn. For young children, having to wait five minutes for a turn can seem an eternity. It isn't that the child is impatient; young children really have no idea of how long a minute is. You can help them deal with the waiting in these ways:

- Use a kitchen timer to time each child's turn.

- Develop a waiting list so that each child can see when his or her turn is coming up.

- Use signs to post information, such as "Jenny gets to use the police officer's hat on Tuesday."

These suggestions help make waiting times more concrete for young children.

Responding to Challenging Behavior

The younger the child, the more adults have to guess what lies behind their behavior. Even adults sometimes can't explain what they are feeling or why they are behaving a certain way. Often, you have to be a good guesser to try to figure out what a child is thinking or feeling. When a child acts out — for example, by kicking, biting, crying, or having a temper tantrum — that child may be giving you a message:

- "I'm crying because I don't like the sun shining in my eyes."

- "I miss my mommy and I'm afraid she won't come to get me. That's why I'm crying."

- "I'm angry. That's why I hit Jamal."

- "I am afraid. That's why I won't let go of your hand."

- "I'm scared I'm not good enough. That's why I keep tearing up my pictures."

- "I need limits. That's why I'm running around the room."

- "I'm yelling because you put on my mittens. I'm big enough to do it myself!"

When a child's behavior tells you that the child is unhappy, confused, angry, or fearful, you still have to stop the behavior if it endangers the child or someone else. It helps if you can do this in a way that acknowledges the child's feelings and helps the child understand what is acceptable as well as what is not.

Consider the following strategies for intervening:

- Give attention to the child who is hurt: "That really hurts, doesn't it, Sally?"

- State what happened: "You kicked Sally and that hurts."

- Acknowledge the child's feelings: "I think you're angry because Sally wouldn't let you sit in the big chair with her."

- State what is not acceptable: "I can't let you kick because someone will get hurt."

- State what is acceptable: "You can kick this ball if you want to kick something, or you can use your words to tell us how angry you are."

- Help children come up with a solution: "If you want to sit with Sally, how can you let her know?" "That's a good idea. You can bring a book over to her and invite her to read it with you."

Guiding children's behavior is an important part of helping them grow and learn to live successfully with others. There is usually a good reason for a child's misbehavior and the more you know about the child, the better you can handle the challenges that inevitably come up when you care for a group of young children.

Guiding the Behavior of Your Own Children

For many providers, one of the nice things about running a family child care home is that you are able to be at home with your own children. Having your own children involved in your profession can also be challenging. It is often difficult for your children to adjust to sharing their home, their toys, and, most importantly, their parent with other children. You can expect this to be an adjustment for your children. They may not be able to say in words how they feel about the other children "taking over" their home. They may try to tell you with their behavior: crying more than usual, clinging to you throughout the day, refusing to share their toys, pushing other children away, or insisting on sitting on your lap. All of these behaviors are normal ways for a child to say, "You are my mommy or daddy, and I want to be sure I am still the most important to you."

One thing that can help your children to adjust to the new situation is to prepare them ahead of time for what it will be like to bring children into your home. Explain that there will be new children coming to play during the day. Allow them to put away favorite toys and special possessions that do not have to be shared with the other children. Once you have started running your program, you might try the following ideas for helping your children adjust to family child care:

- Be sure that your children have a space of their own in the house that can be off limits to child care children.

- Try to have separate toys for the "visiting" children so that your children don't have to share their toys with the others. Your children may enjoy helping you choose toys for the program.

- Set aside some time during the day that is just for your children.

Do not be surprised if at first your children like the idea of having other children around and then seem to change their minds and want everyone to go home. This is normal. A reassuring word from you, an extra story at bedtime, or some time alone together will help your children feel more secure.

Building a Partnership with Parents

For many parents, placing their child in someone else's care—even when they know their child is receiving good care—is a difficult experience. Parents will need reassurance from you that their child is happy, well cared for, and secure. By communicating with parents and involving them in your program, you can help reduce some of their concerns. When you work with parents to provide a warm, supportive environment for their child, you can develop a partnership that will benefit everyone.

Communicating with Parents

A true partnership depends on good communication. It begins before a child even enters your program. Take time to schedule a meeting with new parents so that you can get to know each other. New parents sending their first child to child care will especially need to be reassured that you will protect and love their child but not replace them as parents. Tell parents about your approach to child care, answer questions, and obtain information that will help you in providing care that meets their child's individual needs.

Some topics you might cover in this initial meeting include these:

- How your program operates (you might share a copy of a daily and weekly schedule with them).

- Your philosophy of promoting children's learning through play (you might show parents a copy of *The Creative Curriculum* so they can see firsthand the approach you'll be using).

- Approaches to discipline, mealtimes, toilet training, problem behaviors, and so on.

- Tips on making separation easier for both parent and child.

- Information on their child's eating and sleeping habits, likes and dislikes, fears, favorite toys, and activities.

- Policies and procedures of your family child care program.

The last item is very important. Family child care is a business, and most providers find it helpful to share their policies with parents in written form. By giving parents a written record, you can guard against possible misunderstandings in the future.

Items to put in writing might include the following:

Logistics:

- The hours that you provide child care.

- When the child is likely to arrive in the morning and be picked up in the evening, and how any changes in the schedule should be handled.

- Who will bring and pick up the child, including a list of those individuals to whom you are authorized to release the child.

- What you and the parent will each supply for the child (diapers, food, change of clothes, toys, etc.).

- How many meals and snacks you will provide.

- The holidays and/or vacations when child care will not be provided, and if parents are required to pay for these times.

- Your fees or payment schedule (including late fees).

- The names and ages of your own children who will interact with the children attending your program, along with any other family members that may be present from time to time.

- Termination policies.

Illness and emergencies:

- The name of the child's doctor or clinic.

- What you will do if a child gets sick, including which parent should be called first.

- Any allergies the child may have and what should be done in case of an allergic reaction.

- The need for written authorization if you are to give the child medicine.

- How the parents will notify you if the child is ill or will not be coming to your home.

- How you will notify the parents if you are ill or unable to care for the child, and who is responsible for back-up care—you or the parent.

- A permission slip authorizing walking field trips and/or the transporting of children by car or bus.

- The name and background of an individual you have designated as an emergency back-up for you.

Clarifying your policies and program philosophy with parents at the beginning will ensure that everyone understands what to expect. This will not only help eliminate misunderstandings but will make future communication with parents easier.

Keeping in Touch

Communication with parents is vital at the beginning of, and throughout the child's entire stay with you. You'll find that good communication benefits everyone. Parents can be reassured that their child is being well cared for. In turn, you can be reassured that you are providing children with care that meets their parents' expectations and that your efforts are appreciated. Best of all, children tend to feel more secure when they see that their parents and provider respect each other and are working together.

Here are some suggestions for keeping in regular contact with parents:

- *Arrange a time to talk* when the children are brought in the morning or picked up in the evening. When possible, occasionally stagger arrival and departure times so that you can spend a few minutes with each parent each day.

- *Let parents know when they can call* to talk about nonemergency problems or to discuss the child's experiences in child care. Ask parents if, where, and when they would like you to call them to share information.

- *Agree on the best time* for you and the parents to meet regularly at length to discuss how the child is progressing in your child care home. This should be at a time when the child is not present so that you may speak freely.

- *Encourage parents to write you notes* to share a concern or to discuss matters related to their child's well-being.

Daily informal talks, phone calls, and notes about how the children are doing can make parents feel a part of your program. Keeping in touch with parents on a regular basis will ensure that when problems do come up, they can be handled in a positive and constructive manner.

An effective partnership between you and the parents is sustained with mutual respect and trust. Each party has much to contribute to the relationship. Parents know their own children in a special way, and you can contribute your knowledge about child development. Here are some additional ways to set a positive tone for a partnership with parents:

- *Convey how central parents are* to your program and your curriculum. Let them know that there are many ways for them to be involved in their children's learning.

- *Invite parents to visit* during normal child care hours. Letting them see you and the children in action can help them feel comfortable about leaving their children in your care and will help them appreciate the fine work that you do.

- *Hold a family night or an open house.* Helping parents get to know you and the other families with whom you work can benefit everyone.

- *Ask parents for their advice* about new ideas you'd like to try. When their input is taken seriously, they are more likely to become involved. For example, you might ask for ideas on what style or size your new sandbox should be, or whether they would like to celebrate their child's birthdays.

- *Let parents know how great you think their children are.* Every parent wants to hear that their child is liked and thought of as capable.

- *Always maintain confidentiality.* Never talk about any child with anyone other than that child's parents (unless you are reporting a case of suspected child abuse or neglect to a professional).

- *Set up a parent's bulletin board* to post information of interest, and invite parents to contribute to it.

- *Keep a journal for each child,* jotting down short notes each day if possible. This could also be a place where parents could leave messages for you, but the primary purpose might be to tell parents fun stories about their children.

Getting Parents Involved

Almost all parents have something important to offer. You will benefit and so will the children if you can find a way for parents to make meaningful contributions to your family child care program. Contributions can be in many forms (most of which don't require money): for instance, time spent making materials, gathering supplies, or helping out with an activity. Although parents will have varying desires and abilities to help, most are willing to participate in some way if they feel that they are respected, needed, and valued.

Ways in Which Parents Can Contribute to Your Program

- Collecting materials that the children can use for activities (old magazines, fabric scraps, collections, dress-up clothes, and props).

- Helping with projects such as building a sandbox, making smocks, and constructing easels.

- Helping plan and celebrate special occasions such as holidays and birthdays.

- Accompanying you and the children on a field trip.

- Joining you and the children for breakfast or lunch.

- Having the children visit them at work.

- Attending an informal gathering of your child care parents or a larger meeting of parents from several child care homes to hear a guest speaker or talk about a topic of interest.

When parents can contribute to the program their child attends, they feel that they are really part of a partnership. One of the most effective ways to encourage this partnership is to help parents understand your curriculum.

Sharing the Curriculum with Parents

Sharing your curriculum with parents has two major benefits. First, parents will recognize that you are a professional who understands how children learn and grow. They will appreciate even more the important role you play in their children's lives and will be more likely to give you the respect you deserve. Second, as parents learn more about what you do each day to encourage their children's growth and development, they will be better able to support and extend this learning at home.

All parents want their children to succeed. However, not all parents understand what children of different ages are ready to learn. For example, you may have parents who expect you to teach their preschool children to read or add numbers, or parents who are concerned that you haven't taught their two-year-old to cut with scissors. You need to help these parents understand the value of a developmentally appropriate curriculum. You can do this by explaining the goals of your program and why you do what you do.

Here are some topics you might want to discuss with parents:

- *The daily schedule* you follow and how it helps children feel secure and more in control.

- *How you have organized the toys and materials* within children's reach so they can find, choose, and return what they need on their own.

- *How you talk to children* and ask open-ended questions so they learn new words, have opportunities to express their feelings and ideas, learn to socialize, and have opportunities to develop their thinking process.

- *How you help children develop self-help skills* by encouraging them to pour their own juice, dress themselves, and help care for materials and toys.

When you talk with parents each day, you can tell them about something their children particularly enjoyed and suggest things that parents can do at home to build on what children are learning in your program. To avoid being intrusive, you might first ask parents if they want ideas for home. Otherwise, parents might feel offended, thinking you are making judgments about what goes on in their homes. Also, there are many parents who won't need ideas, and your suggestions may seem condescending. Don't forget to ask parents for ideas — they are in the best position to know what their children might enjoy.

Daily conversations have the advantage of being informal and non-threatening. Here are some examples of things you might say to initiate a conversation with parents at the end of the day.

- "Ever since you told me that John stood up for the first time, I've been encouraging him to pull up on the furniture here. He's so proud of his new ability."

- "Eric really loves to sort things. He organized my whole button collection today. Does he ever help you sort things like the laundry at home? Sorting is an important skill for reading and math, so if you want to encourage that, you might want to help him start some collections at home."

- "Sarah had a great time today dropping things on the floor and watching them fall. I bet she'd have fun at home with some plastic containers and bottle tops."

- "Jenny has a wonderful imagination. She set up a grocery store with some empty food boxes and got two other children to play with her. Have you ever played grocery store at home?"

- "I've been meaning to offer you this recipe for playdough. Andy loves this activity, and it may come in handy some rainy day when you are looking for things to do. This recipe is better than the kind they sell because it doesn't stick to carpets and won't harm children if it's accidently swallowed."

As noted, daily communications can be very effective in helping parents learn more about your program, what their children are doing while they are at work, and how they can support their child's learning and growth at home. Ongoing, informal communications with parents can be improved in these ways:

- *Greet the parents by name* and make them feel as welcome as their children.

- *Ask about experiences* such as what the child did the night before or over the weekend, or any special events that may affect the child's behavior.

- *Solicit parents' advice* about their children in terms of how they would like to participate.

- *Offer support* by saying things like this: "It's hard to say goodbye. If you'd like to give Tyrone one more reassuring hug, I'll give some special attention after you leave. Call us when you get to work, and I'll let you know how he's doing."

- *Be a good listener* and take their concerns seriously.

- *Check out what parents say* to be sure you have understood them correctly.

- *Give clear "I messages"* stating what you feel and need rather than what they are doing in a given situation. Judgmental statements only put people on the defensive.

In addition to these informal communications, some providers like to hold workshops for their parents. The next section briefly discusses how this can be done.

Conducting Workshops for Parents

Planning workshops occasionally with parents can be fun for them and for you. If held on a convenient weekend day or during an evening of the work week, workshops allow you to communicate with parents at greater length in a more convenient forum. Workshops give you an opportunity to share some of the ways in which you both support children's learning and to suggest activities that parents can try at home. Workshops can also be used as a time for doing projects together, such as making learning materials or building equipment. Here are some suggestions for workshops you can offer parents.

Dramatic Play

- Encouraging dramatic play at home: providing realistic toys, letting children try grown-up clothing and jewelry, and promoting doll play.

- Making costumes for the children to use: prince and princess costumes, hospital uniforms, space suits.

- Making prop boxes together: hairdresser, gas station, post office.

Blocks

- Encouraging block play at home: hints for storage include using containers with picture labels rather than dumping blocks into a toy chest.

- Showing parents how blocks can be used to teach math, promote problem-solving skills, and extend dramatic play.

- Assembling props for block play, such as people, animals, cars and trucks.

- Making homemade blocks from foam rubber or milk cartons.

- Saving large cardboard cartons for children to crawl through and play in.

Toys

- Demonstrating how parents can help children use toys at home to develop fine muscle skills, learn to solve problems, match, and classify.

- Allowing children to play with household objects such as plastic containers, pots, and wooden spoons.

- Scouting yard sales for toys.

- Making homemade toys such as Lotto games, self-help boards, and puzzles.

Art

- Sharing your philosophy of art with parents: process is more important than producing a finished product; why you don't use dittos or adult-made models; the value of displaying children's art.

- Assembling supplies for art such as felt, glitter, feathers, shells.

- Allowing children to play with household objects such as plastic containers, pots, and wooden spoons.

- Sharing recipes for art materials such as playdough, finger paint, clay, and soap crayons.

Books

- Sharing tips on how to read books with children: asking open-ended questions, letting the children turn pages, pointing out pictures and words, and responding to what each child says.

- Inviting parents to accompany you and the children to the public library.

- Sharing information on how to select appropriate books for children as well as your recommended reading list.
- Making books together, using the children's drawings or family photos.

Sand and Water:

- Encouraging parents to have sand and water play at home (outside or water play in the tub).
- Assembling props for sand and water play, such as measuring cups and spoons, funnels, sieves, bottles, and basters.
- Making a large sand tub for the children.
- Making smocks for the children to use in sand and water play or art projects.

Cooking:

- Sharing tips for cooking with children.
- Assembling cooking utensils.
- Making a child-sized workstation for cooking activities.
- Making picture recipe cards.
- Sharing family recipes and your own recipe books.
- Sharing nutrition and cooking information with parents.

Music and Movement:

- Encouraging parents to share music times with children at home; listening together, exercising to music, using music for dramatic play.
- Making instruments for use at home and in the family child care program.
- Sharing recommended records and songbooks with parents.
- Having parents accompany you and the children to the library or music store to make selections.
- Recording the children making up songs or chants.

Outdoor Play:

- Sharing with parents how to organize their own backyards for learning.
- Inviting parents to help create a garden.
- Holding equipment-building sessions: making tire swings, securing a log for wood-working, building a sand box.
- Having parents accompany you and the children on walks and field trips.

Not all providers feel the need to offer workshops: however, those who do find that both they and the parents gain from the experience. By spending this time together, you and the parents have an opportunity to get better acquainted. You will have a better understanding of the children's home life, and parents will in turn become more familiar with you and your program. Also, by actively involving parents, you send them the message that they are a vital part of your approach to child care.

Another way to share the curriculum with parents is to send home occasional written communications. In this way parents have something in writing to which they can refer when they want to know more about what is happening with the children in your care. On the next page you will find a sample letter to share with parents that describes *The Creative Curriculum for Family Child Care.* Parent letters for each of the activities are included in Part Two. In using these letters, consider whether you think the children's parents would appreciate communications of this type. Just as you know the children, you probably have a good idea whether their parents would be receptive to these materials. For those parents who are interested, letters can be a wonderful communication bridge.

A Letter to Parents on Our Curriculum

This is the first of several letters I will be sending you about my program. I want you to know a little about the curriculum I am using because together we will be helping your child grow and learn. I want you to feel that you are a part of your child's life here and to understand more about what we do every day.

In my program, I use *The Creative Curriculum for Family Child Care*. Its philosophy is that children should be allowed to grow at their own pace and to learn in ways that help them become confident in themselves as learners. The curriculum has two goals:

• to help children learn about themselves and the world around them; and
• to encourage children to feel good about themselves and capable as learners.

These goals guide everything I do in my program.

For example, I have organized my home to make it a safe place for children to explore and to learn. I keep the children's toys and materials on low shelves, in low and easy-to-open drawers, or on a blanket on the floor. This makes it easy for the children to find and play with the toys they like. It helps them learn how to make choices and be independent. All children also have a place to keep their jackets, blankets, and pictures to bring home. This lets them know they are a valued part of my family child care home.

When you visit, you will notice that we have a schedule that we follow. This lets the children know what comes when. It helps them feel secure when they know that every day I will read to them before naptime or that after snack we go outside. The schedule also allows for the times when we all do things together, such as music and story time, and times when the children are doing things on their own, such as coloring and playing with toys.

I plan many activities for the children. We build with blocks, dress up and make-believe, put puzzles together, read books, tell stories, play with sand and water, draw and paint, cook, dance to music, and play outdoors. All the activities are aimed at helping the children learn new things and feel good about what they can do. I encourage the children to do things on their own and to be curious and interested in all that's going on around them. I talk with them, ask questions, and answer their questions to help them learn new words and to express their ideas and feelings.

I value working in a partnership with parents. Many of the things we do here are activities that you can do at home. I'd be glad to share my curriculum with you and to have you contribute to our program in any ways that you like. To help you feel a part of what we do, I will be sending you occasional letters on the different activities we are doing and why we do them. You are welcome to join us whenever your schedule permits.

Part Two
Activities

Overview and Goals

Part Two of *The Creative Curriculum for Family Child Care* presents nine different types of activities you can include in your program. Each chapter has three sections:

I. Why the Activity Is Important explains how each activity promotes children's growth and development.

II. Setting the Stage provides a list of materials you can purchase, collect, or make and offers practical ideas on creating space and storage for these materials in your home.

III. Helping Children Learn tells you what to look for as you observe children and also helps you plan appropriate activities for each age group. To illustrate how you could involve children of different ages in the activity, we close each chapter with a sample scenario.

Sharing your program with parents is a central theme of the curriculum. In addition to the suggestions for building a partnership with parents in Setting the Stage, in Part Two we offer two additional strategies. First, we have included sample letters at the end of each activity chapter that explain what you do in your family child care program and why. You are free to use these letters or adapt them as you please. However, you should bear in mind that not all parents will appreciate getting a letter telling them what you do and/or suggesting things they can do at home; some parents might feel insulted. Others, though, might really appreciate learning more about your program in this way. On the basis of what you know about each of the parents in your program, you can judge whether these letters will be helpful to parents.

A second way to share the curriculum with parents is to display and use the activity charts for each age group. These charts are meant to be used as a quick reference for you, but they can be equally helpful in showing parents the wide range of activities you offer children.

As stated in the Introduction to Part One, we encourage you to read through the activities that interest you the most, and that are most appropriate for the children in your care, when you have a few free moments. Reading all of Part Two at once may be overwhelming; besides, you can't possibly do everything at once. Begin with Section I, which provides you with an overview of the particular activity. Then flip through the suggestions for how to set up and plan the activities, or use the activity charts to help you decide what to focus on first.

Goals for Activities

The children in your family child care home will be experiencing and learning many things as they play. As you observe and think about the children in your care, you can set goals appropriate for each one of them. Here are some goals for children in programs using *The Creative Curriculum for Family Child Care*.

Goals for Cognitive Development:

To recognize objects, people, and self.
To imitate actions of others.
To develop decision-making capabilities.
To develop problem-solving skills.
To develop language skills.
To develop planning skills.
To develop math skills such as matching, pairing, and classification.
To enhance creativity.
To begin to understand scientific and physical concepts and math concepts such as gravity, cause and effect, and balance; size, shape, and color; and volume and measurement.

Goals for Emotional Development:

To be able to express feelings.
To develop a concept of self.
To develop self-control.
To develop self-understanding.
To develop a positive self-image.
To develop the ability to stick with a task to completion.

Goals for Social Development:

To acquire social skills.
To cooperate with others.
To respect materials.
To respect other people.
To appreciate and value differences.

Goals for Physical Development:

To refine sensory abilities.
To develop large muscle abilities.
To develop small muscle abilities.
To develop eye-hand coordination.
To refine visual discrimination.
To refine listening skills.
To establish reading readiness skills.

You will find more information about what children can learn from this curriculum in each activity chapter.

Dramatic Play

I. Why Dramatic Play is Important

Dramatic play, sometimes called "make-believe play," is one of the most natural ways that young children learn about themselves and others. If you've ever taught an infant to play pat-a-cake, pretended to talk on the telephone with a toddler, provided two preschoolers with dress-up clothes so they could go to a "party," or watched a group of school-age children put on a circus, you have helped children engage in dramatic play.

What children do in dramatic play will depend on their age, their stage of development, and the experiences they have had. Dramatic play has three stages through which children will grow: imitative role play, make-believe play where the imagination starts to blossom, and socio-dramatic play in which children interact verbally with each other.

Children don't need a well-equipped doll house or a stage to make-believe: a shoe box can serve as a baby's bed; a paper towel roll can be a firefighter's hose. Dramatic play helps young children develop an understanding of the world around them, cope with fears and uncertainties, and learn to get along with others. In other words, dramatic play helps young children develop skills they need both now and in the future.

Here are some examples of how dramatic play supports development.

Children develop thinking skills by:

- imitating the actions of others (playing peek-a-boo or pretending to bark like a dog).

- solving problems in play (deciding they will take the sick baby to the doctor).

- using different objects to represent something they need in their play (a block as a bulldozer).

- sorting objects into categories (collecting the cups and saucers, sorting the dress-up clothes).

- remembering their own experiences and replaying them (being a baby or a mommy).

Children develop socially by:

- responding to what other children are doing (joining in a play episode that other children have started).

- sharing props and toys (telling another child, "You wear this hat and I'll take the suit-case").

- trying out different roles (pretending to be a doctor or a mail carrier).

Children develop emotionally by:

- assuming powerful roles (being a policeman or a large animal.

- replaying experiences that scare them so they begin to gain a sense of control (acting out scenes of going to the hospital or getting punished).

Children develop physically by:

- using large muscles (crawling on the floor pretending to be an animal).
- using small muscles (zipping and buttoning dress-up clothes).
- coordinating their hand movements (placing objects in a cooking pot).

These are a few of the many ways in which young children develop and grow through dramatic play. You can encourage this learning and growth by setting the stage for dramatic play in your home.

II. Setting the Stage for Dramatic Play

Children can engage in dramatic play anywhere and at any time. Two children playing with water may decide that they are actually pouring "coffee" and serving it. A child rolling out playdough may declare that she has created a "dangerous snake" and everyone nearby had better "watch out!" Puppets and flannel board figures lend themselves to imaginary play as children take on the role of the character they are holding. When you set up a special place with props for dramatic play, you will see even more imaginary play.

It almost seems as if children will engage in dramatic play without any encouragement from adults. Yet in the examples above, someone valued children's play enough to create the settings—water, playdough, puppets, flannel boards, and a dress-up area—that led to imaginative play. What children do and the amount of time they stay involved and interested depends a lot on the materials you provide and how much time you allow for dramatic play.

Selecting Materials and Props

You don't need expensive furniture and materials to encourage children's dramatic play. Real materials and realistic props tend to interest children the most and inspire them to try out new roles and play out scenes that have meaning for them. Parents can help collect many of these materials. You might be able to get donations such as work "scrubs" from a hospital or a firefighter's helmet from the rescue squad. Other good sources are second-hand stores and your own closets and storage areas. Listed below are some suggestions for props and materials that will interest children in dramatic play.

- *Furniture*
    A stove, sink, and doll bed made from cardboard boxes or wooden crates
    A small table and child-sized chairs
    Full-length mirror

- *Basic props*
    Two or more dolls, preferably male and female and ethnically diverse
    Two telephones
    Blankets and doll clothes
    A box to serve as a baby bed

- *Kitchen equipment*
    Pots and pans
    Wooden spoons, ladles, sifters, tongs, egg beaters, measuring cups, etc.
    Plastic plates and cups
    Dish towels
    An old tea kettle or coffee maker
    Cleaning equipment: broom, mop, dustpan
    Assorted plastic containers

- ***Dress-up Clothes***
    - Jackets, skirts, dresses, shirts, hats—for both boys and girls
    - Shoes and boots
    - Ties and scarves
    - Costume jewelry
    - Hats and wigs
    - Suitcases, pocketbooks, briefcases, lunch boxes, wallets, keys

Making Prop Boxes

One of the best ways to bring new ideas into children's dramatic play is to make some "prop boxes." A prop box is simply a box filled with objects that can be used by children to play out a particular theme. For example, you might have a prop box to play "hospital" or "supermarket." Here are some ideas of the props you might collect on various themes.

Baby
- Diapers and diaper pad
- Baby clothes and blankets
- Empty baby powder containers
- Cotton balls
- Rattles
- Baby food containers
- Baby bottles (plastic)
- Baby back-pack or front carrier
- Baby scale

Hospital
- White or green shirts
- Real stethoscope
- Band-Aids, gauze
- Paper and pencils
- Hospital gowns
- Play thermometers
- White sheet

Supermarket
- Cash register (could be made from a box)
- Empty food containers
- Plastic fruits and vegetables
- Paper bags
- Scale
- Baskets to hold food
- Play money

Laundromat
- Plastic basin to wash clothes
- Empty detergent boxes
- Clothesline and non-pinching clothespins
- Doll clothes to wash
- Play iron
- Washing machine made out of a cardboard box

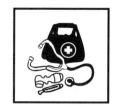

Shoe Store

Assorted shoes
Shoe boxes
Shoe-shine kit with clear non-toxic polish and rags
Foot measure (perhaps donated by a shoe store) or a ruler
Cash register (made from a box) with play money

Barbershop/hairdresser

Combs and brushes
Empty shampoo bottles
Curlers
Hat-style hair dryer without the electric cord
Towels
Basins

Office

Pads of paper
Stapler
Paper clips
Old typewriter
Adding machine or calculator
Telephone
Pencil, pens, and markers
Stamp pad and stampers
Briefcase

Painter

Buckets (with water to paint the house or fence)
Paint brushes and rollers
Painter's caps
Old sheet for dropcloth
Old shirts

Parents can be a great help in collecting the items for a prop box. You might also get together with other providers to make up prop boxes and then share them. That way, children in each program will have many more props to use to extend and enrich their dramatic play.

Creating Space

Although dramatic play can indeed take place anywhere, you will see more of it if you also create a special place for props and dress-up clothes. The most common theme in children's dramatic play is family life because this is what they know best. You can create a setting for playing house by making a corner of the living room or play room the make-believe area. A shelf or a chest can hold props such as dress-up clothes, plastic dishes, pots and pans, and so on. The more enclosed the area, the more children will like it. An enclosed area gives them a feeling of being someplace else, away from the rest of the activities. This is why children like to crawl under a table or behind a sofa to play and use their imaginations.

Furniture in the dramatic play area should be child sized. A cardboard box or wooden crate can be painted and made into a stove, a sink, or a bed for the doll baby. A small table and two chairs are wonderful additions to the dramatic play area. Covered with a bright piece of fabric, the table becomes an attractive setting for serving coffee and dinner.

Imaginative play can also be encouraged by adding props and materials to other activities. Putting out cups and pots when children are playing with sand or water, or adding rolling pins, cookie cutters, plastic knives, and plates to playdough can often lead children into imaginary games. Puppets and flannel board stories in your book area encourage dramatic play, as do small cars and wooden people figures for block building.

Dramatic play can also take place outdoors. By taking a box of props outside, you can encourage children to develop play themes in a new environment. Old towels can become capes; a sheet can be used to create a tent or a picnic blanket.

Storing Materials

For several reasons, it is a good idea to organize materials for dramatic play:

- It makes your job easier. When materials are given a specific place and that place is labeled with a picture to show where each item belongs, it is much easier for you to get children to help clean up after play time.

- It helps you keep props and toys clean and intact. Children quickly lose interest in dolls that are falling apart or in dress-up clothes that are torn or have missing buttons or fasteners. An orderly arrangement of materials tells children that you value their toys and materials and will help them take care of them.

- When materials are stored attractively in places where children can get to them, the children feel invited to play. Good storage allows children to find the things they need, make independent choices, and begin their play without delay.

Here are some ideas for storing props and materials:

- Wooden pegs on a board, for hanging clothes, hats, and bags.

- A shoe rack or hanging shoe bag, for shoes and other small items.

- A small coat tree, cut down to a child's level, for hanging clothes and bags.

- Three-tiered wire baskets that hang from hooks, for storing plastic food, ties and scarves, costume jewelry, and doll clothes.

- A piece of pegboard, for hanging dress-up clothes, pots and pans, cooking utensils, and mops and brooms.

Where you decide to store materials depends on your home setting; every home is different, and you have to use what you have available. A shelf, plastic storage boxes, or dishpans are ideal for holding props and materials. When you place a picture of the items to be stored in each place, children quickly learn where to find the things they need and how to return them to the proper place after play.

You can make labels using poster board or cardboard and magic markers to draw simple pictures of the items. If you cover the label with clear contact paper, it will last much longer. Tape the label on the shelf, the basin, or near the peg where the item will be hung. This helps children find the props they need and return them when they are finished. Matching the real object with a picture not only helps at clean-up time but is an important step in learning to read.

Time spent organizing materials in your home will benefit both you and the children. If you can easily find the things you need when you need them, caring for young children will be easier. If children are able to reach the play materials that they need and return them when they are finished, they become more independent and have more time to play.

Having created the space for dramatic play, we'll now explore your role in supporting children's growth and development through such play.

III. Helping Children Learn Through Dramatic Play

What children do in dramatic play will depend a lot on their ages and stages of development, their past experiences, and whether adults have encouraged and joined in their play. For children who are already skilled in make-believe play, you can encourage them to try out new roles. For children who have limited skills in make-believe, you can teach them how to play. Watching what children do will enable you to provide appropriate dramatic play experiences for each child in your program.

It's not difficult to know how to respond to children if you are aware of developmental stages and take time to observe children at play. As you observe, look for the following:

- What children do.
- What materials they prefer and how they use them.
- What they say to themselves and to other children.
- Whom they play with.

The information you get from observing children helps you respond in ways that support children's thinking, helps them come up with new ideas for their play, and makes them more aware of what they are doing. As the child care provider, you may wish to take on the role of participant. This means getting in and playing with the children in a low-key role—perhaps talking on the phone to a friend and saying, "Yes, we're busy today. Sally is cooking and Raymond is washing dishes." You may choose to help the children play by asking open-ended questions such as these: "Where are you taking your baby?" or "What are you cooking? I bet there are lots of hungry people around here."

It might be helpful to review the information on each developmental stage in the "Understanding Child Development" chapter of Setting the Stage. Then use the charts on the following pages that suggest appropriate dramatic play experiences. With each suggestion, you'll find a rationale for doing this activity that is rooted in child development.

Infants

Infants whose needs are consistently met by caring adults—people who talk to them and play with them—are building a foundation for dramatic play. It isn't long before an infant responds by laughing and trying to imitate your facial expressions, the sounds you make, and your actions. Games such as peek-a-boo, pat-a-cake, and rolling a ball back and forth teach infants how much fun it is to play with others.

Dramatic Play Activities That Help Infants Develop	Why These Activities Are Important
Emotionally…	
As you change an infant's diaper, take time to play peek-a-boo or sing a soothing song.	These daily interactions during routines teach infants that you care about them and think they are special.

Install unbreakable mirrors where infants can easily see themselves and the others around them.

Infants love seeing their reflection and it helps them develop a sense of self.

Socially...

Imitate an infant's babbling sounds to begin a "conversation" and continue as long as the child seems interested.

This teaches an infant about the give and take of interacting with another person and also promotes language development.

Hold an infant on your lap and talk about what older children are doing as they play.

Infants can also learn by watching older children play and seeing that you are also interested in the other children.

Cognitively...

Provide a small basket of kitchen props (small pots and pans, spoon, plastic cups) for infants to handle and mouth.

Infants learn about objects by touching, smelling, holding and tasting them.

Offer infants soft dolls to hold and play with and take turns rocking a baby doll.

This encourages older infants to pretend and to imitate what they see adults do.

Talk with infants on play telephones, encouraging them to talk or make noises with you.

Children learn language by observing you and trying to mimic what you do.

Physically...

Provide mobile infants with a sturdy doll stroller so they can push dolls and stuffed animals around the room.

This will encourage children to develop the strength and coordination to stand, walk, and push.

Let infants play with dramatic play props on their own, trying out hats, banging pot lids together, standing up to be admired in a mirror, etc.

As children learn about these props, they also develop small motor skills and improve their coordination and balance.

Toddlers

Toddlers are often content to play on their own or beside another child. A toddler might cover a doll with a blanket and say "night, night" or pick up a telephone and say "hello, goodbye" to no one in particular. Another child might be playing nearby—even doing the same thing—but the two children hardly seem to notice one another. This type of play is called **parallel play**. Even though they seem to ignore each other, however, toddlers are becoming increasingly aware of and interested in other children. They will imitate something another child does or says and play follow-the-leader. They will observe another child playing with a doll or "cooking" something and want to join in. It doesn't matter to

a toddler who is playing what role; they may both be playing the role of a mother taking care of the baby. Toddlers are pleased when you notice what they are doing and usually like to have you join in their play.

Dramatic Play Activities That Help Toddlers Develop	Why These Activities Are Important
Emotionally...	
Give toddlers real props that adults use: dress-up clothes, briefcases, old telephones.	Toddlers feel more grown-up when they can use the same things you and their parents do.
Introduce only a few dramatic play props at a time. Too many props at once become overwhelming.	Toddlers learn best when they can perform an activity well and show it to you over and over again. If you give children only a few props at a time, they have an opportunity to shine.
Encourage toddlers to act out stories featuring family members or people at the family child care home: "What do you think your daddy would do if he were in this kitchen?"	You help strengthen the bond between children and parents and children and providers when you remind children of all the things you do together.
Socially...	
Let a child who doesn't want to be involved in dramatic play watch from a safe distance. Gently encourage the child to join in: "What do you think we should do with this stethoscope?"	Some toddlers need help in developing social skills. They'll feel "safer" with your guidance.
Provide lots of familiar props and encourage children to imitate activities they've seen adults engage in, such as washing dishes, reading a magazine, mowing the lawn, etc.	Children learn through imitation. Because they admire adults, acting like grown-ups makes dramatic play fun as well as educational.
Cognitively...	
Encourage toddlers who are learning to pour juice for snack to serve you "tea" when they are playing make-believe.	This repetition of skills in different environments helps children learn.
Ask toddlers to describe their actions for you: "Where are you taking your baby doll?" or "Is your baby sad?"	This will help children develop language skills naturally.
Keep on hand prop boxes such as grocery store, hospital, and baby, so that toddlers can try something new when they are ready.	Children like to be in charge of their own learning. Prop boxes allow them to choose their next learning activities.

Physically...

Provide enough space in the dramatic play area so that children have room to move about freely while play-acting.

Toddlers learn when their bodies and minds work together. They also enjoy the experience more.

Encourage toddlers to use props that develop physical skills, such as silverware, an eyedropper, or a stethoscope.

As toddlers have fun and play, they develop small muscle skills at the same time.

Preschool Children

During the preschool years, children's dramatic play is full of imagination. They still enjoy using realistic props but can just as easily use a piece of rope for a fire hose or a ball for a steering wheel. Most preschoolers prefer to play together. They generally have lots of ideas but are also open to your suggestions. If you like to role play, you can have a great time playing with the children. When you do become involved in children's play, you can extend and enhance their skills and understandings about the world around them.

Dramatic Play Activities That Help Preschoolers Develop

Why These Activities Are Important

Emotionally...

Encourage preschoolers to take on play roles in which they can be successful, powerful, or in charge (e.g. teacher, doctor, parent).

Children need to feel successful in order to thrive. By play-acting these feelings, they contribute to their own sense of competence.

Ask questions to find out how a preschooler is feeling: "How does it make you feel when the baby keeps crying?" or "What would you like to tell the doctor before she gives you a shot?"

Dramatic play enables preschoolers to express their angers or fears in acceptable ways.

Socially...

If a child is shy or is never asked to join in dramatic play, find a way of helping that child join the group: "Oh, this baby's sick. It's a good thing I've brought the doctor with me."

Being accepted by peers is important to preschoolers. Some children may need help from you.

Provide lots of adult dress-up clothing for preschoolers to try on.

Dress props encourage children to play act adult roles.

Comment positively on what you see: "That baby doll is lucky to have a mommy who hugs her so much," or "You know a lot about being an astronaut."

Preschoolers thrive on positive reinforcement.

Cognitively...

Ask lots of questions to promote language development: "You look so dressed-up with that pocketbook and gloves. Are you going anywhere special?"

Conversations help children develop language skills naturally.

Have lots of props on hand for a preschooler to examine, such as a stethoscope, kitchen gadgets, or office supplies.

Children learn cause-and-effect relationships by playing with objects and discovering how they work.

Suggest that preschoolers put on a very short skit for younger children. Have everyone applaud at the conclusion.

Helping children accomplish a project helps them learn to see a task as having a beginning, a middle, and an end. Doing all these steps provides a sense of accomplishment.

Use real props whenever you can. An old telephone, for example, is a more effective learning tool than a toy one.

By picking up a real phone, children model your actual behavior and thus learn from you.

Physically...

Have props on hand that will encourage small muscle use: dishes to wash, paper clips to put on paper, doll clothes to change, etc.

At the same time that they are play-acting, children are refining their small muscle coordination.

Take dramatic play outdoors where children can include running and action-oriented activities in their make-believe play.

Preschoolers enjoy "throwing themselves" into dramatic play. At the same time that they are learning cognitive and social skills, they are improving their large muscle coordination.

Provide lots of jewelry, hats, and accessories for children to put on.

As they act on their desire to dress up and be like adults, children develop coordination skills.

School-Age Children

Many school-age children enjoy planning and putting on their own plays and shows. Writing a script, providing background music, and gathering elaborate costumes can all be part of their dramatic play. Such projects may last from an afternoon to several weeks.

Dramatic Play Activities That Help School-Age Children Develop

Why These Activities Are Important

Emotionally…

Encourage school-age children to use dramatic play costumes and props on their own without having to ask you for permission first.

Let school-age children know that it's OK to play dress-up if they want to, and have special props. Help them to make their own props.

Older children need to feel independent. They are more likely to want to do dramatic play if it's their choice, not yours.

If you have props on hand that appeal exclusively to the older children, you send them the message that they are welcome to play with the dramatic play materials whenever they feel like it. Some older children may need help in understanding that dramatic play isn't just for babies.

Socially…

Suggest that school-age children work together with friends from school to develop a skit about a topical subject, such as how to say "no" to drugs.

Encourage children to express their opinions on subjects such as school life, politics, or rock and roll as dialogue for a puppet show or a skit.

Ask a school-age child to serve as the director of a skit involving younger children.

Skits not only give children a chance to work and play together but provide a forum for dealing with issues that may be problematic. A group skit on dealing with peer pressure serves both functions.

Older children need socially acceptable ways of expressing their opinions and feelings about their world.

Some school-age children love being the boss; younger children look up to the older ones. You can help them understand the abilities and interests of the younger children.

Cognitively…

Ask school-age children to help you assemble particular prop boxes, such as ones for playing school or office.

Check out a book of plays for children from the library. Encourage the school-age children to stage a short play for the younger children or their parents.

Ask the children to write a play, puppet show scene, or a skit that could be performed either by the children or by the family child care children.

School-age children enjoy special assignments, especially those that lead to a product everyone can admire.

School-age children are natural performers; they love being directors and stars. You can tap into this motivation by making the stage production a learning experience.

Children will learn to appreciate the uses of drama when they get to decide how it should be enacted. As authors, they can make their voices heard.

Physically...

Set up a puppet theater in which school-age children can perform. Introduce marionettes as well, if appropriate.

If a child shows interest in acting or puppetry, get information from the drama department at the local high school or the public library on how to prepare for this work physically.

Puppetry demands skills of coordination, balance, and muscle control. While having fun, school-age children can improve their physical skills, too.

Building stage sets, setting up lights, controlling the curtain, and painting scenery develop large muscle and physical coordination. Acting skills such as juggling, dance, and mimicry also develop physical skills. By encouraging children's special interests early on, you can truly enrich a child's life.

Amy (4 years)
David (2 years)
Anna (10 months)
Bobby (7 years)

Involving Children of Different Ages

Can you encourage dramatic play when you have to balance the needs of children in different age groups? The answer is yes. Let's suppose that you have brought out a new prop box for playing "painter." Here's what might happen:

Amy pulls out the paint caps and puts one on.

"Ms. Painter," you say to Amy, "will you please come here and paint my dining-room table? It needs some fresh paint. Don't forget to bring your dropcloth. I don't want any paint on my floor."

"What color do you want?" asks Amy.

"What colors do you have?" you ask.

"I have red, blue, yellow, and pink."

"I guess blue would be good. It goes with my curtains," you respond.

David has been watching you and Amy carefully. He pulls out a paint cap and puts it on his head. "Want to paint, too!" he says.

"OK, Mr. Painter," you say to David, "Here's a paint brush and bucket for you. Would you please paint my cabinets?"

While the two children are busy playing painter, one other child is looking at books and another is putting together a puzzle. Anna wakes up from her nap; after changing her, you bring her into the dining room where the painters are still busy. Anna watches the action with great interest. You describe for her what is going on. "See what Amy and David are doing? They are painting my furniture. Aren't they doing a good job?"

Anna reaches for the paint roller one of the children is using. "So, you want to paint too, Anna," you say. Reaching into the prop box, you bring out a paint roller. "Here you are," you say, holding the roller for Anna. You spin it around to show her how it works and Anna repeats your action, making the roller spin. She's delighted by the action and repeats it many times.

"I'll be back in a few minutes to check on your painting jobs," you say to Amy and David. You take Anna and the roller with you as you go to play with the other two children.

Later that afternoon when Bobby returns from school, he looks through the new prop box. You say to Bobby, "Would you like to fill the buckets with water and take them outside to paint the fence?" Bobby thinks it's a great idea and agrees with your suggestion to have two other children join him.

This is an example of how you might encourage dramatic play with children of different ages by bringing out a new box of props. It illustrates several important points:

- Your involvement in children's play is very important.

- You don't have to involve all the children in the same activity at one time. Children can be given choices of what they want to do.

- Each child can participate in the play at his or her own level. An infant may be content simply to play with the props while older children will use them for make-believe.

- Simple materials can provide excellent learning opportunities.

Dramatic play is a very important learning activity for young children. The suggestions offered here should make it easier for you to provide children with experiences that will inspire their interest and engage their minds in meaningful play. You might also share the letter on the next page—modified to suit your program, if you wish—with the parents of the children in your care. It will let them know your approach to dramatic play.

A Letter to Parents on Dramatic Play

What We Do and Why

We do a lot of "make-believe" and "let's pretend" during the day. This is because dramatic play helps children learn to think, to express their ideas, and to become successful learners. The children love to use their imaginations, and I encourage them to do this. I have a drawer with dress-up clothes for both boys and girls—with hats, clothes, jewelry, and shoes. There's an assortment of play dishes and pots so the children can "cook" and enough baby dolls to bathe and rock to sleep.

Children often play "house" because this what they know best. But they also play "ice-cream truck driver" when they are outside with the tricycles and "car racers" with the blocks and miniature cars. They like to pretend about other places they've visited.

As the children play, I watch what they do and say. Sometimes I join in and become part of their play. I try to encourage them to talk about what they are doing by asking questions such as these:

- "Why is your baby crying?"
- "What kind of cake are you making?"
- "Where are you going, all dressed up?"

Sometimes what the children say or do during make-believe play tells me they are worried about something or are trying to deal with something that frightens them. That's why I encourage them to play "hospital" or "school" so that they can work through their fears in a safe environment.

Because make-believe play is so important, I encourage even the youngest babies to play games such as peek-a-boo or pat-a-cake. Sometimes I ask the older children to stage plays for the younger ones so that all the children can have a chance to use their imaginations.

What You Can Do at Home

You can try pretending together with your child at home. Children love to have you join in their play, and both of you will have fun playing and learning together. Here are some suggestions of how you can help your child develop good skills in dramatic play:

- When you are bathing your child, play "tea party" or "ships at sea."

- Dress up and put on a little play with your child.

- Role play doctor or grocery cashier with your child.

- Encourage your child to use his or her imagination and to pretend to be different animals or people.

When you take the time to make-believe with your child, you will both have fun, and you will be helping your child acquire important skills for successful learning in school.

Blocks

I. Why Blocks Are Important

Blocks encourage children to explore, to try out their own ideas, and to recreate the world around them. Whether made of hardwood, cardboard, or soft spongy material, blocks encourage children to build, to make patterns, and even to destroy what they have made and start all over again. From the simple explorations of an infant or toddler to the more complex buildings of a preschool or school-age child, blocks offer children unending learning opportunities.

When children play with blocks, they develop their physical skills. Lifting blocks, moving them around, and making structures help children develop balance and coordination as well as large and small muscle skills. Children also develop math concepts as they build when they notice that two small blocks can take the place of one long block. They solve problems methodically as they try to figure out how to make a bridge or a ramp. They create designs and patterns using blocks as an art material. Children develop social skills, too, as they listen to each others ideas and learn to share materials.

Here are some examples of how block play supports development.

Children develop thinking skills by:

- discovering the physical characteristics of materials (mouthing and squeezing a rubber block).

- learning how their actions affect objects (piling blocks to make a tall tower and knocking it down).

- learning to represent other places and things (building an enclosure of blocks, filling it with animals, and calling it "a zoo").

- solving construction problems (constructing a house of blocks with windows and steps).

Children develop socially by:

- understanding appropriate behavior (building a tower and knocking it down but not destroying another child's tower).

- making friends and developing social skills (working together to create a building).

- learning how to cooperate (sharing blocks).

Children develop emotionally by:

- building self-esteem and pride (showing what they have made to the provider or to their parents).

- replaying scary events so they can control their feelings (creating a setting to play hospital or monsters).

- developing independence (putting blocks away in the correct place when they are finished).

Children develop physically by:

- learning how to coordinate eye and hand actions (stacking cardboard blocks one at a time to make a tower).

- developing large muscles (carrying blocks around the room).

- developing small muscle control and learning to balance (carefully placing unit blocks so that a tall building won't fall down).

These are just a few of the many ways in which young children develop and grow through block play. You can encourage this learning and growth by setting the stage for block play in your home.

II. Setting the Stage for Block Play

Some planning is needed to make block play a part of your program. Most of the work required involves getting the blocks you need and then making a space available in your home. To make block play even more interesting to children, you can add simple props that will spark their creative ideas. And, of course, there is the challenge of finding a place to store blocks when children are not using them.

Selecting Blocks

Blocks come in a variety of sizes, shapes, and materials. There are cloth-covered spongy blocks, cardboard blocks, wooden blocks, small table blocks, and even homemade blocks made of milk cartons and newspapers. Blocks made of soft materials are good for infants and toddlers. Hardwood blocks are ideal for older toddlers, preschoolers, and school-age children. (Small blocks such as colored inch cubes, parquetry blocks, plastic snap-together blocks, and other table blocks are discussed in the chapter on Toys.)

Inexpensive Blocks

Purchasing blocks can put some strain on your budget, but there are alternatives to consider. The most inexpensive blocks are the ones made of soft materials—cloth or rubber blocks, cardboard blocks—and square wooden alphabet blocks. The cardboard blocks are hollow inside and typically painted to look like red bricks. They are quite sturdy and not very expensive. They are ideal for toddlers and young preschool children who like to carry them around, build with them, and create structures they can climb into to pretend.

Handmade Blocks From Milk Cartons

You can also make blocks from milk cartons and newspapers. Milk cartons are good because they come in graded sizes: half-pints, pints, quarts, half-gallons, and gallons. To make blocks from milk cartons, you need the following materials:

- cardboard milk cartons (two of the same size for each block)
- newspaper
- rubber bands
- contact paper to cover the finished blocks, preferably in solid colors

Here are the instructions:

1. Cut out newspaper squares the size of the bottom of the milk carton you will fill. You will need a tall stack of newspaper squares to give the block some weight.

2. Cut off the tops of the cartons so they have a square opening.

3. Slit one of the two cartons down each corner. Then hold the sides together with three rubber bands.

4. Pack the slit carton with newspaper squares stacked flat and pressed down. This fills the carton and allows it to stand up.

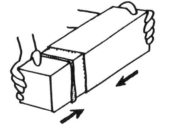

5. When the first carton is filled, put the second carton over the first, upside down. The rubber bands can be removed, as the second carton encloses the first. Finish the block by covering it with solid-colored contact paper.

Unit Blocks

Hardwood unit blocks are expensive to buy but a very worthwhile investment. They are made in specific sizes so that as children play with them, they learn important math concepts. Unit blocks also provide children with opportunities to solve construction problems, to learn science concepts, and to develop small muscle skills. Because they are made of hardwood, they will last a long time. If you can make this investment, it will repay you many times. A set of unit blocks includes a variety of shapes and specific sizes, as shown below.[1]

A less costly way to obtain unit blocks is to make them yourself. It may also be possible to contact a local high school or vocational training program whose shop teacher is willing to organize a student project to make the blocks you need. Be sure they use hardwood (such as oak) rather than a soft wood (such as pine or poplar). The blocks should be cut to very specific lengths and sanded well to get rid of any splinters. The dimensions of the blocks originally designed by Caroline Pratt, Arlene Brett, and Eugene Provenzo (in The Complete Block Book. [Syracuse, NY: Syracuse University Press, 1983]) are as follows:

Units ....1-3/8" x 2-3/4" x 5-1/2"
Half units...1-3/8" x 2-3/4" x 2-3/4"
Double units...1-3/8" x 2-3/4" x 11"
Quadruple units...1-3/8" x 2-3/4" x 22"
Triangles..1-3/8" x 2-3/4" x 2-3/4"
Triangles..1-3/8" x 2-3/4" x 5-1/2 "

Large Hollow Blocks

Large wooden hollow blocks come in five sizes and shapes: a half-square, a double square, two lengths of flat board, and a ramp. Infants will crawl and pull up on large hollow blocks. Toddlers will step on them and jump off. Because these blocks are large and open on the sides, older children like the challenge of carrying them around and building with them. These children often create settings such as a fort, a house with furniture, or a bus. After completing their structure, the children can climb inside and make-believe.

---

[1]From Harriet M. Johnson, *The Art of Block Building* (New York, NY: Bank Street College of Education, 1933), p. 3.

Props For Block Play

Providing children with simple props can add a lot to their dramatic play with blocks. They can use props to wire an apartment house, to create a zoo or farms for animals, or simply to decorate their buildings. Props are easily stored in plastic containers or shoe boxes. Listed below are some suggestions for props that will make the children's block play more interesting:

- Small wooden and plastic figures of people and animals
- Small cars and trucks—metal or wood
- Doll house furniture
- Miniature traffic signs
- Shells and seeds
- Colored inch cube blocks
- Telephone wire
- Empty paper towel rolls
- Bottle caps and other collectibles

When you have set out the materials and prepared a place for children to play, you can step back and watch what children do. You will probably find that the children eagerly explore the materials. What they do with the blocks will give you ideas for encouraging their learning and growth.

Creating Space

It is important to have a secure place for children to use and store blocks. Ideally, it should be an area closed off on three sides to prevent the normal activity and traffic patterns of other children from disrupting or destroying the block building. A corner of a room with a shelf or couch perpendicular to one wall makes a great place to build. It is also important to allow plenty of space for children to spread out and play comfortably. It can be very upsetting for children if they accidently knock down their own or another child's building because there isn't enough space in which to move around.

Children can play with blocks on a smooth surface such as a linoleum floor or a flat, tightly woven rug so the blocks will stand up easily. Wooden blocks tend to create more noise as children build with them; therefore, you will want to provide a space away from where infants and toddlers are sleeping. If blocks are stored in boxes or carts, any area can become a space for block play simply by bringing the blocks to a cleared area.

You will also want to consider the rules that will apply in your family child care home with regard to blocks. Here are some good examples:

- Children can knock down only their own buildings, not someone else's.
- Blocks are for building, not for throwing.
- Blocks remain in the block area. (If children want to use the blocks with other toys or equipment, they can ask permission to take the blocks elsewhere, or they can bring the other prop to the block area.)

A low shelf to hold blocks is ideal because they can be arranged by size and shape. This way children know what is available and can select what they need. At clean-up time it will be easy for children to see where each block goes, and clean-up becomes a matching game as children place similar block shapes together. Using a picture label to show where each block goes makes clean-up a reading readiness activity as well.

If you don't have a shelf, a TV cart on wheels is a good alternative. You can easily move it out when children want to build and wheel it out of sight when they are finished.

Plastic milk boxes can also be used to store soft blocks. The smaller blocks can be stored in plastic dishpans labeled with pictures.

Having created the space for block play, we'll look next at your role in supporting children's growth and development as they play with blocks.

III. Helping Children Learn Through Block Play

Children use blocks in fairly predictable ways, depending on their ages, stages of development, and whether they have used blocks before. Knowing what to expect at each stage and observing how children use blocks will help you encourage each child's development. Block play typically proceeds in stages: children carry blocks; pile them and lie them flat on the floor; connect them to create structures; and make elaborate constructions.

Taking time to talk with children about what they are creating and the discoveries they are making helps reinforce and extend their learning. It's important to pay attention to the ways in which children use blocks. The following questions can guide your observations:

- What blocks do children select?

- How do they use blocks (e.g., as objects to carry around, as "food" for a picnic, to build a structure)?

- Do children tend to play alone or with a friend?

- Do they create designs or patterns with blocks?

- How long do they stay with a block activity?

- Do they name their buildings?

- Do they use their buildings as settings for dramatic play?

One of the most important teaching techniques in working with children during block play is talking to them about their structures. Making nonjudgmental observations and asking questions about their play will enrich their experience. You might say:

- "Billy, I see that you have made all your blocks stand up. That's different from what Jane has done—her blocks are lying flat on the floor."

- "Tell me about that tall tower you've built. How did you get it to stand up?"

Here are some suggestions for appropriate block play experiences for children at different stages of development.

Infants

It may seem strange to think about block building with infants; it's not an activity that infants are likely to undertake. Because they are at the stage of exploring and learning about the world through their senses, infants are just as happy putting a block in their mouth as an older child is in using blocks to build a city. Older babies may enjoy pounding and feeling hardwood or plastic blocks, but you must supervise play to ensure the children's safety. Soft, flexible blocks that can be squeezed, tasted, and thrown are appropriate for infants. As infants develop the ability to move on their own and climb, large cardboard or hollow blocks become an interesting challenge.

Block Play Activities That Help Infants Develop	**Why These Activities Are Important**
Emotionally...	
Talk about pleasurable sensations infants get from play with soft blocks.	Infants learn that we take pleasure in seeing their enjoyment.
Introduce infants to block play in ways that suit their personalities. Some infants will want to sit on your lap and watch block play; others will enjoy crawling around blocks that they can grab.	Children will be more likely to enjoy playing with blocks if you adjust your approach to match each child's personality.
Socially...	
Stay close to infants when you're first introducing blocks. Let children know that this is an activity you can do together.	Infants will learn to associate block-building times with being with you. They will grow to be more independent in their play once they feel secure enough to venture off on their own.
Carry infants to block play by older children and discuss what's going on. Involve infants in the play, but don't allow them to disrupt the older children's activities.	Infants enjoy group experiences. Older children, though, also have a right not to have their block towers knocked over by curious infants.
Cognitively...	
Give crawling infants soft, washable blocks that can be banged, punched, mouthed, and cuddled.	Infants need to learn what blocks are like so that they will know how to manipulate them during play. For infants, this learning takes place through all their senses.
Build a tower of soft blocks with infants. Let them knock the tower down. Keep doing this together for as long as the activity interests them.	Children will learn about cause and effect when they have an opportunity to observe firsthand that certain activities (swatting at a tower of blocks) causes certain effects (the blocks topple). Repetition reinforces the concept.
Drop a cardboard block to the floor from the air. As it lands, make a crashing sound such as "boom!"	Language stems from sounds and noises that infants utter aloud. They learn to associate the sound with the activity.
Physically...	
Place soft blocks at a distance from mobile infants.	You can encourage infants' physical development by placing interesting blocks several feet away.

Encourage infants to play with soft blocks in a space where they can bat at blocks undisturbed.

Free exploration will give infants an opportunity to not only learn about blocks but also to develop small motor and coordination skills as they move them about.

Toddlers

Toddlers will pick up blocks, drop them, carry them around, put them into containers or in trucks, and move them from one place to another. Although this may not seem like block play, toddlers are learning about the weight of blocks, exploring their different shapes, and discovering what kinds of noises they make when they hit the ground. They are developing large and small muscle skills as they learn about blocks. Older toddlers may begin to build with blocks. Typical building at this stage may look like a tower—blocks piled on top of each other—or a flat design on the floor.

Block Play Activities That Help Toddlers Develop

Why These Activities Are Important

Emotionally...

Encourage children to take out and return blocks and block props on their own.

Children will learn about responsibility and become more independent when you trust them to play with blocks on their own.

Introduce toddlers to hardwood blocks before letting them play alone. Show how to stack blocks, match them, and so on.

Provide wood or plastic people figures for block play. Ask a toddler, "Where do you think this Mommy and Daddy are going?"

Socially…

Bring toddlers together for block play: "Let's see what we can make from all these blocks. Sharon and Brian, could you both help me, please?"

Help toddlers notice how older children make simple towers and bridges.

Cognitively…

Give toddlers many opportunities to play with blocks on their own.

Ask questions as the children play: "How do you think we should move the blocks to get around this Stop sign?"

Regularly add new props and materials to the block play to maintain toddlers' interest.

Physically…

Provide a clear, unobstructed space for block play where toddlers can move about freely as they build.

Show toddlers how to even a stack of blocks to keep it from toppling over.

Learning takes place in steps. Toddlers need to feel competent with early tasks before they turn to more difficult ones.

When you talk about the toddlers' parents with them, you strengthen the link in their minds between home life and family child care life.

Toddlers may need your help in learning to share and play cooperatively.

Young children want to do the things they see older children do.

Toddlers need lots of practice using skills. Block building allows children to reinforce these skills as they build.

You can use the children's block play as a natural vehicle for extending their language.

A variety of props will keep toddlers steadily involved with block play. With each new prop, the children can add a new dimension to their play.

Toddlers need space to interact physically with blocks so that they can fully enjoy the experience.

Not only will stacking increase the children's enjoyment of block play, it will also improve their coordination and small muscle skills at the same time.

Preschool Children

It's a lot of fun to watch preschool children use blocks. The piles and floor designs that preschoolers make often suggest something specific to them, and they start using their buildings for a purpose. A line of blocks may become a road for cars, or a tall tower of blocks may become an apartment house. As preschool children gain more experience with blocks, they begin to make enclosures. They arrange the blocks so they surround an area into which they may put other blocks or props. They may make an enclosure and fill it with cars to become a parking lot, or they might take some bottle caps you have put out and use them to represent people in a house. Children at this stage of block building begin to name their structures and use them as settings for dramatic play.

Because preschool children are good talkers and have lots of ideas to try out when they play, there are many ways in which you can help them grow and develop as they play with blocks.

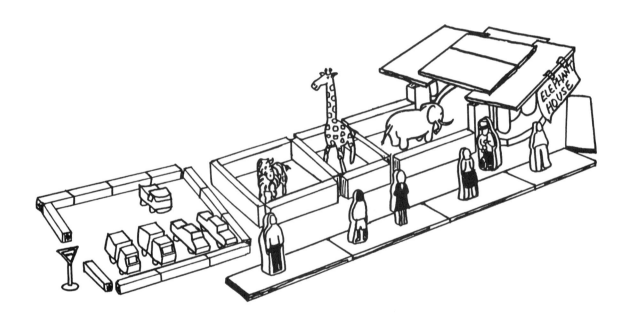

Block Play Activities That Help Preschoolers Develop

Why These Activities Are Important

Emotionally...

Take the time to comment when preschoolers make something with blocks that is especially creative or is impressively put together.

Your admiration will make preschoolers proud and more confident.

Help preschoolers put their feelings into words: "How did it make you feel when you were able to build a tower that didn't fall over?"

Preschoolers can't readily interpret their own emotions; questions like this help children gain self-understanding.

Socially...

Encourage children to work in pairs: "If you run out of gas, you could take your car to the gas station Matthew is building."

Provide preschoolers with block props that promote dramatic play: people and animal figures, cars, and trucks, for example.

Find something positive to say about every preschooler's efforts: "You were able to put every block we have into your building."

Preschoolers enjoy each other's company but may require your assistance in figuring out how best to play together.

By introducing dramatic play, you can help children act out problems and fears and recapture happy moments during block play.

Praise must be genuine if it is to have the desired effect. Look for something constructive to say that will let each child know you value him or her.

Cognitively...

Ask open-ended questions during block play: "You've been working a long time on that building. What can you tell me about your building?"

Introduce preschoolers to new props, such as a pulley with a string, and let them try to figure out how it works: "What ideas do you have about how to use this?"

If a child has built a special structure or spent a great deal of effort on something, preserve the effort: "Why don't we leave Jeff's rocket ship up so we can admire it for the rest of the day?"

Incorporate real props into block play: flags, potted plants, telephone wires, and so on.

Open-ended questions encourage children's language development because they need to respond with more than a "yes" or a "no."

Children enjoy figuring things out for themselves. The child who figures out how to use a pulley will understand how it works far better than the child who is shown how to use it.

By regarding the children's accomplishments as works of art, you build up their self-concepts.

Preschoolers learn best through interactions with objects from their own world. Real props hold special meaning to young children who are eager to behave like the adults they see using these materials.

Physically...

Give preschoolers small objects such as shells, colored inch cubes, buttons, and seeds to decorate the buildings they make.

Encourage children to carry large blocks back to the marked areas on the shelves where they belong.

Challenge preschoolers to construct towers and bridges like the ones they see in picture books or magazines.

Every time they put a decoration in place, preschoolers will improve their small muscle skills.

This activity encourages responsibility and promotes large muscle development, too.

As children build, they develop physical skills. Balancing blocks requires well-developed coordination between eye and hand movements.

School-Age Children

Blocks are as appropriate for school-age children as they are for the younger ones because school-age children love projects. They like to plan what they are going to do ahead of time and are usually quite clear about what they need. If they don't see a prop they want, they'll generally ask you for it.

Block Play Activities That Help School-Age Children Develop

Why These Activities Are Important

Emotionally...

Give school-age children free time to use blocks in whatever ways they want. Refrain from always assigning children a specific project.

School-age children respond positively to being granted free choice.

Praise children frequently but sincerely. Compliment the child's efforts, not just the finished product.

School-age children often seem so poised in their playing that they don't need encouragement. However, a cool exterior often hides self-doubts.

Socially...

Encourage a school-age child to work with a peer on a special construction project.

Older children are more apt to want to play with blocks if you approach the play as a social activity.

Let children decide what a building or construction should look like, even if it goes against your own opinions.

Children need to have their ideas respected if they are to be creative. You may be surprised at how well the children's ideas work out!

Encourage school-age children to work with preschoolers on block building projects. Show the children how to offer assistance without taking over.

Tutoring of younger children by older children serves both age groups well.

Cognitively...

Invite school-age children to assist you in a project to make blocks from milk cartons.

Many older children enjoy working on craft projects. Seeing them being used by the other children becomes an added source of satisfaction.

Ask school-age children to sketch a construction before building it.

This challenge helps children learn to think abstractly.

Show children pictures of bridges and buildings and challenge them to make similar constructions using hardwood blocks.

This encourages children to develop problem-solving skills in a game-like setting.

Give school-age children a building challenge to think through and discuss: "Can you make a bridge that the younger children could use to drive their cars over?" When they have explained their plans, have the children carry them out.

By asking children to explain their approach to you ahead of time, you help them put their ideas into words and plan through their actions.

Physically...

Encourage children to develop increasingly elaborate structures. Find drawings in magazines that will inspire the children.

Offer children a variety of special blocks to test their skills with: a selection of small pattern blocks for making designs and large hollow blocks, for example.

Advanced building techniques require manual dexterity. This activity encourages physical skill development at the same time that it promotes creativity.

Children have different strengths. If you give them a variety of materials to experiment with, most will find at least one type of block they can excel at using.

Using Blocks to Help Children Learn Basic Math Skills

Unit blocks are ideal for helping children acquire a basic understanding of math. Because they are cut to mathematical proportions and can be combined and used in many ways, they are perfect learning materials for young children. Using blocks, children learn concepts such as these:

- More and less: "I have more blocks than you do."
- Taller and shorter: "My building is the tallest."
- Twice as big: "I need two of those blocks to match this long one."
- Names of shapes: square, rectangle, triangle, cylinder.
- Numbers: three squares, four cylinders.

By playing with blocks, children learn important ideas that will help them understand math. For example, they practice sorting blocks by size and shape. This concept is called classification.

Classification: Putting blocks that are alike in a group.

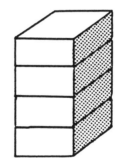
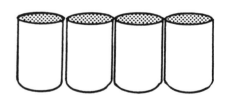

Playing with blocks, children notice differences in sizes and may place blocks in order from large to small. This concept is called seriation.

Seriation: Putting blocks in order—for example, by height from shortest to tallest.

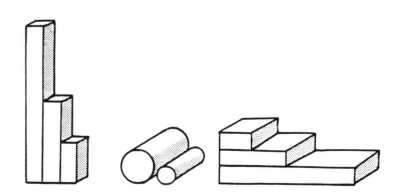

97

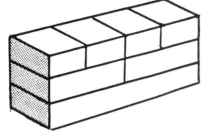

When children use blocks to create a design, they sometimes discover that they can fill the same amount of space with different kinds of blocks. This concept is called equivalence.

Equivalence: Discovering that four squares fill the same space as two units, which fill the same space as one double unit.

Although block play by itself leads to discoveries about mathematics, you can help children learn these ideas by talking with them and describing what they are doing. Here are some examples:

* "You found that *two* of these short blocks make *one* long block."
* "Your building is *as tall as* the shelf."
* "Yesterday you built a *tall* building and today your building is a *long* one."
* "All the blocks in your road are the *same size.*"
* "You used *four blocks* to make a big *square.*"

Involving Children Of Different Ages

Noah (5 years)
Mark (2 years)
Susan (2-1/2 years)
Jill (3-1/2 years)
Angie (9 months)

One of the challenges of offering block building for family child care is learning to include infants and toddlers while protecting the buildings of older children and extending the learning experience for each age group. Here is an example of how a provider might handle this challenge:

It's 3:10 p.m, and Noah comes racing in from the school bus. Excitedly he says, "I'm going to work on my city!" Over the past two days, Noah has drawn a blueprint of a city, showing where each building, road, and tree will be. You have arranged a protected area for him in the play room so that he can continue his "work" over several days.

Moments later Noah comes into the kitchen, visibly upset. "This is too much work," he says. You respond, "Why don't you sit and have snack with the rest of us, and we can talk about your project?" He sits slumped in his chair and eats slowly.

Once the children are settled in their places, you talk with Noah again. "How are you feeling about your block project?" you ask. "There's too much to do," he replies. After a long pause, he adds, "I need some help. I can't do all of this by myself."

"Well, Noah," you respond, "Mark and Susan have been excited about seeing your city. I know they're too young to build with the plans you've made, but I bet you could find a way for them to help you."

Noah thinks for a while, and then his eyes light up. "I know, they could get the blocks I need and bring them over to me. I just need to use my energy for building, not for getting all those blocks."

"OK," you say. "Let's give that a try after snack."

After the children have finished eating, you invite them to play near the block area. Holding the baby in your arms, you ask Mark and Susan to bring blocks to you so that you can hand them to Noah. (He is building his city inside an old refrigerator box to protect it.) Naturally, these two toddlers bring over not only the blocks Noah needs but also an interesting selection of other small toys. You pass the appropriate blocks to Noah and pile the toys nearby. With each delivery you say something encouraging, such as "Oh, you've brought two blocks this time" or "This fuzzy puppy can come over here, too."

Just as you have handed two plastic blocks to the baby, who is delighted to knock them together, you hear one of the toddlers saying "Mine, bock!" Mark and Susan have decided that it's their turn to do some building. Setting the baby down to play on her own, you pull out a dishpan full of soft, stackable blocks and sit back to see what the toddlers will do.

Mark is the first to make a tower of three blocks. He smiles, then cries "Boom!" and knocks them down. The baby looks up, startled at first, and then begins to giggle. The toddlers both scurry to build tower after tower just so that they can knock them down again. (Noah, now totally engrossed in his building, takes no notice.)

In the excitement, Susan starts to knock down Mark's towers. Mark stops and says, "No, mine!" You turn to Susan and say, "Those are Mark's blocks. Here, let me build a tower for you to knock down."

After several more demolitions, the toddlers wander over to the play stove to "cook" a few blocks. You turn to Noah and say, "I'm impressed. It looks like you've finished three buildings already." You hear Jill waking up from a late-afternoon nap. Picking up the baby, you meet Jill in the hallway. "Hi, Jill. Would you like to join us?"

"She can't be in here," Noah shouts. "She'll wreck my stuff."

"I won't let her do that, Noah. Jill, come and sit on my lap until you decide what you'd like to do," you say.

Jill snuggles in for a moment and then says that she wants to build, too. "I want the bricks. I'm going to make the biggest building ever," she replies.

"I bet you are!" you say.

This is just one example of how block play can be incorporated into family child care. Here are some points to remember when offering block play to children:

- Let a child work out the problem alone but with your support if she or he doesn't seem too frustrated.

- Offer assistance if you think a child needs your help: "You're trying to do something that's pretty hard to do. Let's see if we can work it out together."

- Suggest the first step in the solution and then encourage the child to think through the rest: "Maybe Mark and Susan could help you...?" Let children participate in the same activity, but help them find their own skill and interest level so they don't disturb others' play.

- Encourage children to work together cooperatively even if this means they are working on different aspects of the same project.

When you take an active part in children's play, you can have as much fun as the children playing with blocks. Your involvement in children's block play tells them that they are important and valued. And playing with children gives you many opportunities to build on their ideas and help them to learn and grow using blocks.

The following letter is one you can modify or send as is to parents in your program. It is one way of informing them about the block-related activities you provide for the children in your care.

A Letter to Parents on Blocks

What We Do and Why

Blocks are one of the children's favorite learning materials. We have several different kinds of blocks:

- soft, cloth blocks that the babies touch, throw, and stack.

- table blocks for building, putting into containers, and stacking.

- a small set of wooden unit blocks that the older children build with and use for make-believe play.

The children have many creative ways of playing with blocks. They measure different spaces; they create original designs; they use them as pretend "foods"; they use them as doll beds; they create houses and zoos.

When the children are building with blocks they learn about sizes, shapes, colors, amounts, and why it's important to build on a sturdy base. They do this by counting blocks, discovering which ones are the same shape, and learning the names of the different shapes. The children learn to share and develop their language skills as they play together and talk about their block structures.

When children build with blocks, I talk to them about their constructions and ask questions to get them to think about and share their ideas. I might say:

- "How many square blocks do you think you'll need to fill up that space?"

- "You built a tall building. Does anyone live in your building?"

- "I see you made a road for your car. What will happen when the car runs out of gas? What else do you need to make?"

These questions and comments are designed to help the children become aware of what they are doing and to get them to think of ways to extend what they are doing.

What You Can Do At Home

Hardwood unit blocks are expensive, but there are several other types of blocks you might want to have at home to extend your child's learning. For example, you might wish to purchase:

- table blocks or castle block sets
- colored wooden cube blocks
- cloth blocks
- cardboard "brick" blocks

I also have directions for making blocks out of milk cartons and newspaper. I'd be glad to share them with you if you'd like to make a set for your child.

Toys

I. Why Toys Are Important

Toys, games, and puzzles include a wide range of materials that children can explore, put together, push and pull, stack and create—sometimes for long periods of time. Appropriate toys give children opportunities to practice new skills such as putting pegs into small holes, and to develop new skills such as matching pictures that are the same.

Toys are almost a basic requirement of family child care. It's hard to imagine a provider without such materials. A good toy is one that can be used in more than one way. In fact, the more ways in which such objects can be used, the longer they will hold a child's interest and the more value you get from your investment. This is why construction toys, colored pattern blocks, doll houses, and sets of people or animals are so popular. Children tire most quickly of gimmicky toys such as wind-up toys that can be used in only one way and fail to challenge their imaginations.

A good toy can be used by children at different stages of development; children will simply use them in different ways. For example, one-year-olds and four-year-olds both enjoy nesting cubes. One-year-olds typically put these toys in their mouths, drop them to see what happens, or dump them into a container. Four-year-olds, however, will fit the nesting cubes together, make elaborate designs and structures with them, and name the color of each cube.

Many of the skills children learn using toys help prepare them for later schooling. For example, when they play with toys children learn about math, patterning, and direction.

Here are some ways in which children grow and develop by playing with toys.

Children develop thinking skills by:

- using their senses to explore a toy (chewing on a plastic ring).

- identifying colors and shapes (playing with colored toys or using a game with geometric shapes).

- learning directionality (turning puzzle pieces so that they fit together).

- classifying objects according to size, shape, or function (playing with a button box and grouping buttons in a muffin tin).

- being creative and solving a problem (trying to create a space ship with a set of pick-up sticks).

Children develop socially by:

- sharing materials that interest them (using toys, games, and puzzles together during free play).

- playing cooperatively (playing a Lotto game with another child).

- taking responsibility (using materials carefully and returning them to their proper places).

Children develop emotionally by:

- experiencing their own power (pounding a toy with a plastic hammer and seeing it move).

- achieving satisfaction by completing a task (successfully completing a wooden puzzle).

- extending their imaginations and creativity (using parquetry blocks to create unique designs).

Children develop physically by:

- using small muscle skills (picking up colored cubes and dropping them in a plastic container).

- practicing visual skills (playing with a set of stacking rings).

- coordinating eye and hand movements (stringing wooden beads).

When children have time to play with toys, they manipulate, explore and experiment. They learn many concepts and develop important skills while having fun. In the next section we provide suggestions for creating an environment that encourages children's learning as they play with toys.

II. Setting the Stage for Toys

Deciding where children will play; which toys, games, and puzzles you want for your program; and how to make them available are all important elements of setting the stage.

Selecting Toys

High-quality toys for children are appropriate to their developmental stage and abilities. When selecting toys for your children, you can use the recommended ages listed on the packaging to help you decide what is age-appropriate. However, your own observations will be your best guide in determining when a child is ready for a new type of toy. For example, when a child quickly loses interest in a toy, it could be that the toy is either too easy or too difficult. When a child becomes easily frustrated with a toy, it probably requires skills the child does not yet have. Two-year-olds who still put everything in their mouths are not ready for a button collection but could sort colored cube blocks or colored wooden beads.

Another criterion in selecting toys is that they should always be able to "do" what they are supposed to. For example, puzzle pieces should fit precisely so children aren't frustrated by trying to get a piece to fit. Pieces of a construction toy should also fit as intended, or children will soon lose interest and give up. Any toys that are donated or purchased at yard sales should be checked first to see that all the pieces are there and in good working order.

Durability and safety are also concerns. Puzzles should be wooden, rubber, or made with sturdy cardboard to withstand a lot of use. All materials should be nontoxic, safe, and designed to be used by many children. In general, having a few high-quality table toys that can be used by children of different ages is better than having many inexpensive ones that may not last or hold children's interest. You can also add to your collection by making matching games, puzzles, and self-help boards. (For further information on this topic, check the list in Selecting Furnishings and Materials in Part One.)

The toys suggested below are organized by age group. Within each group we have suggested toys that would be appropriate on the basis of what children are like at each stage.

Infants

- *Non toxic toys that can be put safely in the mouth:*

        Plastic rings and keys
        Plastic containers to chew on
        Large plastic blocks
        Wooden spoons and spatulas
        Teething rings of different colors, shapes, and textures
        Stacking rings
        Shape blocks

- **Toys for manipulation** (to grab, turn, squeeze, drop, push, pull, and poke):

  Balls
  Cloth blocks
  Stuffed toys of varying textures
  Cloth dolls
  Large plastic or sturdy rubber animals
  Toys to poke and pull at (e.g., busy boxes)

- **Activity centers** and toys that attach to surfaces with a suction cup.

- **Toys to drop,** hide, or fill a container with, such as cube blocks, nesting boxes, or shape blocks.

- **Toys that make sounds,** such as chime balls, mobiles, music boxes, wind-up radios, ticking clocks, and toy telephones.

- **Toys to look at,** such as mobiles, toys attached to strollers or high chairs, and mirrors for infants.

- **Toys to push and pull,** such as school buses, trucks, or large vehicles.

Toddlers

- **Toys that can be used independently:**

  Busy boxes
  Activity centers
  Snap-together toys
  Toy radios and telephones
  Shape sorters

- **Toys that challenge small muscles:**

  Large pegboards and pegs
  Stringing beads
  Stacking toys
  Nesting cubes
  Sorting boxes
  Snap blocks
  Bean bags and balls

- **Puzzles** with three to five pieces, made of wood with and without knobs, interlocking and noninterlocking.

- **Simple matching games**

- **Toys that encourage cooperative play:**

  Small figures for a doll house, farm, zoo, airplane, or school bus
  Puppets
  Hats
  Table blocks
  Fit-together blocks
  Sets of rubber animals
  Family dolls
  A doctor's kit

- *Toys that hold things:*

    Trucks or wagons
    Boxes and plastic containers
    Purses and backpacks
    Child-sized shopping carts and doll strollers

Preschoolers

- *Toys that stimulate dramatic play:*

    Family and animal sets
    Snap-together blocks
    Construction toys
    Doctor's kit

- *Games to play with others:*

    Go Fish, Old Maid, Hearts
    Lotto games
    Memory
    Candy Land
    Connect Four
    Blockhead
    Bingo

- *Toys that promote muscle and visual skills:*

    Peg boards and pegs
    Sewing cards
    Snap-together blocks
    Interlocking toys or manipulatives
    Plastic shape blocks
    Bean bags
    Self-help skill frames for buttoning, zipping, and tying
    Parquetry blocks or pattern blocks
    Sorting toys and shape boxes
    Magnetic boards with shapes
    Felt boards with shapes and felt animals and people

- *Collections of objects to sort, match, and compare:*

    Plastic bottle caps or baby food jar tops
    Buttons
    Coins
    Keys
    Seashells
    Fabric squares
    Different colored plastic coffee scoops
    Rocks

- *A variety of puzzles:*

    Wooden (about 10 to 17 pieces)
    Sturdy cardboard
    Rubber puzzles and insets
    Floor puzzles

School-Age Children

- *Card games*

    Uno
    Hearts
    Old Maid

- *Board games:*

    Checkers
    Chinese Checkers
    Candy Land
    Monopoly
    Sorry!
    Chutes and Ladders
    Boggle
    Junior Scrabble
    Trivia

- *Manipulatives that require more advanced small muscle skills:*

    Plastic snap-together blocks with small props such as wheels and windows
    Sketch boards
    Pick-up sticks

- *Craft kits*

    Paper dolls
    Colorform sets
    Bead design sets
    Origami

Although the inventory suggested above is given by age group, many of these materials can be used by children older or younger than noted here. Another point to keep in mind is that toys, games, and puzzles should be rotated periodically. A toy that the children aren't using can be put away for several weeks. When it is brought back, the children will probably treat it as a new toy. When rotating materials, however, don't remove them as soon as the children master them. Children find satisfaction in repeating recently learned skills over and over. You're very likely to see a three-year-old playing with an infant busy box or a four-year-old enjoying a simple puzzle.

Creating Space

In a home setting it may be tempting to put all the toys in a toy box. Doing this, though, makes it very hard for children to find what they need. Typically, they will empty the entire box (creating an enormous clean-up job) just to find the toy they are looking for. A

small bookshelf, a shelf in a closet, or a low table, as illustrated here, are good alternatives.

When toys are displayed in this way, children can see what the choices are, select what they want, and return the materials when they are done. This not only encourages them to be independent, it also makes clean-up time easier. Here are some additional tips for storing and displaying toys in your child care home:

- Put out a *manageable selection of toys.* Too many toys and materials can be overwhelming to children; too few toys will lead to arguments and unhappy feelings.

- Try *displaying toys in more than one room.* For example, one shelf in the kitchen could have toys and puzzles the children can use when they first arrive in the morning; the shelves in the free play area can have a larger selection of these materials.

- Toys with *small pieces should be stored in sturdy containers.* The boxes toys come in get ripped and torn, and pieces fall out. Instead, try storing toys in shoe boxes, sturdy cardboard boxes, plastic food containers, or plastic tubs. Child-sized shoe boxes are a good size for some toys. Ask parents to save them for you.

- Display toys so *children can see what is available.* Put puzzle and game boxes on the shelf next to each other, not stacked on top of each other. This makes it easier for children to see what is available. It also prevents pinched fingers and keeps wooden puzzles from falling on children.

- Be *safety minded.* Keep collections or toys with small pieces designed for older children out of the reach of infants and toddlers. It's preferable to have older children ask for these toys rather than putting them on the shelf.

You can make toys, games, and puzzles available in the early morning and again at the end of the day when children are preparing to go home. Like books and art materials, toys are good substitutes for television. They invite interaction, stimulate creativity, and keep children happy and involved for long periods of time.

The sample schedule in Managing the Day, Part One, identifies times during the day for free play. During these periods children can select the toys that interest them and continue playing as long as they like. You can also use these times to observe what children do and to talk with them to extend their learning.

Having set the stage for play with toys, you'll need to focus on supporting children's growth and development through such play. It is to this topic that we turn next.

III. Helping Children Learn as They Play with Toys

One of the advantages of selecting good toys for children and providing uninterrupted time for them to play and explore is that they will learn many skills on their own. As children use the toys you have selected, you can support their growth by observing what they do and talking with them. When you are watching children play, consider the following:

- What toys does the child like best?
- Does the child usually pick the same toys or eagerly try new ones?
- How involved does the child become with a toy? Is the child easily distracted?
- Does the child play for long or short periods of time?
- Does the child stick with a toy until a task is accomplished?
- Does the child usually play alone or with another child?

You can use the information you gather to interact with the children in different ways depending on the needs and interests of each child. What you say and do while children play with toys can help them learn new ideas and concepts. Combining your knowledge of each individual child's personality and interests with your expectations for each stage of development will help you plan appropriate experiences with toys.

Here are some suggestions for how you can encourage children's development through play with toys.

Infants

Infants explore toys by using their senses. They take in new information about their environment not only as they play but also as they watch you and other children. You can help infants grow and develop in many ways.

Toy Activities That Help Infants Develop	Why These Activities Are Important
Emotionally . . .	
During daily routines, talk about the bears in a mobile over the changing table or wind up a music box to lull a child to sleep.	Infants feel more secure when the routines in their lives are associated with pleasant experiences.
Make sure the toys you offer infants are safe to mouth and have no small parts such as buttons that can come off.	Mouthing of objects is a source of tremendous pleasure and one of the primary ways that infants learn about objects in their environment.
Socially . . .	
If separation is becoming difficult for a child, suggest to parents that they bring a special toy from home.	By welcoming treasured toys from home, you help a child feel more connected to the family while in your care.

Show the older children how to play "give and take" games with an infant: handing the infant a ball and saying "Thank you" when the infant hands it back.

This teachers an infant about relationships: sharing, respect, courtesy, and fun.

Cognitively ...

Provide toys for infants to explore and manipulate, such as stacking rings, shape blocks, balls, and rubber animals.

Children learn through all their senses. Toys that can be mouthed, punched, shaken, and easily grabbed are best for promoting learning.

Put out a few toys at a time; when infants tire of those toys, put some away and offer different ones.

If you put out everything at once, infants can be overwhelmed and will find it hard to concentrate on any one toy.

Talk about what an infant is doing: "You have the big red ring in your hand. And now you're holding it with both hands!"

Infants begin to make connections between the words you are using, and the objects and actions. This is important for language development.

Physically ...

Place a few toys (large pop beads, or small blocks) in a plastic sand bucket so infants can carry, dump, and fill the bucket over and over again.

These actions promote development of large muscles (carrying and dumping) and small muscles (filling the bucket) and eye-hand coordination all in the same activity.

Offer mobile infants a large, inflatable beach ball to roll, bat, carry, and climb over.

Responding to the ball's movement and trying to control it allows infants to enjoy lots of large muscle activity.

Toddlers

Toddlers are establishing their independence and want to do things for themselves. They are easily frustrated, often because they want to do more than they can or more than adults will let them do. They enjoy being with other children but are just beginning to learn how to share and take turns and may prefer to play alone. They are eager to please adults and like to be told they've done a good job or tried hard.

Toy Activities That Help Toddlers Develop

Why These Activities Are Important

Emotionally ...

Encourage toddlers to work with some of the simpler self-help boards, such as those with velcro fasteners.

Learning self-help skills will enable toddlers to dress themselves and become more independent from adults.

Choose age-appropriate toys for toddlers (e.g., five-piece puzzles, not ten-piece ones).

Toys should challenge toddlers but not frustrate them. By carefully observing what a toddler can and cannot do, you can provide just the right toys.

Have dolls on hand that toddlers can use for acting out family relationships during dramatic play. Make sure you have dolls that reflect the ethnicity of all the children in your care.

Dolls that children can identify with strengthen the children's self-concepts and make them feel more secure about themselves and their families.

Socially . . .

Provide duplicates of the children's favorite toys. When toddlers do share, reinforce this behavior.

Because sharing is a developmental skill, some toddlers will know how to share and others won't. You need to prepare the play situation to avoid fights over toys for those toddlers who can't yet share well.

Provide toys that imitate adults in action, such as a doctor's kit, sewing card, or fire engines.

Children love acting like adults. Toys that allow children to act grown-up are instant favorites—and ones from which children readily learn.

Cognitively . . .

Have lots of toys on hand that toddlers can use independently: a busy box, activity center, shape sorter, and so on.

This will allow children to play independently and use and reuse those they enjoy.

Ask open-ended questions. If a child is playing with a toy bus, you might ask, "Who's on your bus today? Where is the bus going?"

When you talk with children during their play, you promote thinking and language skills.

Keep a variety of toys on hand. Puzzles, dramatic play items, trucks, wagons, and matching games appeal to toddlers at different times.

Children need variety. You should have enough different materials to meet the toddlers' shifting needs and interests.

Physically . . .

Provide materials that promote large muscle development, such as ride-on trucks, balls, or hula hoops.

Toys and games are a natural way of helping children use and develop their large muscle skills. Throwing a ball through a large hoop helps children develop arm and leg muscles—in addition to being fun.

Select toys that strengthen small muscle skills, such as stacking toys, nesting cubes, and sorting boxes.

Nearly every table toy, game, or puzzle will help toddlers refine their powers of coordination, balance, and hand control. Even if you are using table toys to teach children a skill such as classification, you'll still be helping them physically.

Preschool Children

Preschoolers can express their ideas and feelings in words and like to talk about what they know. They can think up new and creative ways to use toys. They are able to play with a toy for an extended period of time and have the skills to do more things with their fingers and hands.

Toy Activities That Help Preschoolers Develop	Why These Activities Are Important
Emotionally . . .	
Encourage preschoolers to work with self-help boards and then apply these skills to dressing themselves.	By encouraging preschoolers to to be independent, you build their sense of competence.
Lend a helping hand if preschoolers become frustrated or impatient during play: "Why do you suppose some of the pieces fall out of the box when we shake it? Let's see what we can do to make this work."	Preschoolers can be high-strung emotionally. Appropriate intervention can turn a preschooler's fit of exasperation into smiles.
Socially . . .	
Suggest board games that children can play with in pairs to encourage developing friendships.	Children gain social skills as well as knowledge from playing together.
Encourage preschoolers to use materials as settings for dramatic play: "Where do you suppose that bridge you made out of Legos leads to?"	Playing with toys, games, and puzzles often naturally leads to dramatic play. You can derive the benefits of both types of play when you combine the two.
Give sincere praise: "Henry, you put that whole puzzle together yourself! Good job!"	Children respond positively to positive encouragement.
Cognitively . . .	
Ask questions to stimulate use of language: "What kinds of things could we do with this collection of buttons?"	Talking with preschoolers develops both thinking skills and language development.
Give preschoolers collectibles to sort, match, compare, and make designs with, such as bottle caps, seashells, and keys.	Preschoolers will enjoy exploring these collections, sorting, and organizing them.
Provide paper shapes to match pattern blocks so children can make pictures of patterns and designs they create.	Patterning is an important skill in mathematical thinking and for reading. Children can keep their creations this way.

Give preschoolers new objects to explore that have built-in "solutions" to their use, such as sorting toys or shape boxes. Let the children try to figure out how they work before helping out.

Physically . . .

Provide materials that promote small muscle skill development, such as sorting toys, brick and waffle blocks, and sewing cards.

Provide outdoor toys such as scooters, ride-on cars and trucks, skateboards, and tricycles that promote large muscle skill development.

Give preschoolers access to toys, games, and puzzles that refine eye and hand coordination.

Preschoolers learn most when they can actively manipulate objects and discover for themselves how things work. A preschooler who completes a sorting toy without any guidance from you will truly know how this toy operates.

You can help children work on small muscle skills while playing with toys. Whether or not this is your main learning objective, you'll find toys an excellent way of strengthening physical skills.

Outdoor toys are your best means of helping children operate and control their large muscles.

As you encourage their play, you can also help children improve their fine motor coordination and balance skills.

School-Age Children

Older children become interested in board games that have simple rules they can follow. They also enjoy making up their own games using cardboard, markers, magazine pictures, and so forth. In addition, they enjoy games they can play by themselves, such as dot-to-dot, beginner's crossword puzzles, jigsaw puzzles, and word games.

Toy Activities That Help School-Age Children Develop

Why These Activities Are Important

Emotionally . . .

Designate a particular drawer or shelf for toys, games, and puzzles that are specifically for the use of school-age children.

This will send children the message that their independence and interests are valued by you.

Reassure school-age children to build up their confidence: "I really like the type of design you made on the sketch board. The zig-zags give the drawing energy."

Even though they are older, school-age children still need frequent, realistic praise.

Socially . . .

Ask school-age children for suggestions of popular games they'd like you to have at your family child care home.

By so doing, you let children know that you respect their interests. You're also helping children become adept at games they're likely to want to play with their peers.

Let the children know it's OK to let off steam during a board game—but that rules still prevail.

Children need guidance to gain a firm understanding of when it is and isn't permissible to vent their emotions through action.

Ask the children to help you show the younger children how to play Lotto or a simple board game. Help them understand the abilities and limitations of the younger children.

Older children enjoy leadership roles, and younger children enjoy learning from the older ones.

Cognitively . . .

Ask the children to help you make Lotto games that can be used by younger children to learn shapes, colors, or practice classification.

Many children enjoy taking on a teaching role with the younger children. By helping you make learning materials, they can also take pride in their efforts.

Introduce a new board game by reading the directions out loud with the children. Then play the game together, frequently checking with the children to see if you're following the rules correctly.

Part of the fun for children in playing a board game is making sure that the rules are enforced exactly. They'll love being the judge for you.

Stock up on lots of board games such as Monopoly, checkers, and Boggle for school-age children to play with friends or with you.

School-age children can derive hours of pleasure from board games. You'll keep them busy, happy, and learning if you have challenging games on hand.

Challenge school-age children to invent their own board game, complete with a set of written rules.

Inventive children will love developing their own games, complete with rules. By encouraging children to write down the rules, you'll let them know that you think their ideas are worth preserving.

Physically . . .

Provide toys, games, and puzzles that encourage school-age children to exhibit their skills of coordination, such as pick-up sticks, Legos with intricate props, and dominos.

Older children can show real creativity and flair with toys. School-age children who arrange hundreds of dominoes in intricate designs develop physical prowess as well as creativity and problem-solving capabilities.

Encourage children to develop special skills. For example, if a child enjoys building with Legos, show the child some advanced techniques for working with these materials. Check out books from the library or write to Legoland in Sweden for instructions for making Lego designs.

When you encourage children to develop special talents, you enhance their self-image. At the same time, by developing more refined physical abilities, children become more competent in general.

Kate (4 months)	
Meg (4-1/2 years)	
Sandy (8 years)	
Blair (1-1/2 years)	
Doreen (4 years)	

Involving Children of All Ages

Keeping a group of children ranging in age from a few months to many years happily involved with toys can sometimes feel like a juggling act—but it can be done! Here's what might happen:

On the floor of the living room you have placed three ring stacking toys. You haven't said a thing to any of the children and are waiting to see how long it takes them to find the new toys. Soon you have five children sitting on the floor around the toys.

"Look at all these brightly colored rings," you say as you hand one to Kate and Blair. The baby immediately mouths her blue circle, and Blair taps his leg with his red one. Meg and Doreen quickly take ownership of the remaining two stacking ring sets, dump them out, and proceed to stack and restack. They smile and giggle.

"I know what I could do with these," announces Sandy. "I can spin them. My dad used to do that for me when I was a baby. Watch." Then he takes two of the rings and spins them on the floor. They whirl and delight all the children.

It's a nice quiet introduction to the toys, but soon it is clear that the three older children are no longer interested. To Meg and Doreen you say, "What do you suppose you could do with these rings that the babies can't do?" They look puzzled and have to think seriously about that one.

"We could squash them with our foot," Doreen suggests.

118

"Do you think that would be taking good care of our toys?" you ask.

"No, I was only kidding. Hm. We could wear them like hats," she says as she balances one on her head. "No, I guess that's no fun. There isn't anything to do with these."

"Well," you say, "can you think of something you could do with these if you also had some markers and paper?"

"Yeah!" says Meg, who had been thinking quietly. "We could trace these rings and make awesome pictures. C'mon, let's go!" They head off to the art table with several rings to trace.

"Sandy," you say, "why don't you and I play a game while I try to keep the babies occupied with these rings at the same time? It'd have to be a simple game, but I have a fun new twist for it. I'm going to try to cheat, and you have to watch me carefully to see if I'm following the rules. Do you think you want to try that?"

Sandy nods and goes to get a simple board game. While he is gone, you place the young children on the floor next to you with the remaining rings and pull over a few other toys to catch their interest when the novelty of the rings wears off. When Sandy returns with the game, the two of you play quite successfully until the end. (Sandy is delighted, of course, every time he catches you cheating.)

During the game, you have visually checked up on the preschoolers and have seen that they are engrossed in their tracing activities. Not only have they made circles of many colors on their paper, but they've discovered they can use the rings to form wheels for a picture of a car, to make a sun, and to draw a big snowman.

As you play the game, you talk to the baby and the toddler about what they are doing. You say, "I see you've put a red ring on the post, Blair. Can you find another ring to put on there?" Then you add, "You can pick up a ring with each hand. They aren't too heavy for you. It's hard to get the little rings on the post. Why don't you try this big red one?"

Kate stays interested in the toys you already have on the floor; the toddler wanders off to try out the self-help frame board with snaps. The preschoolers are still busy with the stacking rings, and Sandy has decided to play with Legos at the kitchen table.

Here are some things to keep in mind as you interact with children using toys:

- The same objects can be used differently but with equal pleasure by different age groups.

- What you do and say as you interact with children affects their play strongly.

- You can concentrate on one primary activity with one or two children while keeping an eye on what is happening with the rest.

Take time to share these experiences with parents at the end of the day. Some parents may enjoy getting a letter about what you are doing, and you can adapt or use the one that follows this page.

A Letter To Parents on Toys

What We Do and Why

You've probably noticed that there are many different kinds of toys, games, and puzzles in my family child care program. I try to select materials that will interest children of different ages. I also look for items that can be used in different ways. This keeps the children interested and encourages them to be creative.

Babies like toys they can feel, smell, shake, and poke. We have cloth balls, rattles, mobiles, and toys that make sounds when touched. Toddlers like to do things to toys—to push wagons, use a "busy box," or pile blocks into a plastic container and dump them out again. The preschoolers can handle puzzles and smaller toys such as shape blocks, put-together toys, and small wooden people figures. The school-age children enjoy board games and making models. I have a separate shelf with games, toys, and puzzles for them to use after school.

The children learn so many things when they play with toys. Toys with small pieces and puzzles help them recognize different shapes and develop the small muscles in their hands. These are important skills that will help them later in learning to read and write. The children use their imaginations when they play with toy animals and people. They feel successful when they push a ball across the room or hold on to a toy stroller as they learn to walk. They practice language skills as they play together and talk about what they are doing. They learn to share and to play with a friend.

When the children are playing, I often ask them questions or say things to encourage them to think or try out new ways to use the toys. For example, I might say:

- "Where did your ball go? Can you find it?"
- "How did you decide to sort the buttons?"
- "Can you find another card that looks just like this one?"
- "What kind of project could we do with these bottle caps?"

I talk with children while they play because this challenges them to think about what they are doing and to try out new ideas.

What You Can Do at Home

The toys, games, and puzzles you have at home for your child can also be excellent learning materials. Your child will appreciate and benefit from any time you spend together playing and talking. Let your child take the lead. Watch what your child does, comment on it, and ask questions to extend your child's thinking.

You can easily collect and make toys to use at home. Homemade toys are often better than many of the expensive ones you buy. Collections might include:

- buttons or plastic bottletops to sort in groups of similar objects
- plastic measuring cups and spoons
- empty wooden or plastic thread spools to string with heavy yarn

You can also make your own puzzles and games using cardboard and magazine pictures. If you'd like some suggestions or instructions for making these, just let me know. I'd be happy to share my ideas with you.

Art

I. Why Art Is Important

Many of us don't view ourselves as artists. How many times have you or someone you know said, "I can't draw a straight line"? In thinking about art in this way, we are focusing on the final product of an art experience. But art is much more than knowing how to draw or paint or mold clay. It is a means of self-expression as well as a satisfying activity in its own right.

When children splash brightly colored paints onto paper or roll out balls of clay, they are being creative. It doesn't matter if the painting resembles a rainbow or the clay a snake. What matters is that through experiences such as these, art allows children to show how they feel, think, and view the world.

Perhaps art's greatest contribution to any early childhood program is its ability to make children feel good about themselves. When they scribble with a jumbo crayon, fill paper with colorful strokes of paint, or glue a leaf to cardboard, children take pride in their creations. Through art, children learn not only to feel good about themselves but also to think and to refine their physical skills. Art supports children's growth in all areas of development.

Here are some examples of what children learn through art experiences.

Children develop thinking skills by:

- learning the properties of materials (feeling the difference in the texture of velvet and satin).

- identifying colors (mixing blue paint with yellow paint to get green).

- observing cause-and-effect (poking a hole through a ball of clay or adding water to powdered paint).

- labeling shapes and objects (drawing a circle and calling it a "sun").

- learning to solve problems (discovering how to balance objects on a mobile).

Children develop socially by:

- learning to cooperate (working together on a group mural).

- learning to share (waiting to have a turn at the easel).

- learning to plan (deciding who will do what on a group project).

Children develop emotionally by:

- experiencing pride (completing a drawing, painting, or collage and showing the finished work).

- expressing feelings (punching and pounding playdough or selecting paint colors to match a playful mood).

- asserting independence (starting, completing, and cleaning up an art activity on one's own).

Children develop physically by:

- practicing small muscle skills (coloring with crayons or tearing pictures from a magazine for a collage).

- coordinating eye and hand movements (finger painting on paper or drawing circles).

- learning to use balance (hanging objects from a hanger mobile).

These are just a few of the many ways in which children grow and develop through art. With a little planning, you can make sure that these learning experiences take place in your own family child care home.

II. Setting the Stage for Art

Art can take place at almost any time of the day and in nearly every area of your home. Yet like most activities, art is most effective when it is planned for, with specific goals in mind. What and how much children get out of art depends to a great extent on what you do to support children's art experiences.

Selecting Materials

It doesn't require a great deal of money to create a rich environment for art. Here's what you'll need to provide basic art experiences:

- Something to draw or paint on (a variety of papers).
- Things to draw or paint with (crayons, water-based markers, paints, brushes).
- Something to mold (clay, playdough).
- Things to clean up with (mops, sponges, brooms, towels).
- Things to put together (ribbons, fabric scraps, etc.).
- Something to put things together (paste or glue).
- Something that cuts (scissors).

In addition, you'll want to assemble some "extras" to add to the basics. In the list that follows, we offer some suggestions to guide you in selecting materials for your art program.

Item	Comments
Paper	Different types of papers allow children to experiment with texture, color, and absorbency. Newsprint, which is far less expensive than Manila art paper, can often be obtained at a discount (or free) from a local newspaper or a printer. Hardware and wallpaper stores are usually pleased to donate outdated stock books, and offices will probably supply you with used computer paper. In selecting paper for art work, choose large sizes such as 12" x 18" to give children the freedom they need to make bold movements.
Brushes	One-inch brushes with thick handles that are about 5" or 6" in length are easiest for young children to use for painting, but a variety of sizes offer choices of width.
Other painting tools	Sponges, potatoes, cotton balls, paper towels, marbles, ink stamps, feathers, tongue depressors, straws, strings, and eye droppers.
Easels	Although expensive when purchased new, easels provide an inviting and convenient place to paint. Make an easel or tack a piece of plastic to a wall to convert it into a makeshift easel.
Paint containers	Glass casters, muffin tins, baby food jars, Styrofoam egg cartons, orange juice cans, and yogurt containers.

Paint	Most paints sold commercially for young children are called "tempera paint." Tempera comes in two forms: liquid and powdered. Liquid tempera lasts long and produces vibrant colors; however, it is costly. Powdered tempera is much less expensive, but it must be mixed to the right consistency. If you choose to use powdered tempera, try adding a few drops of alcohol or wintergreen to the mixture to keep it from going sour. Ivory Snow improves the consistency of the paint and makes it easier to get out of clothes.
Finger paint	Finger paint can be made by combining 1 C liquid starch with 6 C water, 1-1/2 C soap flakes, and a few drops of food coloring. Good finger paint can be made by mixing 3 T sugar with 1/2 C cornstarch in a saucepan and then mixing in 2 C cold water. Cover the mixture and cook it over low heat until it is thickened. Add food coloring after the paint mixture cools.
Crayons and other drawing materials	A set of jumbo crayons that are easy for young children to grasp is a wise purchase. Make soap crayons for use during water play by mixing 1/8 C water with 1 C soap flakes and adding food coloring. Pour the mixture into plastic ice cube or Popsicle trays and allow it to harden. Offer white and colored chalk, pens, pencils, and water-based markers for further variety in drawing.
Clay and playdough	Commercial varieties are not recommended because they can be harmful if swallowed. In addition, commercial clay and playdough are difficult to remove from carpets. Fortunately, clay and playdough that have neither of these drawbacks can be made inexpensively at home. To make playdough, combine and knead 2 C flour, 1 C salt, 2 T oil, 1 C water and a few drops of food coloring. Adding 1 T cream of tartar or alum to the batch will make a smoother playdough. To make playdough that will harden, mix 2 C corn starch, 1 C baking soda, 1 C water, and food coloring. Cook over medium heat until the mixture forms a ball; cool and knead. The recipe for modeling clay is 1 C salt, 1-1/2 C flour, 1/2 C warm water, 2 T oil, and food coloring. Baker's clay can be made by mixing together 4 C flour with 1 C salt and 1-1/2 C water.
Paste or glue	White, store-bought varieties are inexpensive.
Scissors	If any of the older children are left-handed, purchase special left-handed scissors for them. All scissors should have blunt ends. Poor-quality scissors are frustrating to use. Be sure yours cut the paper without bending or tearing it.
Natural items	Collectibles from nature can be used in collages or for decorating. Collect acorns, leaves, feathers, flowers, pine cones, seashells, seeds, stones, and pebbles.
Sewing items	Household items such as beads, braids, buttons, cotton balls, ribbons, shoelaces, snaps, hooks and eyes, and yarn can be sewn (or glued) onto felt or fabric. Purchase large plastic sewing needles at craft or "five-and-dime" stores.
Fabrics	Material of every color and texture can be used for sewing projects, collages, puppetry, and so on. Excellent choices include burlap, canvas, denim, felt, fake fur, lace, leather, oilcloth, and terry cloth.

Kitchen/ laundry items	Common household items can be transformed into creative art projects. Examples include aluminum foil, bottle tops, plastic wrap, parchment, corks, egg cartons, bleach bottles, empty food and beverage containers, Styrofoam packaging, cans, paper bags, paper cups, paper plates, paper doilies, paper towels, Popsicle sticks, spray bottles, steel wool pads, string, and toothpicks. Food items such as eggshells, uncooked pasta, rice, potatoes, and beans can also be used in projects, although it's best to check that parents don't object to food being used in this way.
Other "artsy" items	Any number of items fit this category: glitter, confetti, broken clock parts, pipe cleaners, wooden beads, stamp pads and stamps, marbles, Styrofoam, shredded paper, old business cards, hangers, and wire.
Clean-up items	Mops, sponges, brooms, and towels are needed to return your home to its "pre-art" status. Store cleaning agents needed for removing glue or paint in locked cabinets.

Creating Space

Almost any area of your home can be used for art activities, but most providers prefer to designate certain places for specific types of art work. If you have a child-sized table and chairs in your home, this is probably the most convenient place for children to draw, paste a collage, or play with clay. Because some art materials can be messy, it is convenient to set up a space for art near a sink and away from carpeting and furniture that could be soiled. The kitchen or dining-room table can also be used for art projects. Cover the floor underneath the table with a large piece of plastic such as a painter's drop cloth.

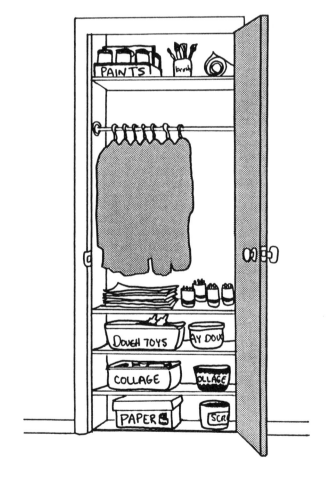

Painting easels can be set up in areas away from furniture, preferably over linoleum, tile, or wooden floors that can be protected with newspapers, a drop cloth, or an old shower curtain. When the weather is nice, easels or tables can be moved outdoors.

To help children readily find the materials they need, arrange art supplies according to how they're used. For example, drawing materials can be stored together in one grouping and collage materials in another. Here's how such a set-up would look inside a closet.

Here are some additional storage suggestions:

- Use egg cartons for storing string, scissors, pencils, pens, or brushes. Tape the carton's edges together so that the lid doesn't open when the carton is carried.

- Use empty coffee cans. Make a scissors holder by punching holes in the plastic lid that fits over the can.

- Use ice-cream containers or newspaper cylinders for paper. Each cylinder can hold a different type or color of paper.

- Staple or bolt ice-cream containers into a pyramid shape. Store collage materials in each of the containers.

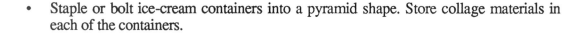

- Make paint caddies from cardboard six-pack cartons. Cover orange juice tins with color-coded contact paper, then fill this with the corresponding colors of paint and place the tins in each of the compartments. Would-be painters can carry these caddies to indoor or outdoor painting sites.

- Store clay or playdough in empty margarine containers, coffee cans, or mayonnaise jars.

- Use baby food jars for individual portions of paste or glue.

- Stand crayons up in frozen juice cans.

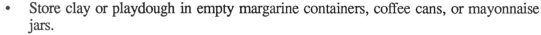

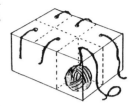

- Make a yarn dispenser from a cardboard box divided into sections by corrugated cardboard. Place individual balls of colored yarn into each divided space. Make holes in the top of the box and draw through the ends of the yarn balls.

- Use empty shoe boxes for art accessories such as scissors, wires, sponges, nails, and so on. Cover the boxes with contact paper for decoration or to color-code materials such as colored paper or felt. Paste a picture label on the outside of each box to identify the contents.

Arranging Time for Art Activities

Art activities are a frequent occurrence in family child care. Keeping paper, crayons, markers, collage materials, and glue available will make it easy for children to express their ideas through art. However, if you care for children of different ages, scheduling a messy activity such as finger painting is no easy task. Here are some general guidelines:

- Individual, nonmessy art activities can take place at almost any time of the day. Many providers use the periods following breakfast or before parents arrive as ideal times for quiet art activities.

- Messy activities are best scheduled for times when infants will be napping. This will allow the older children to finger paint or make collages free from fear that the babies will interrupt or disrupt. The mid-morning nap time is usually an ideal time for such projects. Should an infant wake up in the middle of a project, bring the child into the group. A baby in a high chair can finger paint with pudding while the older children finish their activity.

- Group activities are best scheduled when everyone is alert and eager. The periods following the mid-morning or mid-afternoon snack are good choices. Outdoor play time is another excellent time for group art activities.

We've examined how you can best set up your family child care home to incorporate art experiences into your program. In the next section we'll explore how you can work with children to enhance their growth and development through art.

A Word About Safety

Your careful planning and supervision when children use art materials is important. Keep potentially dangerous materials such as glass containers, small items that could be a choking hazard, and objects with sharp edges or points out of reach of the younger children. Also be sure that any materials you use are non-toxic. This approach will help to keep art time a relaxed, enjoyable experience for you as well as the children.

III. Helping Children Learn Through Art Activities

To build on children's natural enthusiasm and use art experiences to provide learning, you need to observe the children in your care to see what they are doing—so that you can respond in appropriate ways. As children engage in art activities, take note of their individual actions and interests. Here are some things to watch for:

- What art activity does a child seem to like best?
- Does the child tend to repeat the same activity?
- How involved does the child become in a given project?
- How long does the child maintain interest in a given project?
- Is the child able to complete a project?

Being aware of these aspects of a child's behavior will help you interact with that child in productive and individual ways. This is important because what you say and do with the child may have a significant effect on his or her development. Knowing that children go through stages in their art development is also helpful. Disordered scribbling will become controlled scribbling if children have the opportunity to use art materials. Similarly, the last two stages (naming a picture that is not planned, and representational drawing) flourish when children can explore art.

Here are some suggestions for appropriate art experiences for children at various stages of development.

Infants

Infants approach art as they do all activities: by using all their senses. They coo at the feel of velvet, delight in swirling pudding "paint" with their fingers, and find that playdough is even more fun to punch than to chew. By allowing infants lots of opportunities to explore art materials with their senses, you help them learn about these materials and what happens when they are used in different ways. Your encouragement also sends infants the message that art experiences are important.

Art Activities That Help Infants Develop	Why These Activities Are Important
Emotionally…	
As you stroke a piece of soft satin or a fluffy stuffed animal across an infant's cheek, talk about how soft and fluffy it feels.	Your words and the soft sensations will be soothing and comforting to the child.
Allow an infant to freely explore edible materials such as pudding or yogurt.	The sensory pleasure becomes associated with the act of being creative.

Socially…

As infants play together, talk about the way they look, the colors of their clothes, their favorite toys, and so on.

This helps infants become more aware of individual differences and similarities in themselves and others.

Provide a large sheet of butcher paper for infants to crumple, shake, and explore.

Infants will enjoy the sounds they can make as they explore and manipulate the paper and will have fun playing together.

Cognitively…

Use materials with a variety of sensory properties as art materials: add flavored gelatin to edible play dough; add food coloring to whipped cream or pudding "paint."

Each new sensory experience adds a new dimension and inspires infants to explore and learn about their world.

Hold a prism so it catches the sun's rays and creates rainbows on the wall. Show infants the rainbows and how they dance.

This nurtures an appreciation for beauty and an increasing awareness of the world around them.

Physically…

Offer infants rattles and small objects they can hold and grasp in their hands.

Grasping and manipulating objects develops their small muscle skills which they will use later in art activities and for drawing.

Tape a large sheet of sturdy paper on a table so older infants can freely color using stubby crayons.

This promotes large and small muscle development.

Toddlers

With their rapidly developing physical skills, toddlers are naturally drawn to art activities. Having learned to grasp a crayon and a paint brush, they soon discover that they can create something with these tools. They can tear paper and glue feathers to form collages. They can spread finger paint over a large area and stand at an easel creating circles and lines. Art experiences are an important part of a toddler's daily life.

Art Activities That Help Toddlers Develop	Why These Activities Are Important

Emotionally...

Tape drawing paper to the table so they can scribble, rub, and paint without being frusted by the paper moving around.

Children learn best when they are in charge of their own learning. By being allowed to draw on their own, they become both independent and motivated to use art materials.

Plan age-appropriate activities for toddlers. For example, show them how to tear paper for a collage if they are not yet ready for scissors.

Because art projects are fun, we sometimes forget that many art skills are too advanced for toddlers. However, if you choose activities that match the children's skills, you'll keep them eager to do art.

Ask toddlers which of their pieces of art they would like to take home with them.

Most parents and most children are proud and admiring of children's art. By letting children select, they get an opportunity to preserve the creations they like best and most want to share with their parents.

Socially...

Set up a two-sided easel for painting so that children can play together but not have to share.

This is a perfect solution for toddlers who want to share company but not art materials.

Invite toddlers to join older children for group projects such as painting a mural or making costumes for a play.

Young children can benefit from both the guidance and the social experience of working with older children on a project.

Cognitively...

Provide opportunities for toddlers to draw or paint every day.

Toddlers never tire of art. It's a perfect learning opportunity because motivation is built-in.

Encourage toddlers to talk with you daily by asking open-ended questions: "Tell me about your picture" or "How did you make the clay do that?"

Art is an excellent forum for helping toddlers develop language skills. Focus on questions that deal with the process of art, not the products created.

Let toddlers have a say in their art projects. Even if you've carefully planned a group activity such as making puppets, don't force toddlers to participate if they prefer to do something else.

Children learn best when they're responsible for their own learning, so it makes no sense to force a reluctant child to join in. Let toddlers focus on what's exciting to them.

Physically...

Take art outside. Let toddlers paint a fence with water or draw a mural on butcher paper taped to the side of the house.

Outdoors, toddlers can move freely as they create. This helps them use pent-up energy effectively and also enables toddlers to improve their large muscle skills as they paint with broad strokes.

Select art activities that will enable toddlers to improve small muscle skills they've been working on. For example, in tearing and pasting paper for a collage, children strengthen eye-hand coordination.

Art provides a natural opportunity for helping toddlers improve their fine muscle skills. For example, if a child has been having problems doing self-help boards, the toddler will probably enjoy finger painting more than being drilled on the boards over and over. Art provides a "fun" context for physical skills development.

Preschool Children

During the preschool years, children love to apply their newly learned skills to art experiences. They enjoy making things. They like to experiment to see what happens when they mix all the shades of paint together in their painting. They take pride in their accomplishments and want the adults in their life to share this enthusiasm.

Art Activities That Help Preschoolers Develop

Emotionally...

Respond to artwork in terms of the children's efforts, not what they've produced. "What wonderfully bright colors you've used in your painting!" is preferable to "That's a nice house you've painted."

Question children to get them to express their feelings: "What made you decide to do your painting all in blue?"

Socially...

Schedule group projects such as making candles or casting molds so that children can help each other.

Encourage preschoolers to incorporate their artwork into the dramatic play area. "How do you think this mobile you made would look over the baby doll's crib?"

Display children's artwork in prominent places at the children's eye-level.

Why These Activities Are Important

Preschoolers are not adept at representational art. If you focus on what it is that the child has painted, there's a good chance you'll embarrass the child. Your goal is to encourage the child by focusing on how the child made the painting, what colors were used, where it should be displayed, etc.

One of art's main purposes is to express the artist's feelings. Your questions can help preschoolers understand how they're feeling about people and things.

Group projects are wonderful opportunities for working and playing together.

By bringing art into dramatic play, you can help children tie together different activities of their day. They can pretend how the baby would play with the mobile and enjoy its bright colors.

Because preschoolers are prolific artists, it's easy to have a rich supply of drawings to choose from. Children feel that you value them if you place their work where it can be admired by everyone (especially them).

Cognitively...

Ask lots of open-ended questions: "Tell me about this sculpture you've made of clay."

Talking about art with preschoolers encourages their language development and thinking skills.

Provide materials that preschoolers can experiment with. For example, encourage children to mix paint colors to see what happens.

Preschoolers are natural scientists. If you let them discover things for themselves, they'll understand the fundamentals of science and math.

Print the children's names on their completed work. Ask children where on the paper they would like their names written.

Children take great pride in authorship and creation. When you identify them as artists who create particular drawings or paintings, you strengthen their self-concepts.

Give preschoolers opportunities to use real materials in their work: buttons, wood chips, feathers, and Styrofoam packing materials, for example.

Children need first-hand experiences manipulating objects to learn about how things work, cause and effect, how to solve problems, etc.

Physically...

Select art activities that allow preschoolers to utilize their physical skills. Weaving, for example, makes use of hand muscle control.

By encouraging children to put their physical talents to work in art, you can introduce children to exciting new projects. At the same time you are helping children practice using their small muscles so that they can refine their skills further.

Do art activities outside where children can use their large muscles. For example, spread some butcher paper on the lawn and have a preschooler step into some finger paint and then walk, hop, or jump across the paper.

Taking art outdoors allows children to put some of their physical energies into art. A byproduct of this activity is that children learn to improve their muscle coordination and balance.

Encourage a preschooler to do art activities that encourage eye and hand coordination: sewing, beadwork, printing, and making etchings, for example.

Children having difficulties with these physical skills can work on them unconsciously by doing art. In stringing beads, a preschooler concentrates on making a necklace, not eye-hand coordination. The fact that in stringing a bead the child improves coordination is a bonus for the child.

School-Age Children

School-age children can begin and complete almost any art project. Most children of this age enjoy undertaking challenging craft projects that show off their skills. At the same time, they view art as a means of relaxation. They will doodle or sketch in their notebooks as they chat with their friends or listen to music. School-age children begin to think of art in the same way that many adults do—as a way to express themselves and escape the stresses of their day.

Art Activities That Help School-Age Children Develop

Why These Activities Are Important

Emotionally...

Let the children undertake art projects on their own, without assistance from you.

By giving children permission to do art on their own, you help them assert their independence.

Stress the children's efforts and creativity.

Art can be a great opportunity for building children's confidence.

Socially...

Find out what types of crafts are popular with the children's peer group and arrange a craft-making session.

When you undertake a popular craft project, you let children know you value their preferences. You also help children gain acceptance with their peer group.

Encourage the children to tell you what they like or dislike about particular paintings, sculptures, or other work of art.

Encourage children to openly air their feelings. Art is one area in which there is no right or wrong.

Ask the children to help you set up a group art activity such as finger painting or making molds of plaster of Paris.

Older children like both doing crafts and taking on leadership roles.

Cognitively...

Ask the children to assist you in making a bubble frame or a loom that can be used by other children.

School-age children enjoy helping out, especially in doing things about which they are able to feel a sense of accomplishment.

Check out some craft books from the local library. Point out activities that the children could do on their own by following the instructions. Macrame and papier-mache are good choices.

One reason why school-age children enjoy craft projects so much is that they like following directions that lead to an end result. They can take great pride in making a macrame plant holder themselves.

Suggest that the children make up a board game and design the materials for playing it.

Children love board games and may enjoy the challenge of creating their own.

Provide some biographies of famous artists for the children's reading pleasure.

Biographies are popular with school-age children who think a lot about what they want to be when they grow up. Linking art to reading helps children think about art as well as create it.

Physically...

Suggest craft activities that you think children might enjoy trying—sewing costumes for dolls or doing embroidery, crewel, or needle work. If you have a special skill, share it with the children.

If a child shows a particular interest in a specific artistic area, work with that child to determine what physical skills are most helpful for becoming proficient in this area. Develop some exercises for the child.

By providing children with opportunities for doing specialized art work, you also help them develop more refined physical capabilities.

You can help children see the relationship between the body and the creative mind by assisting them in pinpointing and developing physical skills that will help them in their art.

Special Activities

As you work with children, you'll find that art provides many wonderful opportunities for growth and development. Just including basic art materials in your program ensures that children will explore and learn through art. Yet sometimes it's fun for you and the children to try new and special activities. In the remainder of this section, we've picked some of the most popular art activities for family child care. Depending on the ages and stages of the children in your care, some activities will be more appropriate than others.

Painting Experiences

Have the children experiment with a variety of painting techniques such as these:

- Blow painting (using a straw to blow a glob of paint across the paper).

- Spatter painting (using a toothbrush and screen to paint stencils of leaves, feathers, etc.).

- Crayon resist painting (painting over crayon designs with diluted paint).

- Folded painting (placing globs of paint on a piece of paper, folding it, then unfolding it).

Printing

Even very young children can experiment with design printing. Using a thick consistency of poster paint, pour paint over a sponge until it is soaked with paint. Then, using this sponge as a paint source, let the children experiment printing fruit and vegetable designs on paper. Printing tools might include slices of fruits and vegetables such as carrots, potatoes, apples, and corn on the cob.

Printing works best when the fruits and vegetables are cut into chunks or wedges that are comfortable to hold. You can also print with nonfood items such as shape-sorter pieces, pieces of sponge, lengths of string, or odds and ends. You are limited only by your imagination and your willingness to clean up.

Printing with Body Parts

Being involved physically with art is especially helpful for very young children. Here are some body printing activities:

- Make footprints with wet feet on the sidewalk on a hot day.
- Walk or dance across mural paper after stepping in paint.
- Have each child make a hand- or foot-print mural on brown wrapping paper.

Etchings

Another fun and easy printing activity is to scratch out a surface on a printing "block" and then use this for making prints. Here's what to do:

- Give each child a printing "block" such as a Styrofoam food tray.

- Using forks, bottle caps, empty ballpoint pens, or nails (for older children only), let the children etch a design.

- Have the children paint over their "blocks" and then lay blank paper across the top. When the paper is carefully peeled off, it will carry a printed design.

Collages and Assemblages

A collage is made by gluing all kinds of objects onto a flat surface. An assemblage is a three-dimensional piece of art made by putting various things together. Assemblages and collages are wonderful opportunities for creative expression. When children are offered a variety of materials, each child creates something original. New creations can be made by adding materials such as fabric scraps, ribbon, wood scraps, macrame, or feathers.

When first introducing children to these activities, give them time to explore the materials and try out ways of attaching one to another. If children will be using fabric or yarn in their projects, water down the glue for a better result.

Puppets

Puppets are not only fun to create, they're also useful for developing body awareness, language concepts, and spatial relationships. They lend themselves readily to dramatic play and can serve as moral support for a shy child. There are many styles and ways of making puppets. Here are some of the more popular:

- Sock collage puppets: Invite the children to cut and glue collage materials onto a sock "head," forming facial features for people or animals. Alternatively, use gloves or paper lunch bags as puppet bases.

- Newspaper puppets: Using rubber bands and rolled newspaper, have the children make a puppet body that can be decorated and dressed.

- Papier-mache puppets: Have the children place strips of paste-drenched newspaper all over an inflated balloon. When dry, the papier-mached balloon can be painted to resemble a human or animal head. Clothing can be sewn around the "neck" of the balloon head to make a complete puppet or animal.

Necklaces

Both boys and girls enjoy making things to wear. This activity can be tied into dramatic play or table toy play that involves stringing beads. To make necklaces, children need string or yarn, some wax, glue or nail polish for stiffening the stringing end, and something bright and interesting to string. Here are some suggestions:

- Colored macaroni (if parents have no objections to using food in art projects); dye for the macaroni can be made from a mixture of rubbing alcohol and food coloring.

- Plastic straws that have been cut into various lengths.

- Dry cereal (if parents have no objections).

- Shells with natural holes in them; buttons.

Weaving

Weaving is a challenging but rewarding activity for older preschool or school-age children. To weave, children need the following:

- Something to weave on, such as:
  - Chicken wire
  - Mesh vegetable bags
  - Scraps of pegboard
  - Berry containers
  - Styrofoam containers into which holes have been punched

- Something to weave with, such as:
  - Pipe cleaners
  - Straws
  - Rug yarn
  - Ribbon
  - Twine
  - Florist wire

- Tools for weaving, such as:
    Stiffened yarn
    Plastic needles
    Tongue depressors with holes drilled in the ends

Some weaving materials, such as pipe cleaners or wire, are stiff enough to not require a guiding tool.

A Word About Coloring Books, Dittos, and Adult-Directed Projects

Many providers wonder if coloring books, dittos, or pre-cut models have any place in the curriculum. The answer is that they don't.

For one thing, it's nearly impossible for young children to "stay in the lines" of a ditto or coloring book figure. This sets up children for failure. In addition, these types of art experiences deny children an opportunity to use their imaginations, to experiment, and to express their individuality. Using coloring books, dittos, and models goes against the most important values of creativity. Simply put, they are not art experiences.

What should you do if parents want their children to use these materials? Take the time to explain to parents up front why you feel that these structured materials are not in the children's best interest. Most parents who look forward to seeing colored dittos and professional-looking art work really just want to know that their children are doing well while at family child care. What they want to see are signs of "progress." Completed dittos with their child's name on them seem to be proof that their child is accomplishing something during the day. By sharing your approach to art with the children's parents, you can offer them the reassurances they need that even without dittos, important things are happening for their children during the day. It doesn't usually take very long to convince parents that their child's green and purple version of a pumpkin is more of a treasure than a perfectly round orange pumpkin that an adult cut out and wrote the child's name on.

Displaying Children's Art

One of the most important reasons for including art in your family child care program is to make children feel good about themselves. And one of the easiest and most effective ways of doing this is to display their art prominently. Throughout your home you can decorate walls, bookcases, and the refrigerator with samples of the children's art. Be sure to include something produced by each child. Try to place the pictures or constructions at the children's eye level but not so low that infants can tear them down. You can also slip artwork behind clear acrylic panels fastened to the wall, or cover it with clear contact paper, to protect it from infants.

You might also ask children which of their art creations they would like to display in your home and which they would like to take to their own home. This lets children know that their judgment is respected.

Jeff (3 years)
Nancy (7 years)
Mary (2-1/2 years)
Barbara (7 years)
Joe (1 year)

Involving Children of All Ages

In addition to individual art experiences, it is also possible to have group projects if each child's interests and abilities are accounted for. Here is an example of how one group art experience was initiated and carried out:

It's a pleasant spring day, and you are just finishing a snack with the children while sitting on blankets in the backyard. The conversation has shifted to the puppet show that the group is going to present to the parents on family night. Jeff, Mary, and Joe come in and out of the conversation that Nancy and Barbara are having.

The two older children have led the younger ones through the preparations for the show, complete with making puppets. Now they have decided that they need a colorful, "nature-y" backdrop for the show.

"How about using some of the butcher-block paper we have on that large roll?" you say.

"Great idea! But what should we color it with?" they respond.

"Ler, ler," pipes in Joe.

"He means color," says Mary.

"Yes, I know. What do you suppose he wants?" you ask.

"Oh, he wants to color with crayons," they all chime in at once. "Let's get them," say Barbara and Nancy, getting the giggles at saying the same words at the same time. They go to find the large paper, and when they return they also have their pockets full of markers and crayons. You help them lay the paper on the patio and weigh down the corners with large stones. Quickly, the three younger ones have made their way to the paper, chosen their color, and begun to draw.

Having worked (with your guidance) with the younger children on this entire project, Nancy and Barbara know that the younger children are going to color in their own way. But still Nancy expresses her concern: "How are we going to get this to look good?"

After debating several ideas, they finally decide that a "modern-art-looking nature collage" would be best. That way, the younger children's scribbles and drawings would blend in. Nancy and Barbara go off looking for things from around the yard to glue onto the paper. When they begin the actual gluing, the younger children become interested. At this point, you suggest that they too look around the yard.

Each of the three children find pieces of rocks and sticks that they think would be good additions. "You've each found interesting things to put on our collage. Now, how should we get these things to stick onto the paper?" you ask.

The younger children have already noticed the older girls using glue, and they are waiting for it. "How about if we get some containers so that each of you can have some glue?" you ask. They think that's a great idea.

All four of you troop into the house (you are carrying Joe) to find containers to fill with glue, and then you return to work on the puppet show backdrop.

By showtime, the younger children have pretty much forgotten their coloring and gluing, for the afternoon of creating was what was really important to them. Nancy and Barbara are proud of using their creation, yet they also talk about how much fun it was just to make it in the first place.

As a provider, you can work with children to help them join in a collaborative effort to get a project done. Here are some things to remember when working on art projects with children of different ages:

- Focus on process, not product.

- Children can get excited about doing things together if you make fun suggestions and are easy-going about collaborative efforts.

- Working together on a project provides many opportunities for children to solve problems, develop social skills, and be creative.

You can help parents appreciate the importance of process-oriented art and its role in a child's development by sharing with them what you are doing. Discussing a child's work with each parent is one way to share your approach. The letter that follows may be helpful for some parents and can be adapted to suit your needs.

A Letter to Parents on Art

What We Do and Why

Art activities are an important part of my family child care program. Children love to draw, paint, play with playdough, and make designs with scraps of paper and glue. During the day, I set out crayons, paper, blunt-tipped scissors, waterproof markers, and playdough for the children to use during play time. I also plan a special art activity a few times each week, such as finger painting, making collages with glue and paper, or weaving.

When the children are using art materials, I am interested in giving them a chance to express their own ideas. I know that this is more important for their development than having them fill in a coloring book or make a particular product. I encourage children to pull and poke playdough, paint an entire paper with different colors, or just see how it feels to move a crayon around and around the paper. For the older children who are more interested in projects, I set aside many materials for them to use when they come home from school.

I try to avoid asking children what they have made because most young children have difficulty making pictures that represent specific objects. Instead I say things that help children think about what they've done. For example, I might say:

- "Tell me about your picture" instead of "What did you make?" This gives the children an opportunity to talk about anything they want without having to say that they made something.

- "You've used so many different colors in your picture. I see red, yellow, purple and green." This tells the children I have really looked at their picture and also helps teach them the names of the colors.

- "It looks like that playdough is sticking to your fingers. What could we do to make it less sticky?" This encourages children to problem solve and come up with their own solutions.

Sometimes the children like me to write on their picture what they have said—so you may see a drawing one day that says "the sun is smiling" or "this is my Mommy and Daddy."

What You Can Do at Home

You can give your child many hours of art fun at home by simply providing crayons, markers, paper, and paint. Pictures can be cut up from old magazines. One of our favorite activities is playdough. We make our own playdough so I can be sure that it is safe even if children put it in their mouths. Here is the recipe, in case you'd like to make it at home:

- In a bowl, mix 2 cups of flour, 1 cup of salt and 2 tablespoons of cooking oil.

- Add food coloring to about 1 cup of water, add to the flour mixture, and knead it into a ball.

You can keep homemade playdough for about two weeks if you seal it in a plastic bowl or coffee container. Clean-up is easier if you put a plastic tablecloth on the table first; the playdough hardens when it dries and is easy to sweep off the floor.

I'd be happy to share with you other recipes and ideas for art activities from *The Creative Curriculum for Family Child Care*.

Sand and Water

I. Why Sand and Water Are Important

Children are naturally drawn to sand and water play. These activities let children be messy in a world that usually demands neatness and order. Think back to your own childhood. Can you remember how much fun it was to blow bubbles through a straw or bury your feet in cool, wet sand? These experiences were enjoyable, and they were times of learning as well.

When splashing in a tub full of water, an infant learns what water feels like and how it moves. By sifting, pouring, and poking sand, infants also learn about sand's special qualities. As they grow and develop, children apply their knowledge of what sand and water are like in their play. Instead of just splashing water, they create a rhythm of splashes to propel a toy boat through a tub of water. Instead of just filling and emptying pails of sand, they'll form the sand into a castle and in time will refine their activities to add such things as tunnels and a moat.

Through their play, children learn many things. By burying a shovel and digging it up again, children learn about object permanence. By counting as they empty four cups of water into an empty quart-size milk carton, children gain a foundation for math. By pouring sand through a funnel, they learn coordination skills. When digging a tunnel into a sand hill, they use their imaginations to create a toll booth and run cars through the tunnel they've created. The skills children learn through sand and water play help them think, improve their physical powers, and get along with other children and adults.

Here are some ways in which sand and water play support children's growth and development.

Children develop thinking skills by:

- noticing how things are the same and different (sticking their hands into tubs of dry and wet sand).

- discovering how things change (adding food coloring to water).

- observing how their actions affect things (splashing water to move a toy duck; digging a hole in wet sand).

- gaining the foundations of math (pouring the same amounts of water into different size containers and comparing them).

Children develop socially by:

- practicing social roles (washing baby dolls and toy dishes in a wading pool).

- making friends (inviting another child to help build a castle in wet sand).

- sharing (letting another child have a turn with the water props).

Children develop emotionally by:

- seeing a task through to completion (mixing up and using a bubble solution).

- building self-confidence and pride (asking that a sand creation be left intact to show parents).

- developing independence (starting outdoor sand projects on their own).

Children develop physically by:

- developing small muscles (using a baster to transfer water from one container to another).

- learning to move eyes and hands together (using a tongue dispenser to trace figure eights in the sand).

- improving coordination (pouring water from a plastic bottle into a measuring cup).

By including sand and water activities in your family child care program, you can set the stage for learning. In the next section we'll suggest some ways to include these activities in your home.

II. Setting the Stage for Sand and Water Play

Without a doubt, sand and water play can be messy. Yet with planning, you'll find that you can keep messes and germs to a minimum. Children should wash their hands before playing together with water, and basins, sinks, or tubs should be disinfected after water play. Doing that and using the following suggestions will make the activity fun for them and low-fuss for you.

Selecting Materials

It isn't necessary to provide a large amount of either material to make sand and water play an enjoyable experience for young children. A miniature sandbox made from a dishpan with no more than an inch of sand in the bottom and small objects such as coffee scoops, marbles, plastic animals, and straws can hold a young child's interest and lead to all sorts of creative play.

For indoor sand play, sterilized play sand (which can be purchased from a lumber yard) is recommended. Fine-grain, sterilized sand holds its shape better than coarse sand or dirt and thus gives the children more flexibility in their play.

In addition to setting up areas where children can play freely with sand and water, you'll want to assemble materials that encourage children's learning during their play. For example, plastic measuring cups enable children to transport, pour, scoop, mold, and measure sand and water. Most props can be found right in your home. There is no need to purchase expensive play materials; household props are just as effective and often more fun to use.

Props for Sand Play

Buckets and shovels	Colander
Cookie cutters	Feathers
Funnels	Gelatin molds
Ladles	Magnifying glass
Measuring cups and spoons	Muffin tin
Pebbles and rocks	Plastic dishes (regular and doll sized)
Rake	Rolling pin
Rubber animals and people	Seashells
Seeds	Sieve
Sifter	Sticks
Straws	String
Toy cars/dump trucks	Whisk broom

Props for Water Play

Bubble-blowing materials (straws, soap flakes, glycerine)	Buckets
	Corks

Egg beater
Food coloring/vegetable dye
Ladle
Measuring cups and spoons
Plastic or rubber bottles
 (with and without holes punched in them)
Siphon
Sponges
Squeeze bottles

Eye dropper
Funnels
Paintbrushes
Scale
Scoops
Soap (bar, liquid, flakes)
Strainer
Whisks.

Many of the items suggested for water play can also be used for sand play and vice versa. In addition, you'll probably have many other items to add to these lists.

Creating Space

Sand and water play activities can take place outdoors as well as in your home. Both options are described below.

Outdoor Space

The easiest place to offer sand and water play is outside. A bare spot of ground can be used for digging. Buckets filled with water and large paint brushes can lead to an activity of "painting" the house or fence. A windy day makes blowing bubbles a different and exciting activity.

Ongoing water and sand play can be centered around plastic dish tubs or wading pools. Of course, sandboxes are natural centers for sand play. Another idea is to use an inner tube or tractor tire as a sandbox frame.

Providers who are handy with tools (or good at getting the children's parents to help) may wish to build their own sand and water tubs for use outdoors, using metal drums or wooden frames lined with plastic. Five by five feet for each tub is a good size to consider if you're building or purchasing your own equipment.

Indoor Space

What is the best way to set up sand and water play indoors? Most providers turn to the kitchen or the bathroom as natural answers. Not only do these rooms have sinks that can be used for water play, but it is relatively easy to mop up the messes there.

Once you have selected a site, your next step should be to prepare ahead in order to keep spills to a minimum. A sheet of plastic, an oilcloth made from old tablecloths, or crib sheets will protect the floor. A sheet under a sand table works well, as it is easy to fold up, carry outdoors, and shake out. Several layers of newspapers or old towels can be placed on top of the ground cover as further protection against spills. Children's aprons can be made from old shower curtains, heavy-duty garbage bags, or old raincoats. Some providers like children to wear rubber boots or plastic bags over their shoes to keep them dry. Of course, bare feet and swimsuits are always an option. Even with all this, it's wise to arrange with the children's parents to have a change of clothes on hand.

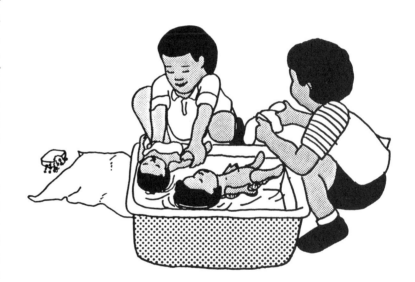

If you are using the kitchen or bathroom for water play, make sure that these areas have been child-proofed. This means that all hazardous items such as razors and chemicals have been locked away. Nearby outlets must be covered, and electric appliances such as hair dryers should be removed to guard against wet hands coming in contact with electricity. Step-stools with rubber slats should be provided for sinks that are out of the children's reach. To prevent the children from being burned by hot water, take special precautions to make sure that the hot water faucets cannot be turned on accidentally. Also, never leave younger children alone during water play.

Plastic dishpans work well for use by individual children. To provide opportunities for children to play together, you will need somewhat larger containers such as plastic tubs used for washing infants.

Storing Materials

Because sand and water play require your ongoing supervision and attention, tubs used for play should be stored out of the children's reach. Empty the water from the tubs or sink immediately after each use. Cover the sand tubs and store them on a high shelf or in an area to which the children do not have access.

Props, though, are another matter. Although you don't want children to set up sand and water play tubs without your assistance, you do want them to have ready access to the props they'd like to use during play times. By allowing children access to the props, you encourage their independence and growth. Here are some ideas for storing sand and water props in your home:

- A heavy plastic dishbin can be a storage container.

- Nylon fruit bags hung on hooks at the children's height can hold props, including kitchen-related items.

- Props can be grouped into smaller boxes or tubs by function, such as filling props (shovels, scoops), floating props (corks, squeeze bottles), or measuring props (plastic spoons and measuring cups, scales, gallon bottles).

- Collectible props such as shells and seeds can be kept in shoe boxes.

Draw or paste a picture of the items being stored on each box, storage bin, drawer, or hook. Cover these picture labels with clear contact paper to protect them from wet or muddy fingers.

Also, children should have access to a broom, dustpan, mop, sponge, and paper towels so that they can clean up their messes. After all, clean-up is an important part of sand and water play learning.

Timing

Because sand and water play are messy and require advance preparation, many providers are reluctant to include these activities in their programs. Sometimes they feel that even though sand and water play are obviously important for children, they don't have the time to schedule these messy activities into an already busy day.

Yet with just a little extra attention, most providers find that sand and water play can easily be accommodated into any family child care program. Because sand and water play also has a marked calming effect on children's behavior, it is well worth the effort it takes. Consider offering sand and water play for a fixed time of the day, such as the mid-morning hours. This time period is suggested for these reasons:

- The children will have eaten breakfast, had their diapers changed, hands washed, teeth brushed, and so on. Morning routines are over.

- There is a large block of time available for set-up, play, and clean-up.

- Older children are energetic and in need of an activity to channel their enthusiasm.

- Providers are ready to handle the day's activities.

Choosing a time slot such as the mid-morning allows play to take place without many interruptions. As infants or young toddlers wake up, they can be brought into the kitchen or bathroom to join in the play activities. If an infant wants to participate by touching the water or holding a toy, you can hold the child up so that he or she can reach the tubs and join in the play experience.

Planning for sand and water play sets the stage for learning. In the next section we'll focus on what you can do to promote children's learning through their play.

III. Helping Children Learn Through Sand and Water Play

What children learn through sand and water play depends a lot on how old they are and what skills they have. By thoughtfully observing each child in your care, you can provide experiences that match the children's individual skill levels. How, you may be wondering, do you go about doing this in a group situation? The best answer is to closely observe each child at play:

- How does the child explore sand and water?
- What does the child do during sand and water play?
- What props does the child use?
- What does the child say out loud during play? To you? To other children?
- What types of play settings does the child prefer?

Using what you observe, you can then respond to each child in ways that will help that child learn best. Here are some suggestions for how you can encourage children's development and learning as they play with sand and water.

Infants

Babies approach sand and water with all their senses. However, babies' personalities differ; one child may be uninhibited about touching, smelling, or tasting the sand and water, but another may be cautious. Allow each child to experience things in his or her own way. Many babies will clap their hands in water, run sand through their fingers (and hair!), splash waves, and level sand buildings with one broad swoop of their arms. Through their explorations infants learn what these materials are like, how they differ from each other, and how they change when combined.

Sand and Water Activities That Help Infants Develop	Why These Activities Are Important
Emotionally . . .	
As you wash an infant's hands or splash his/her feet in a puddle, show your enjoyment in the activity.	The infant will make emotional connections between the pleasurable sensation of the water and your love. This helps the infant to learn that exploring new sensations is a good thing to do.
Bathe a fussy infant or allow her/him to splash in a basin of water, or a puddle on the high chair tray.	Water play is experienced as a soothing, calming activity that helps the child to regain control and feel a sense of peace.
Socially . . .	
As you bathe infants, share your favorite lullabies, as well as their family's favorites.	Repetition of these familiar songs helps promote warm relationships with infants and helps provide continuity with their home experiences.

When putting out a sprinkler for active play, also provide a hose trickling in a grassy area at a distance for quieter play.

This offers a safe retreat area for infants to have fun together, while giving the older children a place to play more actively.

Cognitively...

Put out a variety of tools (funnels, spoons, strainers, and cups) for older infants to use during water play.

Children will discover how tools and water interact, and begin to plan small experiments with new ways of manipulating the water.

Add a variety of objects that will sink or float near a basin of water for water play. Describe what happens when the infant places them in the water.

The infant begins to perceive that objects have different properties in water, and learns to associate the objects with their names.

Imitate the sounds objects make when an infant drops them in the water ("Plop! Squish! Drip! Splat!") until the child takes over and imitates the sounds.

Infants will begin to make connections between actual events and words that describe the events. This is the foundation of meaningful speech.

Physically...

Provide different textures of wet and dry sand for older infants to enjoy.

Patting, molding, and sifting sand allows many opportunities for children to have fun as they develop strength in their muscles.

Set out small pitchers and plastic measuring cups so infants can pour water into containers and dump it out.

The pouring activity calls on small muscles to work in coordination and develops children's ability to plan and carry out a purposeful action.

Toddlers

Toddlers can mold and unmold a paper cup of sand into an anthill or mountain. They can add soap flakes to water to make suds. They can paint a fence with water and sift sand into a mound. Although they often like to play next to another child, most prefer to explore sand and water play on their own, seeing what their own actions and imaginations can produce.

Sand and Water Activities That Help Toddlers Develop

Why These Activities Are Important

Emotionally...

Encourage toddlers to help themselves to available props.

Toddlers like to make their own choices. Giving them this free choice helps them develop a secure sense of power and independence.

Introduce toddlers to only a few props at a time. Measuring cups and spoons and a funnel are a good beginning.

Giving toddlers too many props is overwhelming. The goal is to keep children interested but not frustrated.

Use routine water encounters during the day—washing hands and faces, for example—as times for water play and closeness.

These routines are excellent times for strengthening the bonds between you and toddlers.

Socially...

Arrange sand and water tubs in back-to-back positions so that toddlers can play near one another without interfering with each other.

This set-up is good for toddlers who desire friendship but don't yet know how to play cooperatively.

Encourage toddlers to play make-believe while they are at the sand or water tub: "Can you make some mud pies for us to serve the baby dolls for dessert?"

Sand and water play are natural arenas for dramatic play. You can extend the benefits of dramatic play by incorporating the two.

Cognitively...

Let toddlers play with familiar props for as long as they remain interested. For some, a sieve never loses its fascination.

Toddlers need lots of repetition and practice to master new skills. Take your cues from the children, and let them play with a prop over and over if they still find the activity captivating.

Talk with toddlers about their play. Find out what they are thinking by asking open-ended questions: "What is that you're doing with the comb in the sand tub?"

By asking questions, you can help toddlers learn to express their thoughts in words.

Regularly add new props with unfamiliar uses.

Toddlers should be allowed to play with familiar props repeatedly, but they still need access to other props so that they can try something new when they are ready for it.

Physically...

Cover the play area with newspapers or oilcloth and allow children to play freely.

Active splashing and broad arm movements assist physical development and add to toddlers' enjoyment.

Include props that develop coordination and fine muscle skills: funnels or measuring cups and sifters, for example.

Sand and water play provides an excellent opportunity for you to work with toddlers on developing physical skills in a fun environment.

Preschool Children

Preschoolers use all sorts of props in their sand and water play. They mold wet sand to make a city and add dye to water, delighting in the color change. They like to use buckets, muffin tins, and Jell-O molds to help them create fanciful houses, castles, and space stations from sand. They freeze water into ice and then watch it melt into a puddle of water. Preschoolers use sand and water play to learn about science (how matter changes) and math (how many tablespoons of water it takes to fill a measuring cup) and to solve problems (how much water needs to be added to sand to make it keep its shape).

Sand and Water Activities That Help Preschoolers Develop	Why These Activities Are Important
Emotionally . . .	
Allow preschoolers to play at the sand and water tubs independently. Let them know that, because they will be cleaning up after themselves, they don't need to worry about making a mess.	By so doing, you send children the message that they and their play adventures are valued.
Steer a child who appears unhappy or frustrated to the sand or water tubs where the child can vent feelings acceptably through play.	The soothing nature of these natural materials can be very comforting to an unhappy child.
Socially . . .	
Suggest group projects that the children can do together, such as painting the house with water.	Preschoolers enjoy group exercises and will be more eager to play when they can team up.
Encourage preschoolers to use sand and water play as a setting for dramatic play: a ship can hit an iceberg and leak oil on the beach.	Dramatic play is a natural accompaniment to sand and water play. You can encourage children to use the tubs to recreate what they hear and see in the real world.
Make your praise frequent but sincere: "I like how you used the butter mold to make designs in the sand today."	Children will be more eager to play with sand and water when you give them encouragement.
Cognitively . . .	
Ask lots of questions: "What happened when we added the soap flakes to the water in the tub?"	By asking questions, you can help children learn to solve problems, express feelings, and form questions of their own.
Give preschoolers props that they can explore: for example, an eggbeater, a colander, a funnel. Once they've had a chance to look them over, ask what they could use these objects for.	Let children become inventors. Left on their own, preschoolers may come up with some innovative functions for these props.

If a preschooler has made an elaborate construction in the sand tub, suggest that you leave it for the rest of the day so everyone can admire the child's work.

By preserving the children's creations, you let them know that you value their efforts. Admiring comments from other children and parents will give sand-builders added pride.

Give the children natural objects to experiment with. For instance, provide preschoolers with corks, bottle caps, stones, and sponges. Ask the child to put the objects in the water tub and see whether they float or sink.

Children love experiments. When they are allowed to conduct experiments on their own, the learning has real meaning for them.

Physically . . .

Suggest play activities that will develop small muscles: pouring, emptying pails of water and sand, molding objects in sand, squeezing water from plastic bottles, etc.

You can make good use of sand and water play to help children practice physical skills.

Provide props that develop eye-hand coordination: sieves, funnels, sifters, and basters, for example.

Nearly every prop will help children improve their eye-hand coordination.

Set up water activities in a small wading pool outdoors where children can use their whole bodies during play.

Active water play develops large body muscles.

School-Age Children

For school-age children, sand and water play usually focuses on projects. Many older children love to make elaborate sand creations that show off their skills. Often they enjoy leading younger children in craft projects, too. Making bubble frames and blowing bubbles, for example, easily captivates an older child's fancy. Here are some ideas for school-age children.

Sand and Water Activities That Help School-Age Children Develop

Why These Activities Are Important

Emotionally . . .

Let school-age children know they are free to play with sand and water on their own.

Older children need their independence; if you give them choices, they'll appreciate it.

Praise the children: "I wouldn't have been able to manage making the plaster of Paris molds with the younger children if it hadn't been for your help."

School-age children need praise to enhance their self-concept.

Socially . . .

Encourage school-age children to participate in a group activity such as blowing bubbles.

School-age children need the comfort of their peers. By giving them permission to include their age mates, you let the children know that you respect their desires.

Ask the children to let you know which sand and water activities they enjoy participating in, and focus on these.

Children will be more eager to participate in sand and water activities when you solicit their opinions and then respect them.

Invite the children to help you set up and oversee an outside area where younger children can dig and do sand play.

Many older children like the authority of overseeing the younger children's play activities.

Cognitively . . .

Have school-age children help you make props for sand and water play, such as a mesh screen for sifting sand or wire shapes for blowing bubbles.

Older children often enjoy taking on a task, especially ones like these that result in products they can take satisfaction in seeing completed.

Write on a card the recipe for making glycerine bubbles, and ask the children to mix the solution with you.

Older children will like the challenge of preparing the solution from scratch.

On a warm day, set up a water slide outside. Have the children work with you in developing a list of safety rules for using the slide.

This activity appeals to the children's love of rules as well as their love of enforcing these rules to the letter.

Suggest that interested children check out books on making sandcastles from the library.

Many children love doing research and will find it fascinating to know that there is such a thing as sandcastle art.

Physically . . .

Encourage school-age children to combine their sand structures with block constructions or art collectibles.

This activity will enhance fine muscle coordination at the same time that creativity is spurred.

Provide different types of sand, cardboard, and glue, and invite the children to create sand designs.

Intricate designs require good small muscle control and enable the children to refine these skills.

Special Projects

Most children will enjoy doing special activities with sand and water. Here are some ideas you might try in your family child care home.

- *"It's Freezing."* This experiment is best done following a snowstorm or on a very cold day. Encourage children to discover how frozen water differs from liquid water by filling a plastic baby bottle to the brim with water and placing it uncovered in the freezer or outside (if the temperature is below 32° F.). While younger children can discuss the hardness, coldness, and smoothness of frozen water, older children can observe that frozen water also expands.

- *"The Sands of Time."* Older preschoolers who have a beginning understanding of time can construct their own sand timers. Younger children, who do not really understand this concept, can still enjoy using a timer to let them know when it will be their turn to use a popular toy.

  Help the children glue together the tops of two identical jars. Using a hammer and a thin nail, punch holes through both lids. Have the children add sand to one of the jars. Screw the double lids onto this jar, and then screw this jar on top of the empty one. Once the jars are turned over, timing can begin. Older children can use a stop watch to see how much sand should be added for one-, two-, or three-minute activities. All children can use the finished timers to help play games, to keep track of turns, and to assist in cooking preparation.

- *Casting Molds.* Children of all ages like to use their bodies in art activities. Help the children wet a small box of sand. Then, one at a time, have the children press their hand prints into the wet sand. Using plaster of Paris, assist the children in filling the hand prints. After 40 to 50 minutes (the plaster of Paris will feel cool and hard), the children can carefully lift their hand molds out of the sand. The hands can be painted or left as they are. Children can use this same technique to make molds of their feet or of objects such as shells and keys. Older children might use these molds to hold rings or soap pads.

- *Sand Combs.* Using posterboard or stiff construction paper, help the children design and cut out combs that can be used to make patterns in the sand. Younger children will need your assistance in cutting, but older children might even be able to make combs out of 1/4" plywood. The children can preserve their designs using plaster of Paris, as described above.

- *Water Music.* Children can use water play to determine the unique sounds that pots, pans, and plastic containers make when they are sprayed with water. Help the children select pots and pans that can be taken outside and leaned against a wall or tree. Using squirt bottles, have the children blast the "instruments" with a steady stream of water to make "music." While younger children may be absorbed with the spraying process itself and the resulting noises, older children may try to create musical tones and rhythms to accompany songs such as "Twinkle, Twinkle, Little Star."

- *Water Slides.* On a warm day, spread an old shower curtain on a grassy hill, anchoring the corners with stones or heavy objects. Spray a fine mist of water all over the curtain, and invite the children to jump and slide down the hill.

- *Washing Rocks.* This is fun to do outdoors. Toddlers especially love to wash things, and this activity allows them to discover how water changes the color of objects. Soft sponges and a bucket of water are all the props you need.

- *Blowing Bubbles.* Children of all ages enjoy this activity. Older children can make frames using empty eyeglass frames, coat hangers, pipe cleaners, plastic lids of margarine containers, or plastic berry baskets. Children can dip the frames into the bubble solution and blow bubbles or move the frames swiftly through the air so that soap film moves through the frame, forming a bubble. The following recipe is suggested for bubble play:

  - 1/2 cup liquid detergent
  - 2/3 cup water

Stronger, longer-lasting bubbles can be made by adding corn syrup, gelatin crystals, liquid pectin, or glycerin to the bubble solution. Through experimentation, children will develop their own bubble blowing techniques. Let children discover for themselves that bubble blowing works best when both their hands and the bubble frames are wet.

These activities are, of course, just a starting point. You'll find that the more children play with sand and water, the more discoveries they make and the more ideas you will have for sand and water play.

Involving Children of All Ages

In the following story, you will see that one way of balancing different age groups engaged in sand and water play is to time certain activities so that only children of the appropriate ages are present. Although sand and water play can take place with different ages at the same time, it is sometimes easier if only 1 or 2 children are involved at a time—when the rest of your group is already engaged in other activities. Here's what might happen:

Gisela (2 years)
Jackie (4 years)

"Chair chair," says Gisela as she pushes a kitchen chair over to the sink. She's halfway up when she starts saying "on, play, on." It is clear that water play is on her mind.

Quickly you assess whether this is a good time for this event. The two babies are sleeping; Jackie is sitting at the little table doing puzzles, and your school-age children are not yet home. Yes, you decide, now is a good time.

"OK, Gisela, I understand you want to play with the water," you tell her.

"Ya, play," she says enthusiastically.

"First we must get a towel. Follow me." Cooperating, Gisela follows you to the closet where you pull out two towels and a plastic apron. "Here you go, you can carry these," you say as you hand her the towels. She marches back happily to the sink.

You then spread one towel out on the floor, keep one on the counter for spills, and help Gisela put on her apron. After setting the chair firmly in front of the sink, you turn on the cold water just a bit. "We'll save the water in the sink so you can play with it," you say as you close the drain. "Would you like some toys to play with?"

"Ya," says Gisela, "poon" (spoon). As you hand her a spoon you ask, "What does the water feel like?"

"Code (cold), ya…nice," she responds. Already she has quite a few descriptive terms and ideas about water even though she is still in the early stages of verbalization. You then ask, "Do you need more toys?" When she replies "ya," you hand her two plastic cups. Immediately she begins to fill one with the other.

You decide Gisela is all set up and turn to Jackie. "Jackie, would you like to play with the water, too? You could use the sink next to Gisela."

Jackie says, "Yes, but I'll need more toys because I'm bigger."

"That's an interesting idea, Jackie. What kinds of things will you need?" you ask.

"I need soap!"

"Well, I think that would be OK. Where do you suppose you could get some soap?"

"From you!" she shouts. You smile, and then she goes on to say, "And from the soap bottle."

Within a few moments, Jackie is set up next to Gisela at your double kitchen sink. They play contentedly for a long while. When you think its about the time that the babies will awaken from their naps, you lead the girls through clean-up time, and then they are off to another adventure.

Water play can take place quite naturally as part of your family child care program, even with children of different ages. Here are some points to keep in mind:

- Try to pick up on children's interests as they arise and plan activities they like.

- Prepare for spills ahead of time to make clean-up easier.

- Talk with children as they play to develop their language and make them aware of what they are learning.

To help parents understand more about the value of sand and water, you may want to discuss some of the ideas covered in the letter that follows, which you can share with parents if you choose.

A Letter to Parents on Sand and Water

What We Do and Why

You may be surprised to learn that sand and water are important activities in our program. We have water play indoors, using the kitchen or bathroom sink and small plastic tubs of water for the toddlers who can't reach the sink. Outdoors, during warm weather, we use the wading pool and plastic tubs for water play. We also have a place for sand play outside.

When the children play with sand and water, they stay involved for long periods of time. With water, they like to bathe the doll babies or find out what will float or sink. They like to pour the water into different-sized containers and add food coloring or soap to see what happens to the water. With the sand, they poke, mold, and push to see what happens. The older children build with the sand. I have props for the sand box, including shovels, sieves, buckets, small plastic containers, and plastic cars and trucks.

Children learn a lot of things when they play with sand and water. They discover they can make bubbles by adding soap to the water. They learn that they can mold sand into a castle when they add water to dry sand. They have a chance to practice pouring and spilling things without worrying about the mess.

The children can't always tell me all they are learning when they play with sand and water, so I say things to help them put their ideas into words. For example, I might say:

- "Look how cloudy the water is with the soap in it. You can't see the toys."
- "You discovered a way to make the wheel turn by pouring sand through the top."

Sometimes I ask them questions to encourage them to think about what they are discovering:

- "Why do you think the wet sand won't turn the wheel?"
- "How does the wet sand feel when you touch it?"
- "How many cups of water will you need to fill the gallon jug?"

What You Can Do at Home

You might like to try some of these ideas at home. Although sand and water play can be messy, here are some ideas for making it more manageable:

- Put a towel or plastic tablecloth on the floor so your child can play at the sink.

- Let your child help clean up when finished. Have ready towels and sponges ready.

- Use a small plastic dishpan for sand play in the yard, on the front steps or porch, or in the basement.

There are many good ideas in *The Creative Curriculum for Family Child Care,* and I'd be happy to share them with you.

Books

I. Why Books Are Important

Sharing books with young children can be one of the most pleasurable times of your day. Holding a child in your lap while one or two others snuggle next to you gives the children and you a chance to relax, talk, look at illustrations, and share an intimate moment. Books open up the world to children. Through pictures and stories, children clarify ideas and feelings. They hear about people who are just like them and people who are different. They are introduced to new worlds, ideas, and places. Books can soothe an upset child, make a child laugh, and excite a child's imagination.

Books also play a major role in helping children grow up to be readers. Research tells us that children who are used to being around books when they are young are likely to become good readers when they get to school. They're also likely to enjoy reading throughout their lives. By sharing books with children when they are very young, you can set the stage for success in school and a lifetime of good reading habits.

Here are some examples of the ways in which children learn from books.

Children develop thinking skills by:

- learning to understand symbols (pointing to a picture of a boy, learning the written "boy," and relating both to a real-life boy).

- learning vocabulary (naming an object "dog" when you point to a picture of a collie in a book).

- anticipating events (telling you what's about to happen in a story you are reading together).

- learning to count (pointing to objects while you read a counting book out loud).

- learning to recognize colors and shapes (pointing to objects and labeling them for you as you are reading out loud).

- applying knowledge (making up nonsense rhymes after reading verses together).

Children develop socially by:

- learning to share (inviting another child to hear a story you are reading out loud).

- trying out different roles (acting out stories through dramatic play).

- showing concern (discussing books about people who are differently abled, have suffered prejudice, who are hurt in some way, or who face a challenge).

Children develop emotionally by:

- working through fears (listening to a story about children or animals going through rough times such as their parents' divorce, sibling rivalry, a death in the family, a friend moving away, being angry, etc.).

- feeling good about themselves (discussing how they like characters who are strong and happy).

- showing compassion for others (identifying strongly with story characters and their problems).

Children develop physically by:

- developing their small muscles (turning pages in a book).

- strengthening their eye muscles (following pictures and words in a book).

- coordinating their eye and hand movements (pointing to objects as you name them in a picture book).

As you read to children and encourage them to look at books, you'll find that there are any number of ways in which books can be used to encourage children's growth and development. In the next section we'll focus on choosing appropriate books and how you can set up the environment in your family child care home to support children's development.

II. Setting the Stage for Using Books

Reading to children is an activity that can take place almost any time and in any room of your house. It is also something that can be planned for and looked forward to. In addition, young children need opportunities to look at books by themselves. Even though they can't yet read, children can learn what books are like and enjoy looking at the illustrations. Time alone with books helps children become comfortable with them and shows them the special joys that books offer.

Selecting Books

The first place to begin in selecting books for your family child care home is to consider the ages of the children in your care. In general, the following guidelines will apply.

For Infants:

The best books for infants are those with people and with colorful illustrations of familiar objects such as balls, dogs, and cars. Because infants are not yet verbal, wordy books will only frustrate them. And because infants learn with their hands, mouths, and toes—as well as their eyes—sturdy books made of thick cardboard, soft vinyl, or washable cloth are highly recommended. Hinged books with stiff pages that are easy to turn are also good for infants.

For Toddlers:

Most toddlers enjoy simple stories about events and things they know. Plots that feature activities of daily life, such as Margaret Wise Brown's classic bedtime story, *Goodnight Moon*, are very popular with this age group. Picture books that deal with familiar experiences and animals are usually of high interest, too. Toddlers in the "why?" stage love simple books that show how things work and why things happen as they do. They also like seek-and-find books where the reader is asked to find a child or animal hidden in the picture. Although the hidden objects are often obvious to the adult who is reading out loud, the child reader will delight in discovering them and pointing them out each time the book is read. Toddlers also enjoy books that feature rhymes, word play, and repetitive sounds. Books with rhymes, such as the class *Mother Goose*, or newer books such as *Ride a Purple Pelican*, help toddlers develop their speech. Bright, bold illustrations of realistic settings that show things from the child's (rather than the adult's) point of view are favored by most toddlers.

For Preschool Children:

Preschool children like many of the same picture books that toddlers do. And because they can sit still for longer periods of time than toddlers, they also enjoy hearing more involved stories. They love stories with a sense of humor, word play, and puns. Nonsense rhymes are often very popular with this age group. Stories that include lots of repetition, imagination, and surprises appeal to most preschoolers. Although some preschoolers

enjoy fairy tales, myths, and legends, many do not. Giants and "big bad wolves" can trigger nightmares in some preschoolers, so select such books carefully. Preschoolers, like toddlers, enjoy bold, colorful illustrations. However, preschoolers (much more than toddlers) enjoy illustrations with details, especially those related to the plot. Finding hidden details in drawings is especially appealing to these children.

For School-Age Children:

Because this span covers so many years, the interests of school-age children will vary greatly. Young school-age children enjoy many of the same books that preschool children enjoy. This is especially true of stories with humor or irony. Books known as "early reading books" are, as their name implies, good for children who are beginning readers. Children in the middle grades especially enjoy adventure stories and mysteries. Biographies and stories of friendship and pets are always popular. Older school-age children like reading about the teenagers they will soon be. Plots that deal with romance, family relationships, and school are usually appealing. Better readers will prefer books that rely more on text than illustrations.

Don't assume that children who know how to read no longer want to be read to. Reading out loud is a pleasant experience for people of all ages, so have story time for the older children as well as the younger ones. It is a good way to introduce them to a new author or more challenging classic books such as *Tom Sawyer* or *Anne of Green Gables*.

Take Your Cues from the Children

The children you care for have many interests and concerns. What are these interests? Is one of the children fascinated by firefighters? Do the children ask you questions about nature? About time? About how things work? If you look for books on topics suggested by the children, you are more likely to gain their interest and attention.

Another helpful approach is to select books that deal with problems or issues being faced by the children. Books on friendship, for example, are always appealing. If any of the children are facing problems such as divorce, death, the birth of a sibling, or moving, look for books on these topics that will help them through these rough times. Sometimes, however, a child will not want to read about a subject that is too closely connected with his or her experience. If you encounter this, don't force the issue, and pick a different book. Reading can function here as a low-stress get-away for the child.

Other Sources for Suggestions

Think back on your own childhood. Can you remember any books that you loved? The chances are good that these same books will also be treasured by the children you care for.

Parents are an excellent resource in selecting books. Ask them if their children have any favorite books at home. By providing a copy of the children's favorite books for their use in family child care, you make the children feel valued and important. You can also surprise the children with another book by their favorite author. For example, if a parent tells you that Doug's favorite book is *Curious George* by H. A. Rey, you can delight Doug with a copy of *Curious George Rides a Bike*.

The children's librarian at your local public library can also be a very helpful source in selecting appropriate books. The librarian can steer you to the classics, point out the newest children's literature, and tell you which books seem to be most popular with children of particular ages.

Another way to select books is to look for those that have received children's book awards. Every year since 1938, the American Library Association has awarded a Caldecott Medal (named in honor of the English artist Rudolph Caldecott, a pioneer in children's illustrations) to the picture book nominated as outstanding for that year. Since 1952 *The New York Times* has also given annual awards for outstanding illustrations in children's books. The Newberry Medal (named for a famous eighteenth-century London bookseller) is awarded each year to authors of distinguished books for school-age children. The books that have won these awards have medallions on their covers.

Once you've picked out individual books for your family child care home, take a moment to look at the collection as a whole. Do the books touch on a variety of subjects? Do they show people of all ethnic backgrounds? Do men and women take on a variety of roles? Are people of all ages, differing abilities, and various economic classes represented? Are there both fiction and nonfiction books? You will probably want to update your collection frequently with books borrowed from your local library. However, it's a good idea to keep a basic core of, at the very least, 10 to 20 books in your home for the children to look at and read together with you. This way, children can always return to their favorites. Be sure to include both hard- and soft-covered books in your collection, as they offer very different reading experiences. Having books in a variety of sizes and shapes will also enhance your library. To help you in putting together your own collection and to assist you in checking out books from the library, the Appendix to this unit lists some highly recommended children's books.

Creating Space

The key to helping children develop a love for books is to make their use inviting. If you have areas in your home where children can readily find a book to look at and then settle down with, you'll find this goal easy to meet.

In deciding where in your home you'd like to make room for the the children's use of books, here are some ideas to consider:

- Books should be stored on low shelves that children can easily reach. If you don't have a bookcase available, you might try building some shelves in a closet.

- Display the children's favorite books in a standing position. Because younger children can't yet read titles, it's easier

for them to identify a book by its cover. If you don't have the space to display covers, do be sure to store books loosely on shelves so that children can flip through and see their covers easily.

- Place some large pillows, old couch cushions, or a bean bag chair in a quiet spot not far from where the books are stored. If a sofa or cushioned chairs are nearby, they will do fine. The goal is to have a cozy place where children can nestle up with books, either by themselves or with you. Children may also want to snuggle in with blankets, dolls, stuffed animals, or pacifiers.

- Make sure that the area children will be using is well lit. Natural light is always best, but you may need to bring a lamp close by so that children don't have to strain their eyes.

In this section we've focused on setting the stage for reading books with children. The time you spend in organizing your home and selecting books will be time well spent. In the next section we'll look at ways in which you can support children's growth and learning through books.

III. Helping Children Learn Through Books

All children can benefit from books. Because young children are nonreaders, much of their experience with books depends on you. For this reason it is especially important that you interact with children in ways that will help them grow and learn through books.

Here are some ideas you can use with children at each stage of development.

Infants

Infants learn about books with every one of their senses. They look at the pictures, smell the pages, swat at the covers, shake the pages together, and almost always try to put books into their mouths. From these explorations infants learn what books taste, touch, smell, sound, and look like. Gradually, they begin to piece together the idea that books can show them things about themselves and the world they live in. Older infants will learn to turn pages and follow along with short, simple stories, especially those with sound effects. Reading to infants doesn't have to mean just reading the text. You can also explore the pictures, describing what is happening in them to the child.

Book Activities that Help Infants Develop	Why These Activities Are Important
Emotionally…	
Read to tired or fussy infants in a soft voice, while stroking or cuddling them on your lap.	This calms infants and leads them to associate warm and comforting feelings with books.
Provide infants with books that can be handled and mouthed as well as looked at.	Infants learn that the same pleasure they get from other play materials can also be associated with books.
Socially . . .	
Hold an infant on your lap as you read to the older children.	The infant learns that reading and exploring books can be done as a part of a group.
Make books for infants that include pictures of home, family, the infant, you, and the other children in the group.	This creates a connection to the child care group and promotes a sense of belonging
Cognitively . . .	
Provide infants with cloth and laminate books. Books that let them feel textures, such as *Pat the Bunny* by Dorothy Kuhnhardt, are good selections.	Infants learn through all their senses. Their reading experiences should involve more than looking at pictures and listening to words.

Read books to infants that have lots of repetition and simple rhymes.

Infants enjoy the rhythmic sounds of language. The more language they hear, the more they understand and the larger their vocabulary.

Encourage infants to repeat rhymes and sounds from stories. Animal picture books are especially good for echoing sounds.

Talking begins with sounds and babbles. By encouraging infants to repeat sounds, you help stimulate their language development.

Physically . . .

Put "babyproof" cloth and laminated books on a low shelf.

As infants reach up to a shelf to grab a book, they also develop physical strength.

Give infants books with laminated pages and let them practice opening and shutting the book and turning pages.

When infants put books in their mouths or turn pages, they are also improving their coordination and small muscle skills.

Toddlers

Toddlers know what books are like. They enjoy hearing simple stories and following along as you read to them. Active toddlers are also active listeners. They'll point to the people or animals in an illustration as you read aloud. Toddlers will turn the pages for you even before you're ready to go to the next page. They may even recite favorite stories word for word. They'll laugh at the funny parts of a story each time, as if it is the first time they've heard them, and they'll point out the sad parts for you in case you missed them. They're enthusiastic about books in every way. Many toddlers will listen and "read" books for a surprisingly long time. Remember, though, that toddlers' enthusiasm may end after five minutes.

Book Activities that Help Toddlers Develop

Why These Activities Are Important

Emotionally . . .

Let a toddler be responsible for turning the pages of a book you are reading together.

Because toddlers need you to help with the reading, they enjoy being in charge of the page-turning.

Ask the librarian for suggestions for books that deal with typical frustrations felt by toddlers, such as *I'm Telling You Now* by Judy Delton.

Reading toddlers books about frustrations lets them know that all children their age share these same feelings.

Toddlers love to hear books about families like theirs. If a toddler is going through a family crisis, reading a book such as *Dinosaurs Divorce* by Marc Brown and Laurane Krasny can be very helpful.

Toddlers identify strongly with the characters in books. Seeing other families like their own dealing with problems like their own can be very reassuring.

Socially...

Take time every day to read to the group. This brings children of all ages together in a noncompetitive setting.

Group reading allows toddlers to socialize without having to test sharing skills.

If you're trying to get toddlers to adopt appropriate social behaviors, books such as *Going to the Potty* by Fred Rogers can be helpful.

Toddlers love to imitate adults. Books that show adults acting appropriately can serve as strong role models for toddlers.

Cognitively...

Be prepared to read a favorite story to toddlers repeatedly; encourage their participation as you read together.

It may seem like endless repetition, but children learn something new from a book each time it is read.

Take time to discuss each story you read with a toddler. Ask questions such as this: "How would you have felt if you had lost your dog like the boy in the story did?"

Books provide a wonderful opportunity to promote language development. They also enable children to reflect on what's been read and relate it to their own lives.

Take regular trips to the library so that toddlers can select books of interest to them.

Children learn best when they take charge of their own learning. New books from the library keep them excited and eager to learn.

Physically...

Don't make toddlers sit still for long periods of time to hear a story. If they seem restless, suggest that they act out a role from a book you are reading together. Let them make themselves comfortable as they listen to books by stretching out or lying down.

You may need to let toddlers incorporate physical activities into reading times to keep them engaged.

Encourage toddlers to point things out in the illustrations as you read books to them.

At the same time that you are assisting children in understanding the story, you are helping them refine their powers of eye-hand coordination.

Preschool Children

Preschool children love listening to stories with you. Their longer attention spans enable them to sit through a longer story, and their increased vocabularies allow them to discuss stories at length with you. They often want to hear the same stories over and over and soon can tell you what the pages say word for word. During the preschool years, children are learning about sequencing—that stories have beginnings, middles, and ends; that stories involve both the pictures and the text in books; and that the pictured text represents the words that make up the story. Children of this age may also want to experiment with writing symbols (letters to them, scribbles to us) and with making their own stories.

Book Activities that Help Preschoolers Develop	Why These Activities Are Important

Emotionally...

Read preschoolers books about self-concept that reinforce the idea that others worry about the same things they do. Two good choices: *I'm Terrific* by Marjorie Sharmat and *The Carrot Seed* by Ruth Krauss.

Preschoolers may need help in developing a strong self-concept. Books can be an excellent way of doing this.

Have books on hand that will help preschoolers deal with the many emotions they feel—some of which they know are not socially acceptable. Some suggestions: *The Hating Book* by Charlotte Zolotow and *I'll Fix Anthony* by Judith Viorst.

Children may not know what to do or how to handle emotions they've been told aren't "nice." Books can help them find ways of handling their emotions. They also let children know they aren't alone in their feelings.

Socially...

Encourage a preschooler to invite another child to hear a storybook you are about to read together.

Books don't have to be a solitary experience. Reading a story to a preschooler and the child's best friend can be an intimate experience for both children.

Encourage preschoolers to act out parts of a book as you read aloud. For example, urge children to roll their eyes, show their claws, and gnash their teeth like the monsters in Maurice Sendak's *Where the Wild Things Are.*

Children can often appreciate the magical or whimsical parts of a book more when they incorporate dramatic play into the reading experience.

Praise a child for developing good reading habits: "It makes me happy to see you taking books from the shelf to look at, Elaine."

Good reading habits start early. If you praise a child for reading, you help children develop a love for books.

Cognitively...

Continually ask and answer questions as you read: "Why do you think the doggie got hurt?" or "What made the mommy rabbit so sad?"

By discussing the story with children as you read, you encourage them to express through language what they are feeling and learning.

Check out books from the library that tap into the preschoolers' natural curiosity about the world. Popular themes include transportation, machines, weather, and farms.

Preschoolers love hearing about how trucks go, why thunder happens, or how milk gets from a cow to their dinner table. By reading children books about things that interest them, you send them the message that you respect their ideas and preferences.

Let the children "author" their own books by gathering their drawings into a picture book. Staple or sew the left-hand edges together to make the books look real. Be sure to include title and author pages.

Preschoolers delight in having their work preserved. You strengthen their self-concept as well as their pleasure in reading by doing this activity.

Encourage preschoolers to check out books themselves so that they can see for themselves how libraries operate.

Visits to the library help children learn about both books and libraries.

Physically...

Let preschoolers hold the book you are reading together in their laps. Ask them to turn the pages for you and to point out objects as you read.

This not only gives children an opportunity to act independently but also enables them to refine the small muscles in their hands.

Incorporate dramatic play activities into reading, whenever appropriate. For example, *The Little Engine That Could* (a 1930 classic by Watty Piper) encourages readers to act out the part of a struggling train.

Dramatic play enables children to act out feelings and gives them opportunities to develop their muscles as they move in their enactments.

Ask the children to point out objects hidden in the background of illustrations of participatory books. *Where's Waldo?* by Martin Handford and *Each Peach Pear Plum: An "I Spy" Story* by Janet and Allen Ahlberg are excellent choices.

Participatory books develop both cognitive and physical skills. In learning to discriminate details and parts of a whole, children strengthen their eye-hand coordination.

School-Age Children

During the school years, children's relationship with books changes significantly. They, not you, become the readers, although they still enjoy having you read to them. Reading becomes a much more personal activity for these children. The best support you can give to a school-age child is to suggest new books, answer questions, and discuss ideas.

Book Activities that Help School-Age Children Develop

Why These Activities Are Important

Emotionally...

Encourage school-age children to get library cards in their own names (if allowed) and to visit the library and check out books of their own choosing.

Regular library use not only instills a love of reading but promotes independence as well.

Keep books on hand that deal with self-esteem. *Tales of a Fourth-Grade Nothing* by Judy Blume is one good choice.

Many school-age children struggle with insecurities. Books are a terrific way of helping them deal with problems and letting them know how universal their fears are.

Socially...

Suggest that school-age children form a reading club with friends so that they can swap popular titles.

Reading clubs serve the dual purpose of promoting reading and allowing children to participate in group activities, which are very important at this age.

Encourage the children to write reviews of books they've read in which they can express their likes and dislikes.

School-age children enjoy airing their viewpoints. Book reviews are a socially acceptable forum for such self-expression.

Encourage the children to occasionally read storybooks to the younger children.

Many older children like reading storybooks aloud to younger children and "hamming up" the roles. Younger children love the attention from the older children.

Cognitively . . .

Use books in conjunction with other activities. Have school-age children make up their own stories and then record them on tape. Or see a magic show and then use library books to help the children put on their own show.

Storytelling lets older children put into words the ideas and feelings they are grappling with. By encouraging them to produce these stories, you send them the message that you value their efforts.

Check out "how to" books from the library on topics of interest to the children, such as building model airplanes or doing science experiments.

You can help older children turn their curiosity into hobbies or projects by steering them to appropriate books.

Check with the librarian, or consider purchasing or borrowing some of the newer mystery book/ jigsaw puzzle combinations that children can solve together.

Older children enjoy solving mysteries, following elaborate board games, and working on projects together. You can promote both cognitive and social growth through group projects.

Ask the children to write a poem or limerick that they then might read to the younger children.

Through this activity you let children know that you value what they have to write and say.

Physically . . .

Have older children put together books of their own photographs or artwork.

Not only does this activity preserve the children's efforts and let them know their work is valued, it also gives children practice in refining their physical skills as they paste the pages, sew the bindings, and decorate the book.

Encourage the children to check out books from the library on their favorite sports.

You can promote children's interests in various sports through books. You can also help them learn techniques that will improve their skills by reading books by experts.

Some Guidance On Reading With Children

Nearly all the experiences suggested above depend on one key factor: that you know how to read and discuss books effectively with children. On one level this is very simple: just read and talk about a book with a child. However, there are some strategies you can use to make reading books particularly effective. Here are some pointers that should help in reading books to each age group.

Reading to Infants and Young Toddlers

Very young children may find it difficult to listen to a story or look at a picture book from start to finish. For them, the shared experience is what's important—not finding out how the book ends. To help children get the most from this experience, try doing the following:

- Settle the child comfortably in your lap.

- As you look through a book together, stop frequently to ask questions such as "what's that?" Give the child time to respond with a sound, a word, or a pointed finger. If the child doesn't respond, try asking the question in another way or answer the question yourself.

- Give feedback to any response from the child: "Yes, that's the Mommy you're pointing to. It looks like she is playing with her baby."

- Be prepared to stop reading at any point and start again when the child is ready so as to keep the reading experience fun and exciting for the child.

Reading to Older Toddlers and Preschoolers

Older toddlers and preschool children can enthusiastically listen to stories read over and over. They love books, illustrations, and the closeness of having you read to them. Here are some suggestions for making reading to older toddlers and preschool children a fun and productive experience:

- Make sure that the child is seated comfortably in your lap or beside you.

- Examine the cover together with the child and discuss what's illustrated.

- Ask open-ended questions as you are reading: "What's happening in this picture?" or "Why do you think the little girl was sad?" Give the child time to respond. If there's no response, try asking the question a different way: "What happened to the little girl's dog that made her so sad?" If there's still no response, you can answer the question yourself in a matter-of-fact tone of voice.

- Give feedback to a child's verbal and nonverbal cues. For example, if a child points to a glass of milk being knocked over, you might comment, "Uh-oh—the glass is falling off the table."

- Encourage the child to anticipate the story line: "What do you think will happen next?"

- Pause to allow the child to anticipate dialogue or join in repeated phrases.

- Point out words in the text as you read. Encourage the child to point to the words, too.

- Relate what is happening in the story to the child's own life.

- Discuss the completed story with the child. Ask the child for his or her opinions about characters, feelings, and concepts.

- Provide follow-up to the story by reminding the child of the book during related activities or when the child is experiencing feelings similar to those dealt with in the book. For example, at nap time you might repeat the goodnight phrases from Margaret Wise Brown's *Goodnight Moon.*

- When possible, try reading a story straight through. Children will learn from the rhythm of the words as you read the book from page to page. Take your cues from the children when deciding if a particular story time is good for hearing the entire book or for examining individual ideas.

- Be prepared to read favorite stories again and again.

Reading to School-Age Children

Although most school-age children can read to themselves, this doesn't mean that they don't sometimes enjoy listening to an adult read. Reading aloud chapters of a book, particularly classics such as *Peter Pan, Huckleberry Finn, Treasure Island,* and *Gulliver's Travels,* can be a special time you share with school-age children. You will find that the children look forward to having this time with you even if you have time to read only one short portion a day.

Special Activities

Reading and discussing books with children is probably the number-one activity you'll be doing to support children's growth and development through books. However, there are other activities you can try doing to extend children's learning. You can make available materials such as paper, writing tools, a typewriter, and other office supplies; a tape player and book/tape sets; and dramatic play props, puppets, and so on to encourage children's play beyond reading. Here are some additional thoughts:

- Have preschoolers and school-age children try their hand at storytelling. By encouraging children to tell a story in their own words, you help them build their vocabularies and learn to think logically. You can begin this activity by asking children to retell a favorite story. With practice and confidence, they can move on to create their own stories. Storytelling can be enhanced by the use of props, costumes, puppets, and flannel boards.

- Make your own picture books for infants to "babyhandle." Paste photographs or magazine pictures to cardboard, cover the cardboard with clear contact paper, and fasten the books with string or yarn strung through holes in the margin. Make indestructible cloth books by drawing illustrations of everyday objects on muslin sheets, using indelible markers or nontoxic embroidery paint. Pictures of dogs, cats, birds, rabbits, balls, bottles, and other familiar objects are good choices for illustrations.

- Make "feelie" books for infants by sewing different fabrics or unbreakable objects such as a rattle or pacifier onto cloth "pages." Sew the pages together to form a book.

- Help the children make their own "me" books using photographs or crayon-drawn self-portraits. Ask the children to describe each picture or photograph so that you can record a text for each page in the book.

- Together with the children, write your own books based on their experiences at family child care and at home. Discuss with the children topics of interest such as a visit to the fire station, a trip to their grandparents' house, how they grew vegetables in the garden for snack, and so on. Sit with each child and discuss the topic at length. Then record the child's thoughts in the simple language you find in picture books: clear, short, and to the point. For illustrations you can use photos, the children's art work, magazine pictures, or a combination of all three. The pages of these books can then be covered with plastic and bound together as described earlier.

- Plan regular field trips to your local library. Library visits are the easiest and least expensive way of providing children with a rich variety of books, and are also fun excursions. Letting children help pick out books ensures that you are selecting books of interest to them and that you respect their opinions and choices. Before planning a group trip, it's wise to check first with the children's librarian to arrange a convenient—and perhaps regular—visiting time when the librarian will be available to assist your children in selecting books. (Be prepared to assist in selection by helping the children find stories of particular interest or by helping them choose among books. The number of books available can be overwhelming—especially for enthusiastic children.

| Charlie (5 years) |
| John (8-1/2 years) |
| Jorie (6 months) |
| Samantha (18 months) |
| Sandra (2 years) |

Involving Children of Different Ages

Books can be used in a variety of ways, at different times of the day, and with all age groups. Here's what might take place in your family child care home:

Charlie and Samantha arrive at your home at 6:45 a.m. After some friendly greetings, they are both off to the book corner. (Near the couch you have several containers of books for the children to select from.)

"Read, read," says Samantha as she toddles off to pick out her favorite book. Charlie follows her to the couch and sits down. She hands him the book, and he begins to tell the story. Samantha's favorite book is a simple picture book with just one line on each page that Charlie has memorized. Although not yet a word reader, Charlie can sight-read from pictures. These two children enjoy this transition routine, and Charlie reads to

Samantha every morning when they arrive. You talk to their parents for a few minutes before they gently interrupt the story to say good-bye. After one or two books, both children are ready to play at a different activity or to join the other children who are now arriving.

Later that day . . .

"I need two red bricks," calls John as he and the other children build with Legos. They have been building for 20 minutes now, and it is clear that Sandra is getting tired of this activity.

"Sandra," you say, "It seems to me that you aren't as interested in the blocks as you were before. Is that so?" (She nods yes.) "How would you like to get a book and sit on my lap? You could read, and I could still be near the other kids."

"Okay," replies Sandra. She chooses a book she has never looked at before and snuggles in to examine every detail of the illustrations.

Later on . . .

"Growl, growl, somebody's been sitting in my chair!" says John as he pretends to be the papa bear from *Goldilocks and the Three Bears*.

"Sunduddy been my chair," says Sandra, pretending to be the mama bear.

"Somebody's been sitting in my chair and now it's broken," you say in your highest baby-bear voice. The children giggle at hearing you talk.

"And the three bears went upstairs," reads John, an accomplished reader who is acting as the narrator of this story. All the children are using this book (which you have read to them many times) to act out the story, complete with props and "bear" voices. They have included Jorie as part of the story; she is examining vinyl-covered books, but she is nonetheless part of the story line. The older children occasionally interrupt to tell mama or papa bear to remember to bring the baby on the walk, too.

Later still . . .

The day is almost over, and everyone is tired. You gather the children around you on the floor—some sitting, some lying down, one with the baby in her lap—and begin to read a few shorter books. As parents arrive, they follow the agreed-upon routine of letting themselves in, checking their information boxes, and quietly joining the group for the few minutes it takes to finish the story. Then, as you say good-bye to the children and parents who are leaving, you let the remaining children browse through the books on the floor.

The foregoing scenes have highlighted some of the important points to remember when offering books to children:

- Books are extremely useful at transition time or when you want to encourage children to relax.

- Books can be used independently or in groups, providing a rich array of learning experiences.

- Because there is usually no preparation required and no clean-up needed (other than putting the books away), reading can be done any time and any place—in addition to any formal story time you may have in your schedule. Reading or looking at books is a good choice for children who do not want to do a group activity, and you can encourage that choice even when you need to be supervising another activity.

- Using books is one of the easiest ways in which to bring together varying age groups.

Parents will be pleased to see that your have a good supply of books in your home and that you read to children often. If a letter to parents is something you want to share, consider adapting the one on the next page.

A Letter to Parents on Books

What We Do and Why

Reading is essential for success in school. It's also a wonderful source of enjoyment. One of the best ways to interest children in reading when they are six or seven is to read to them every day when they are young. I believe in getting children interested in books from the time they can sit in my lap and focus.

I encourage the children to look at books any time during the day. We also have a special story time together. Sometimes I choose a story to read to the children; at other times I let them pick their favorites. Here are some of the things I do during story time to help children learn to love books:

- We look at the pictures together and I ask them questions such as these: "Can you find where the caterpillar is now?" or "What is that silly dog doing?"

- I point out the pictures for babies and say, "There's the ball" or "Here's the baby's bottle."

- I ask the older children, "What do you think will happen next?" or "Why do you think she is smiling?" so they can tell the story with me.

- I let all the children help me tell the story by repeating words or phrases they have memorized.

I keep some of the children's books in a plastic milk crate turned on its side. This way the children can get a book easily any time they like. We keep our library books on a low shelf in the play area. I keep the cloth and laminated cardboard books on the floor for the babies so they can get them when they crawl around.

I also take the children regularly to the library for story hour and to check out new books. The children's librarian helps us find excellent books to borrow for each age group.

What You Can Do at Home

The most important thing you can do to help your child become a reader is to read together every day. A special story time before bed can mean so much to your child and can bring you closer together. There are many wonderful books for children at every age. Your local library is a great source for new books, as are a children's bookstore staff; if you can, take your child there to pick out new books regularly. In *The Creative Curriculum for Family Child Care,* there is a list of recommended children's books on many of the topics that interest young children. I'd be glad to share this list with you if you are looking for new books for your child.

Recommended Children's Books

Books for Babies and Toddlers

Most of the following are board books. Some are available in board and paperback formats.

Black on White, White on Black, What Is It?, and more by Tana Hoban
Country Animals, Farm Animals, Pet Animals, Maisy Goes Swimming, Maisy Goes to Bed, Maisy at the Farm, Playtime: First Words, Rhymes, and Actions, and more by Lucy Cousins
Dressing, Family, I Can, I Hear, I See, I Touch, Clap Hands, Tickle, Tickle, and more by Helen Oxenbury
Forest and Pond by Lizi Boyd
Goodnight Moon (available in English and Spanish), *Runaway Bunny*, and more by Margaret Wise Brown
Guess How Much I Love You, by Sam McBratney
Max's First Word, Max's Breakfast, Max's Bath, and more by Rosemary Wells
Pat the Bunny, by Dorothy Kunhardt
Shake Shake Shake, I Smell Honey, and *Pretty Brown Face* by Andrea Pinkney
Where's Spot?, Spot on the Farm, Spot's First Walk, and more by Eric Carle

Wordless and Almost Wordless Picture Storybooks

Anno's Journey by Mitsumasa Anno
Changes, Changes and *Rosie's Walk* by Pat Hutchins
Two Bear Cubs by Ann Jonas
Have You Seen My Duckling? and *Do Not Disturb* by Nancy Tafuri
Good Dog Carl, Carl's Afternoon in the Park, and others by Alexandra Day
Good Night Gorilla by Peggy Rathman
Let's Go Visiting by Sue Williams
Oink by Arthur Geisert
The Snowman by Raymond Briggs
Zoom and Re-Zoom by Istvan Banyai

Concept, Alphabet, and Number Books

Alphabestiary: Animal Poems from A to Z by Jane Yolen
Animalia by Graham Base
Anno's Alphabet by Mitsumasa Anno
Chicka, Chicka, Boom Boom by Bill Martin
Color Dance by Ann Jonas
Freight Train by Donald Crews
How Are You Peeling: Foods with Moods by Saxton Freymann, Joost Elffers
I Spy Little Book, I Spy Little Wheels, I Spy Little Letters, and more by Jean Marzollo
Is It Larger? Is It Smaller, I Read Signs, Shapes, Shapes, Shapes and more by Tana Hoban

Mouse Paint by Ellen Walsh
Ten Rosie Roses by Eve Merriam

Books of Rhymes, Songs, and Poetry

Animal Crackers: A Delectable Collection of Pictures, Poems, and Lullabies for the Very Young by Jane Dyer
Arroz Con Leche: Popular Songs and Rhymes from Latin America by Lulu Delacre
Diez Deditos: 10 Little Fingers and Other Play Rhymes and Action Songs from Latin America by Jose-Luis Orozco
My Very First Mother Goose and *Here Comes Mother Goose* by Iona Opie
Street Rhymes Around the World by Jane Yolen
20th Century Poetry Treasury by Jack Prelutsky
When We Were Very Young by A. A. Milne
Where the Sidewalk Ends, The Giving Tree, A Light in the Attic, and more by Shel Silverstein

Books with Repetitive Words and Phrases

Brown Bear, Brown Bear, What do You See? (available in English and Spanish) and *Polar Bear, Polar Bear What Do You Hear?* by Bill Martin, Jr. and Eric Carle
I Love You, Little One by Nancy Tafuri
The Very Hungry Caterpillar, The Very Busy Spider, The Very Clumsy Click Beetle, and more in this series by Eric Carle
We're Going on a Bear Hunt by Michael Rosen (available in English and Spanish)

Picture Storybooks

And if the Moon Could Talk by Kate Banks
The Babies Are Coming! by Amy Hest
Bunnycakes and others in the Max and Ruby series by Rosemary Wells
Chrysanthemum by Kevin Henkes
Cleversticks by Bernard Ashley
The Cow Buzzed by Andrea Zimmerman and David Clemesha
Dogzilla and Kat Kong by Dave Pilkey
Joseph Had a Little Overcoat by Simms Taback
The Little Red Hen (Makes a Pizza) by Philemon Sturges
Lon Po Po: A Red-Riding Hood Story from China by Ed Young
Margaret and Margarita (Margarita Y Margaret) by Lynn Reiser
Minerva Louise, A Hat for Minerva Louise, and more by Janet Morgan Stoeke
Piggie Pie! by Margie Palatini
Stone Soup by Tony Ross
Too Much Noise by Ann McGovern
Wolf by Becky Bloom

Families, Friends, and Feelings

Adam's Daycare by Julie Ovenell-Carter and Ruth Ohi (this is a very special book about daily life in an FCC home)
Bedtime for Frances, A Baby Sister for Frances, A Bargain for Frances, and more in this series by Russell Hoban

The Colors of Us by Karen Katz
dear juno by Soyung Pak
Hello, Shoes! by Jean Blos
Families by Meredith Tax
Just Like Me by Miriam Schlein
The Kissing Hand by Audrey Penn
L is for Loving, An ABC for the Way You Feel by Ken Wilson-Max
Red Light, Green Light, Mama and Me by Cari Best
Tar Beach, Dinner at Aunt Connie's House, and more by Faith Ringgold
Tell Me a Story, Mama by Angela Johnson
When Sophie Gets Angry—Really, Really Angry by Molly Bang

Information Books for Young Children

Here are a few examples of books that provide information on various topics. Through ongoing observation and conversations with children you will learn what topics spark their curiosity. You can then provide library books that support and expand their special interests.

Animal Seasons by Brian Wildsmith
Bread, Bread, Bread, Houses and Homes, Hats, Hats, Hats, and others in this series
    by Ann Morris
Bugs, Bugs, Bugs by Bob Barner
Cars and Trucks and Other Vehicles by Claude Delafosse
From Seed to Plant by Gail Gibbons
In the Small, Small Pond and In the Tall, Tall Grass by Denise Fleming
Silver Space Shuttle, Little Red Plane, Big Yellow Taxi, and more by Ken Wilson-Max

Books for Early Readers

*Alexander and the Terrible, Horrible, No Good, Very Bad Day, Alexander, Who Used
    to Be Rich Last Sunday* and others by Judith Viorst
Amelia Bedelia and others in this series by Peggy Parrish
Arthur and others in this series by Marc Brown
Curious George and others in this series by H. A. and Margaret Rey
Frog and Toad are Friends and others in this series by Arnold Lobel
Harold and the Purple Crayon and others in this series by Crocket Johnson
Lily's Purple Plastic Purse by Kevin Henkes
Little Bear and others in this series by Else Holmelund Minarik
Madeline and others in this series by Ludwig Bemelmans
*One Fish, Two Fish, Red Fish, Blue Fish, The Cat in the Hat, Green
    Eggs and Ham* and others by Dr. Seuss

Books for School-Age Children

There is a large storehouse of titles from which you can choose any number of excellent books for school-age children. This listing offers some of the more popular fiction and nonfiction titles suggested for children in grades K-6. Because of wide range of reading abilities and interests that exist in school-age children, not all of these titles will be appropriate for all children. Use this list as a starting point and consult with the children's

librarian at your nearest public library for further assistance. You might also want to supplement this list with general reference materials that would be of interest to school-age children, such as a dictionary, the *World Almanac*, and the *Guiness Book of Records*.

Fiction for School-Age Readers

Are You There God? It's Me, Margaret and others by Judy Blume
Big Men, Big Country: A Collection of American Tall Tales by Paul Robert Walker
Bud, Not Buddy by Christopher Paul Curtis
Bunnicula: A Rabbit Tale of Mystery by Deborah and Hames Howe
Dicey's Song, The Homecoming, and others by Cynthia Voigt
The Giver by Lois Lowry
The Harry Potter series by J.K. Rowling
Holes by Louis Sachar
The Indian in the Cupboard by Lynne Reid Banks
Island of the Blue Dolphins by Scott O'Dell
Maniac Magee: A Novel by Jerry Spinelli
The Queen's Own Fool by Jane Yolen
Roll of Thunder, Hear My Cry by Mildred Taylor
Sarah, Plain and Tall by Patricia MacLachlan
Shiloh by Phyllis Reynolds
Stuart Little by E. B. White
Tuck Everlasting by Natalie Babbitt
26 Fairmount Avenue and Here We All Are by Tomie dePaola

Non-Fiction for School-Age Readers

The Century for Young People by Peter Jennings, et al
The Century That Was: Reflection on the Last One Hundred Years by James Cross
Honest Pretzels and 64 Other Amazing Recipes for Cooks Ages 8 and Up by Mollie Katzen
If You Lived in Colonial Times by Ann McGovern
It's Disgusting—And We Ate It!: True Food Facts from Around the World—And Throughout History! by James Solheim
Underground, Mill, and others by David MacAulay

Cooking

I. Why Cooking Is Important

Cooking is a daily happening in a family child care program. Children need lunch, snacks, and very often breakfast, too. This means that cooking is already part of your curriculum.

But cooking can be more than just a chore you have to do—it can also be a teaching activity. Through cooking experiences, children learn how food helps their bodies develop and how it keeps them healthy. Cooking can also provide children with a wealth of learning experiences, from the scientific to the creative.

Cooking is one of the best ways that providers have to make use of everyday routines to teach children. Moreover, by letting children participate in an activity they see you and their parents doing daily, you invite children into the world of grown-ups. This can be very exciting for children, and it provides built-in motivation for learning. Of course, cooking also involves activities and ways of learning that children love: pouring, dumping, mixing, stirring, scooping, smelling, testing, feeling, hearing, and tasting.

Here are some of the many types of learning experiences that can take place through cooking.

Children develop thinking skills by:

- Learning about nutrition (participating in preparing balanced meals and snacks).

- Solving problems (remembering to fill a muffin tin only halfway to keep batter from spilling over when cooked).

- Sorting and classifying (searching for bananas that are soft and darkened to use in making banana bread).

- Gaining a foundation in math (filling a quart pitcher with four cups of water to make lemonade).

- Understanding scientific principles (watching cream turn to butter).

- Expressing creativity (decorating muffins with cream cheese "faces" or folding napkins into shapes while setting the table).

Children develop socially by:

- Developing responsibility (helping in chores of daily life by preparing meals).

- Learning self-help skills (setting the table for lunch).

- Developing consideration for others (asking another child what she would like to drink during snack time).

- Working cooperatively (baking a cake together).

Children develop emotionally by:

- Showing pride (serving pudding they've made themselves to the younger children for a snack).

- Having fun (enjoying cooking and eating as a group).

Children develop physically by:

- Strengthening hand muscles (sifting flour).

- Coordinating eye and hand movements (pouring water through a funnel).

- Learning directionality (using a whisk to beat egg whites).

These are just a sampling of the many ways in which cooking can be used to support children's growth and development. With just a little planning on your part, you'll find that you can easily provide children with learning opportunities such as these. In the next section we'll look at how you can set up the kitchen in your family child care home to support the development of children in various age groups.

II. Setting the Stage for Cooking

The materials and space needed for cooking with children already exist in your home. All you need to do to make cooking activities successful is to plan an approach to using these materials that meets the children's needs. Here are some suggestions for doing this.

Selecting Materials

What follows is a sample inventory of cooking supplies and equipment. Supplied with these utensils, you will be able you to conduct just about any cooking project with young children. Don't be alarmed, though, if you don't already have all of this equipment. The same equipment you ordinarily use for your own cooking activities can be substituted, as long as it poses no danger to the children. This list is presented merely as a starting point; you'll want to alter it to reflect your own preferences.

Plastic mixing bowls of various sizes
Plastic measuring spoons
Plastic measuring cups
1 and 2 C Pyrex measuring cups (so measuring can be observed)
Wooden spoons
Funnel
Wire whisk
Egg beater
Potato masher or ricer
Colander
Manual sifter or strainer
Pastry brush
Knives (paring and plastic serrated)
Cutting board
Spatulas

Rolling pin
Ladle
Cookie cutters
Tongs
Cheesecloth
Pastry bag with coupler and tips
Large slotted spoon
Cookie Sheet
Muffin tin
Cake pans (round or square)
Saucepans with lids
Electric frying pan or wok (optional)
Blender (optional)
Trivets
Potholders

In assembling materials for the children, try to use ones made of rubber or unbreakable plastic. Accidents are bound to happen, so you'll need to protect children from being hurt by broken bowls, glasses, or utensils. In some cases, though, Pyrex utensils are recommended, as they allow children to see what is going on during the cooking process.

In selecting recipes, be safety conscious. Large chunks of food, too-sticky peanut butter, nuts, large raw pieces of carrot, popcorn, and so on are choking hazards. Clean, thorough cooking is required for many foods. Certain foods such as eggs must be used with care, as some children are allergic to them.

Creating Space

Finding a space for cooking is rarely a problem, for you already have a kitchen equipped with the materials children need for cooking activities. There are, however, certain things you can do to make your kitchen more functional for the young cooks who will be sharing it with you. Here are some suggestions:

- Store materials for use by the children in one area of the kitchen so that children can easily find them and know what is available. This will enable you to incorporate cooking activities into your daily schedule without a great deal of advanced preparation time.

- Place all knives and sharp instruments (e.g., cheese slicers, meat forks, meat thermometers) out of the children's reach. To play it safe, use plastic serrated knives or blunt-edged scissors instead of steel knives.

- Store items that the children are likely to want to reach on their own in cabinets under the counters or on low, open shelving elsewhere in the kitchen. This arrangement encourages independence and promotes clean-up, too. If the items are stored behind cupboard doors, think about displaying picture labels on the outside doors of the cabinets.

- Set up a table for work preparation that is no taller in height than the children's waists. To share in the cooking activities, children need to experience everything. If you don't have a child-sized table available, consider cutting down the legs on an old wooden table or placing an unused door on blocks or bricks. These approaches are better than having children use a step ladder or booster chair to reach an adult-sized table or counter. Children need to be able to move freely around the work area to enjoy the cooking experience fully.

- Place the work table near an electrical outlet so you can plug in a mixer, blender, or electric frying pan. Keep the outlets covered until needed, and then make sure you are the only one who plugs in and unplugs appliances. If this arrangement is not feasible, be sure to block off the area where cords are hanging to prevent children from tripping over them.

- Consider using an electric frying pan or wok as a substitute for the stove. These appliances are more manageable for young children, especially if they're used on a child-sized work table. If you don't own one of these appliances, you can probably buy one at yard sale. Make sure, however, that it is safe to use: no frayed cords or loose switches.

- Draw and display signs that help teach safety in the kitchen. For example, you can post a picture of dirty hands over the sink to remind children to wash their hands before cooking. Next to the stove, you can post a picture of pots with their handles all pointing inward to prevent accidents. You can also post a diagram next to the burners on the stove that will remind the children which switch controls which burner.

- Have cleaning supplies such as mops, sponges, and toweling on hand and within the children's reach. Any cleansers should be locked away.

- Provide aprons or smocks made of old shirts for all children. In cooking, much of the pleasure comes from rigorous stirring of batter and enthusiastic beatings of eggs. Messes are inevitable.

With a relatively small amount of effort, you can set up your kitchen to make it easier to cook with young children. In the next section we'll discuss some strategies you can use to encourage children's growth and development through cooking and other related experiences.

III. Helping Children Learn Through Cooking

There are many opportunities for learning through cooking. However, because cooking activities need to be carefully supervised, your involvement is very important. Unlike playing with toys or books, cooking is not an activity that children can do on their own. It is rather an activity that demands your full support and participation. To make the most of your time, therefore, it's important to be aware of what the children in your care are likely to learn from food experiences, so you can plan activities that will best meet their needs. Here are some ideas for each age group.

Infants

Infants don't possess the physical skills to perform cooking tasks, but they can be a part of the cooking experience. They can use all their senses (not just taste) to learn about different foods. They can dip their hands in a bowl of batter and observe how different the mixed ingredients feel from the individual flour, butter, and sugar that were added. They can also gain a foundation for healthy eating as they observe and help prepare meals and snacks.

Cooking Activities That Help Infants Develop	Why These Activities Are Important
Emotionally . . .	
Feeding time provides an opportunity to talk with infants, soothe them, and help them associate food with pleasant times.	This is a basic element in teaching children good nutrition habits. Children who have pleasant associations with meals grow up to be healthier eaters.
Feed an infant according to his or her individual needs and schedule.	By responding to the infants' unique needs, you make them feel secure.
Socially . . .	
Use feeding times as an opportunity to be one-on-one with infants.	This will make infants feel bonded to you as well as to their parents.
Bring an infant into a group cooking experience by holding up the child to see the action or letting a child hold onto a whisk with you as you beat an egg.	These activities allow an infant to reap the benefits of group experiences without interfering in what older children are doing.
Cognitively . . .	
During cookie-making, give infants a small amount of dough to touch, smell, shake, and touch.	Infants need to use all their senses to learn.
Let infants poke at bread dough as you knead it. Describe what's happening as you do this together.	By participating in the action with you, infants can discover cause and effect for themselves.

Encourage infants to mimic the sounds of popping corn or the whirring of a blender.

Cooking experiences provide terrific sounds for infants to imitate. Making sounds provides the foundation for later talking.

Physically...

Allow infants to begin to handle their food during feedings as soon as they are ready.

Small muscle development and control, as well as eye-hand coordination, are all advanced during this activity which also generates a high level of interest and enjoyment in the infant.

Provide opportunities for mobile infants to help during cooking activities by kneading or rolling dough, mashing vegetables, spraying vegetables with water, and stirring batter.

These activities require the use and control of larger muscles, and offer a chance to practice using these muscles.

Toddlers

Toddlers may be more ready for cooking experiences than you are to provide them. Equipped with the newly learned physical skills needed to hold and use utensils, they can be off and running in the kitchen. Your greatest challenge will be to channel toddlers' energy and enthusiasm into meaningful experiences. Begin by letting toddlers help set up and clean up after meals. Let them become involved in food preparation activities that involve a limited number of ingredients and skills, such as squeezing oranges for juice at snack time. This will cut down on messes while allowing them to refine their physical skills.

Cooking Activities That Help Toddlers Develop

Why These Activities Are Important

Emotionally...

Encourage toddlers to practice self-help skills such as setting the table, using a fork and spoon, or pouring milk from a small pitcher.

Preparing and eating meals and cleaning up afterward gives toddlers wonderful opportunities for asserting independence. Having the children's help makes your day easier.

Initially, introduce cooking projects that require only one or two tasks such as peeling a carrot or hulling strawberries.

Children love to cook because it's a grown up activity, but giving a child a complicated task will cause frustration. Start simple and let the children advance to more complex activities.

Because cooking demands constant adult supervision, this is a good time to work and play side by side.

Children associate cooking with their loved ones, whom they see engaged in this activity daily. When you cook with children, you strengthen the bonds between you.

Socially . . .

Assign each child a specific role to avoid a tug-of-war over who gets to whip the cream and who gets to stir the batter.

Planning can defuse potential conflicts. At the same time, children get the benefits of participating in a group experience.

As you cook, remind toddlers, "You're making soup just like Daddy does," or ask, "Do you like baking bread like Mommy does?"

Cooking is a rare opportunity for children to do exactly the same things adults do.

Cognitively . . .

Give toddlers a chance to excel at cooking tasks they've mastered, such as punching down bread dough.

Children learn through repetition. Cooking activities, with their built-in repetition of tasks, are ideal for learning.

As you cook, ask toddlers, "What happened to the corn when we popped it?" or "What did the butter do when we put it in the microwave?"

Language skills can be promoted naturally during cooking.

Don't ask toddlers to spend a long time on any one task. If egg yolks and sugar need to be beaten for seven minutes, have two or three children take turns.

Toddlers have limited attention spans.

Physically . . .

Encourage toddlers to throw themselves into cooking tasks enthusiastically—stirring using their whole bodies, jumping up and down as they knead dough, etc.

You can make use of the toddlers' energy by channeling it into cooking activities. Children love the physical aspects of cooking.

Assign kitchen tasks that toddlers can readily perform, such as sifting flour, whisking an egg, or dropping dough from a spoon to a cookie sheet.

Cooking activities provide a wonderful opportunity for helping children develop small muscle skills and eye-hand coordination.

Preschool Children

During the preschool years, children can become very interested in both cooking and nutrition. They delight in being able to eat something that they have helped make. Cooking together is both fun and creative for these children. Preschoolers also like learning about how the foods they eat affect their bodies and their health. You can tap into this natural interest in nutrition to lay a foundation for healthy eating.

Cooking Activities That Help Preschoolers Develop	**Why These Activities Are Important**
Emotionally . . .	
Respond favorably to the preschoolers' choice of nutritious snack foods. Let them know that eating well shows maturity and responsibility.	Praising children for their good choices helps them develop self-confidence.
Don't force the children to eat when they are unhappy or angry or when they are not hungry. Help them associate mealtimes with pleasant emotions.	By being sensitive to children's moods, you help make appropriate associations between eating and emotions. You also let children know that they are more important than the meal being served.
Socially . . .	
Encourage children to pair up on a specific cooking task such as grating carrots for carrot cake.	Preschoolers enjoy each others' company. Cooking is a great activity for working in a group or in pairs.
Extend cooking activities into dramatic play time. For example, save some of the muffins you've baked for the dolls in the dramatic play area to enjoy.	This helps children to bring a touch of the fanciful into the otherwise "serious" task of cooking.
Praise children for their help, enthusiasm, and skill—not just for the finished product.	You want children to feel valued for who they are, as well as for what they do.
Cognitively . . .	
Ask questions as you cook together: "What happened to the chocolate chips when we put them in the saucepan on the stove?"	Cooking is a natural environment for promoting language and thinking skills.
Give preschoolers an eggbeater or a potato peeler and have them guess what the gadget is used for.	Preschoolers learn best when they discover things for themselves. If they come up with an original idea for using a gadget, you might try using it that way regularly and crediting the "inventor."
Be sure to comment on the children's contribution to each snack or meal that they help prepare or serve.	Children can take pride in contributing to the well-being of their family day care home.
Use the kitchen as a science lab. Let a preschooler try making bread without letting the yeast proof, or whipping egg whites with dirty beaters. Then let the child do those activities with proofed yeast and clean beaters to see the difference.	Children learn through experimentation. When they're in charge, learning is a natural outgrowth.

Physically...

Provide lots of activities in the kitchen to develop small muscle skills: pouring, stirring, and kneading, for example.

Although the development of small muscle skills many not be your primary goal in planning a cooking activity, it's a wonderful result.

On a nice day, have an outdoor picnic so that children can stretch and move about fully.

Use outdoor eating experiences as opportunities for children to stretch and use their large muscles.

Encourage children to participate in cooking activities that strengthen eye-hand coordination: tearing lettuce, grating carrots, peeling potatoes, or arranging cookie dough on a baking sheet.

You can help children develop physical skills while doing normal cooking routines.

School-Age Children

Many school-age children enjoy cooking activities, viewing them in much the same way they do craft projects. For these children, baking bread or decorating a cake is fun, relaxing, and a source of pride. Other children tend to view cooking more as a means to eating and not as an activity that is interesting in and of itself. These children shouldn't be forced into the kitchen. However, by allowing them "creative control" over their own snacks, you may find that even otherwise reluctant children will take to cooking.

Cooking Activities That Help School-Age Children Develop

Why These Activities Are Important

Emotionally...

Encourage school-age children to prepare after-school snacks of their choice.

By letting older children take on this responsibility, you encourage independence.

Positively reinforce the children's healthy food choices.

Reinforcing proper nutrition habits makes children feel responsible and mature.

Socially...

Suggest that school-age children prepare something special that they can share with schoolmates—a cake, muffins, or brownies.

By bringing a treat to school, older children become popular with their age mates. You'll be doing them a big service if you use family day care time to help them deal with school.

Encourage the children to try new foods, but respect the children's preferences.

School-age children are quick to adopt their peers' preferences for food (and everything else). Encourage experimentation in eating, but don't expect the impossible.

Ask the children to help you supervise a group cooking activity such as baking bread.

Cognitively . . .

Encourage school-age children to prepare a snack that everyone in family child care might enjoy.

Write on index cards recipes for the children's favorite foods. Store these cards in a place where the children can get them whenever they want.

Arrange a group cooking activity for the children to prepare something they can bring to scouts or serve their families for dinner.

Have the children try their hand at inventing their own recipes. Once they work out recipes they especially like, encourage them to record each recipe on an index card.

Physically . . .

Encourage school-age children to develop specialized cooking skills that require advanced physical coordination, such as making vegetable garnishes.

If a child shows interest in a cooking skill such as cake decorating, provide the child with opportunities to refine this skill. For example, make a pastry tube from parchment and give the child cardboard cutouts to practice decorating.

Many older children enjoy taking on a leadership role. It helps them feel more confident, and the younger ones love being with the older children.

Many older children enjoy cooking for a group and taking satisfaction in everyone else's enjoyment.

By doing this you will promote independence as well as providing children with an opportunity to read and carry out a project.

Cooperative activities with peers are all-important during the school years. When you recognize and make use of this, the children will be more enthusiastic about their time at family day care.

Older children love to invent their own concoctions and experiment with foods. By having them record their favorites, you let them know that you value their creative efforts.

You can use cooking activities to help children refine physical skills such as coordination and small motor movements.

Older children already know that practicing physical skills can lead to proficiency. By helping children develop this proficiency you make them more confident and competent.

Special Activities

As you cook with the children, you'll find that you can use your time with them in the kitchen to introduce specific topics and give the children opportunities to practice various skills. Here are some ideas you might wish to try:

*   Have the children prepare a meal or snack from start to finish. This includes planning a menu based on sound nutrition, assembling ingredients, preparing the food, eating the meal family-style, and cleaning up. To make this exercise "complete," children can even grow some of the ingredients. Mung beans or alfalfa sprouts that can be used in salads, stir-fries, or sandwiches are especially easy to grow at home.

- Develop picture recipe cards that the children can use in cooking. These will make the children feel more independent and confident about what they're doing. By labeling the pictures with words, you can also help the children develop pre-reading skills. Cover the recipe cards with clear contact paper to protect them from spills and fasten them together like a book. Here's a picture recipe for making applesauce.

Applesauce

6 Apples

Peel apples

Core apples

Slice apples

Put apples in pot

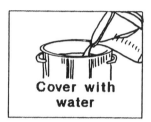

Cover with water

Add honey

Add cinnamon

Cook 30 minutes

Cool

Eat!

- Have the children experiment with finding different uses for foods. For example, at Halloween the children can make pumpkin soup, pumpkin bread, and pumpkin pie. Soak the seeds in a solution of salt water and bake them until dry for a different taste treat.

- Build cooking activities around studies of other people, cultures, and holidays. For example, children can help you cook egg foo yong, pizza, tacos, hummos, or curried chicken. Before cooking these meals, read the children a story about people from the countries where these foods are traditionally eaten. You might also try playing appropriate music to accompany the eating of these foods, such as Indian sitar music for chicken curry or mariachi band music for tacos.

- Tie food into other learning activities. Just as you can use cooking activities to reinforce concepts being learned with table toys or blocks, you can also use food such as tacos, hummus, or curried chicken to teach concepts in these other areas. For instance, consider making food Lotto games in which children match foods by color, shape, or food groups.

- Literature is another excellent tie-in to cooking. What better link could there be to reading "Little Miss Muffet" than to have the children make "curds and whey" (cottage cheese, as we know it)? Actually seeing the curds separate from the liquid whey brings a literal understanding of this nursery rhyme that is new even to many adults.

- Science, too, is a natural extension of cooking. You can discuss the physical changes that occurred in making ice cream or letting dough rise. The effects of heat can be explained by relating them to cooking activities.

- Cooking ties in readily to music as well. Songs that mention foods, such as "Toast and Jam," "Here We Go Around the Mulberry Bush," and "Little Green Apples," are always fun to sing. Food seeds and dried peels can also be used in making instruments such as maracas and tambourines. Throughout the day you'll find countless opportunities to relate cooking to other learning activities.

- Take the children on field trips to food-related sites. Here are some possibilities:

Farm	Cannery
Bottling plant	Dairy
Orchard	Bakery
Hatchery	Grocery store
Mill	Cafeteria

- Consult with your local children's librarian or your county U.S. Department of Agriculture Extension Service Agent for particular references or recipes. Some books that will be helpful for finding recipes suitable for children include:

  Adventures in Cooking (Florence Foster)
  Cook and Learn—Pictorial Single Portion Recipes: A Child's Cook Book (Bev Veitch and Thelma Harms)
  Creative Food Experiences for Children (Mary Goodwin and Gerry Pollin)
  The Good for Me Cookbook (Karen Croft)
  The Good Goodies (Stan and Floss Dworkin)
  Kids Are Natural Cooks (Roz Ault)
  More Than Graham Crackers (Nancy Wanamaker, Kristin Hearn, and Sherrill Richarz)
  Science Experiments You Can Eat (Vicki Cobb)

- You can also write to the Consumer Affairs Department of major food-related companies for suggestions. Associations that serve food producers, such as The National Dairy Council, will provide you with excellent educational materials for use with young children. They will supply you with games and activities as well as (usually) free recipes.

If an activity holds great appeal for the group—the preparation of a snack made from vegetables grown in the family child care garden, or a holiday treat, for example—you'll want to schedule the cooking event as a group activity in which everyone can participate.

You can also ask the children's parents for suggestions for cooking projects. By cooking the children's favorite foods at family child care, you give children the message that they and their families are important. This also allows you to introduce the concept of family traditions into your program.

Using Cooking To Teach Nutrition

One of the most important reasons for cooking with children is to help them gain a foundation for proper nutrition. Even the youngest children can begin to learn that "we are what we eat." The types and choices of foods you and the children's parents introduce during these years will form the foundation for the children's eating choices later on. In family child care you can teach children that snacks of carrots or apples are more nutritious than cupcakes and cookies, and that meals that make use of lots of vegetables and fruits are better for them than meals heavy on red meat and sweets.

Thus, every cooking activity becomes a lesson in good eating habits. Discuss the nutritional value of the different dishes you prepare with the children, and point out the elements from each of the four basic food groups in the food pyramid that make the meal a balanced one. Because young children are fascinated by their bodies and by the changes they are going through, most love hearing how the foods they eat contribute to their growth. For instance, the fact that carrots help them see better or milk helps their bones grow strong are ideas most young children can relate to. Knowing this information helps them enjoy healthy foods all the more.

What kinds of dishes and meals should you prepare in these cooking sessions? This is a very individual choice. Most providers turn to the menus they would be serving even if they were not including cooking with children as part of their family day care curriculum. Dietary guidelines for preschool children recommend that children receive two to three servings of dairy products, two to three protein servings (meat, poultry, fish, beans, eggs, nuts), three to five vegetable servings, two to four fruit servings, and six to eleven servings of grains (bread, cereal, rice, pasta) daily. By consulting with the children's parents, you can make sure that children are receiving balanced meals. From these meal selections you can then choose cooking activities for you and the children to prepare together each day.

For more specific information on nutrition that can help you talk with children about the subject, you'll find a number of resources. Both your local public library and your county Department of Agriculture Extension Service Agent can steer you toward helpful resources. In addition, as mentioned earlier, the National Dairy Council, which has both local and regional offices, produces excellent free materials on nutrition.

Involving Children of All Ages

Cooking and food-related activities require your close supervision and attention; even older children can't do them completely on their own. But with some planning, you can undertake satisfying activities with a group of children of different ages—and everyone can benefit. Here's what might happen:

Sarah (3 months)
Nancy (6 years)
Joe (6-1/2 years)
Doug (3 years)
Karen (7 years)
Joshua (6 years)

As you bend down to pick up Sarah, who is lying on a blanket, you say to Doug, "Come on kids, let's go get snack ready." Since this is a favorite activity, Doug is more than willing to stop his play and head into the house with you. You let the older children know that the three of you are going inside.

Doug is quite adamant about announcing that everyone must wash up and he'll be first. You wash Sarah's hands right along with the others, and you are all ready to prepare a snack.

"Doug, would you please set out napkins? We'll need at least one for everybody," you ask, knowing that Doug cannot yet count but that he's getting pretty good at putting a napkin by each chair (along with a few extras scattered around).

Next, you ask Doug if he would like to prepare the juice. "Ya, I'm good at making juice," he says with obvious pride. You have already set out the pitcher; the frozen juice is now soft, and Doug has found a long-handled spoon in the drawer. "One, two, three, four," you and Doug count together as he pours in cans of water. Then you say to both Doug and Sarah, "Look at the water swirl as Doug stirs. Doesn't that juice smell good?" The baby coos and gurgles. As Doug finishes stirring, you add a box of crackers and sliced cheese to the table. The older children come in to join you for snack.

A little bit later, nap time has arrived for Doug and Sarah, and you have planned a cooking activity for the school-age and preschool children. Nancy, Karen, and Joe are eager to prepare their choices for lunch. Yesterday, they made up the menu, prepared picture recipe cards, and confirmed that you had the necessary foods on hand. Today, they are going to do this cooking activity on their own. One of their menu items is tacos, and they have decided that Joshua can grate the cheese. With your careful supervision, he is pushing a large chunk of cheese along a large sturdy grater.

"I can see you using your strong muscles to grate that cheese, Joshua. Is it really hard to do?" you ask.

"Boy is it! But I'm a really strong kid," he replies.

"Oh? How did you get so strong?" you ask.

"From playing and eating cheese," he answers with certainty. (He is starting to understand the concept that exercise and nutrition make his muscles strong.) After struggling with the cheese for about five minutes, he begins to get tired. "I'm finished with this stuff," he announces.

"OK," you say. "Do you have a plan for something to do while I continue cooking with the others?" (He shakes his head no.) "Well, here are some choices. The books and puzzles are out, and so are those two new toys we have. You can pick from any of those."

He's halfway out the door as he excitedly says he's going to choose one of the new toys. You turn to the school-agers, who have been deciding which food to fix next.

"I think it's time to get started on browning the hamburger while it's easy for me to be here with you," you say. "Whose job is it to do that?" Karen is going to brown the hamburger while the other two finish cutting up tomatoes and lettuce. Nancy tears the lettuce into pieces, and Joe uses a paring knife to slice the tomatoes. Knowing that the other children are safely occupied, you can give your attention to Karen and the task of browning the hamburger.

To include children of all ages in successful cooking activities, as in the scene just described, consider these points:

- Always include children in some aspects of food preparation—no matter how small—to develop self-help skills, to improve small muscle coordination or cognitive skills, and to share in the responsibilities of daily living and the social aspects of cooking.

- Pay attention to skill levels and design activities accordingly. Consider individual children's interest in cooking and the rest of your daily schedule.

- Work individually with children during cooking for closeness and safety.

- Sometimes schedule a cooking activity so that only older children participate. This allows for more complex cooking and is a time when the older children can feel special.

Parents may be very interested and concerned about the types of food and cooking-related activities you provide. If you wish, you can share the following letter—or a version of it—with parents of the children in your care. It will help them understand your approach to cooking and food.

A Letter to Parents on Cooking

What We Do and Why

Cooking is as natural in family child care as it is in your home. I involve the children as much as I can in the preparation, serving, and cleaning up of our meals and snacks.

When we cook together, I put out everything we need on the table and give each child a turn to pour in the ingredients, stir, and observe what's going on. We talk a lot about what we are doing:

- Measuring the water
- Cutting the bread in half
- Mixing the tuna with mayonnaise
- Whipping the egg whites
- Spreading the jelly

This way, the children learn new words and how to talk about what they are doing. They are also learning math and science concepts. When they set out napkins for each person, they learn about correspondence. They also see how the ingredients change when we add milk or take something out of the oven.

The children like to help set the table at lunch and for snack. They practice pouring their own milk and juice from small pitchers. As soon as the babies start to grab a spoon, I let them feed themselves. I try to give them finger foods such as dry cereal and crackers so they can do things for themselves. I serve food family-style so that everyone can participate in this group experience.

Helping me in the kitchen makes children feel important. They take pride in being able to prepare something they will eat later on. They also like being allowed to do a "grown-up" activity.

What You Can Do at Home

It takes a little more time and patience to involve your child in meal preparations at home. But if you make cooking a family activity, you can build positive attitudes about food and helping out at home. At the same time, your child will be learning. Here are some things you might point out and discuss as you cook together:

- The names of different foods
- How they look, smell and taste
- How many teaspoons/cups/pinches of each item you need in a recipe
- Where different utensils belong in the kitchen
- Why some foods need to be kept in the refrigerator or freezer

Children who are still in high chairs can feed themselves as they watch and listen to you preparing dinner. Older children can take responsibility for preparing one particular part of the dinner.

If you and your child want to prepare a special treat for our program, it would be a nice way to share something from home. Please let me know ahead of time. Also, I'm now in the process of collecting simple recipes to use with the children. Let me know if you have any ideas you'd like to share. Family favorites and recipes that reflect your family's heritage would be most welcome.

Music and Movement

I. Why Music and Movement Are Important

From a very early age, children respond to music. Infants smile when adults sing to them. They turn their heads toward toys and mobiles that make sounds. They react to noises in their environment. As children grow, their interest in music continues, and they begin to hum, sing, and create their own rhymes and chants.

Young children respond to music with their entire bodies. As children develop coordination, they sway, dance, bounce up and down, clap hands, and stamp their feet to music. When provided with props such as pots and pans, wooden spoons, and (later on) musical instruments, they discover ways to create music and sound and to combine music with movement.

Music can also affect children's moods. Quiet, comforting music can help them relax and fall asleep, whereas a lively march can invite them to parade around the room and sing. Music gives children many opportunities for creative self-expression. Children naturally connect movement with music. Listening to music allows them to explore what their bodies can do and to become aware of how their bodies move in space. For all ages, music and movement experiences enhance language development and listening skills, physical coordination, and the ability to put feelings into words or actions.

Here are some ways in which music and movement activities support growth and development.

Children develop thinking skills by:

- Linking sounds to their source (turning toward a musical mobile while resting in a crib).

- Discovering cause and effect (banging a pan with a wooden spoon and saying "I make noise!").

- Distinguishing sounds (making different sounds with musical instruments and recognizing differences in volume, tempo, and tone).

- Applying knowledge (replicating the sound of a drum beat on a record by beating on the bottom of a pan).

- Solving problems (learning how to shake maracas or bang a xylophone to produce musical sounds).

Children develop socially by:

- Sharing experiences with others (playing "Ring Around the Rosy").

- Making friends ("dancing" together).

Children develop emotionally by:

- Expressing emotions (reacting in different ways to music and sound).

- Forming a sense of personal taste (beginning to recognize the types of music they like best and experimenting with movement).

Children develop physically by:

- Becoming aware of what their bodies can do (moving arms and legs when music is played).

- Coordinating eye and hand movements (imitating simple finger plays).

- Practicing large motor skills (hopping, swaying, and leaping during creative movement).

- Developing rhythm (clapping and stamping feet in time to music).

These are just a few of the many benefits you can expect when you include music and movement in your family child care program. In the next section we'll look at how you can tailor your environment to provide positive music and movement experiences for the children in your care.

II. Setting the Stage for Music and Movement

One of the nicest things about music and movement experiences is that they are "portable." You and the children can sing, dance, have a marching band, or do a finger play indoors or out, at almost any time of the day. With a little advanced planning and some thought to displaying materials and arranging space, you can use music and movement activities to liven up the children's day and yours as well.

Selecting Materials

Children respond to a wide variety of musical experiences. Here are some ideas regarding how you can select materials that will make music and movement a vital part of your program.

- Children like to listen to many different styles and types of music. Have a record or tape player available for use. The children's librarian at your local public library can help you select records and tapes that are appropriate for young children. In the Appendix to this chapter, we've recommended various children's songs, folk music, exercises, and quiet listening music. If you'd like to start your own collection, you'll find that many record and toy stores carry children's music in records, cassettes, and compact disc formats.

- Use some of your own family's music collection with the children. Children enjoy the same folk songs, classical music, jazz, and rock music that adults do, as long as the lyrics are appropriate for them.

- Provide the children with a variety of musical instruments to play with so that they can learn about sounds, tones, and rhythms. To start with, consider assembling some of the following:

    Instruments that produce sound when hit or shaken (drums, cymbals, rattles, bells, triangles, xylophones).

    Instruments that produce sound when blown (recorders, kazoos and harmonicas, which are especially good for young children because they make noise when air is blown in or out of them).

    Instruments that produce sound when plucked or scraped (guitars, autoharps, banjos, ukeleles, violins).

Although all of this sounds wonderful, you may rightly be worried about the cost. Records and cassettes can be expensive (not to mention compact discs or instruments). However, with a little imagination and resourcefulness you can keep costs under control.

For one thing, as already noted, most community public libraries lend out records, tapes, and compact discs free of charge. You can ask the children's librarian for recommendations. In addition, you can often find records and tapes at reduced prices at yard sales, publisher's close-outs, or second-hand record stores. Stores selling used compact discs are also becoming common. Don't neglect the radio either—different stations offer a wide variety of different musical options.

As for instruments, you'll find that many can be made at home by you or the children's parents. Because the primary function of instruments is simply to produce interesting and varied sounds, you don't need to invest in expensive, professional instruments to gain children's interest.

Percussion instruments such as drums, rhythm sticks, triangles, and bells are most commonly used with young children, as they are relatively constant in pitch and not difficult to play. They are also easy to make at home. For example, drums can be made from oatmeal boxes: cymbals can be made using tin pie plates; and rattles can be made by filling containers with macaroni, rice, or buttons.

Here are the instructions for making your own musical instruments.[2]

Drums and Sticks

Materials for drums:

> Large oatmeal box
> Paint (red or blue, nontoxic)
> Rubber inner tube
> Scissors
> 40" shoestring

Directions for drums:

Cut the oatmeal box in half and paint it. Cut two round drum covers from the rubber inner tube, 4" in diameter. Use scissors or a hole punch to make 10 to 12 small holes around the edges of both drum covers.

When the paint is dry, place one piece of inner tube on each end of the oatmeal box and lace the holes with the shoestring.

Materials for drum sticks:

> 2 dowels (10" to 12")
> 2 wooden beads with holes
> Glue (nontoxic)
> Scissors

Directions for making drum sticks:

Sharpen the ends of both dowels to fit the holes in the wooden beads. Make sure the pointed ends are hammered in tightly after you apply the glue.

Bell Band

Materials:

> 6" of elastic, 1" wide
> Small bells
> Needle and thread
> Velcro (optional)

---

[2]Adapted from Tapp Associates, *Learning Experiences for Young Children* (Atlanta, GA: Tapp Associates).

Directions:

Sew the elastic to make a small circle, or attach velcro to the ends of the elastic strip. Sew several bells on the outside of the band.

Kazoo

Materials:

Empty toilet paper tube
Contact paper or paint and brush
Rubber band
Scissors
Wax paper (2" by 2")

Directions:

Cover the paper tube with contact paper or paint. Punch 3 holes in the tube with scissors. Cut a small square of wax paper. Fit it tightly over the end of the tube. Secure it with a rubber band.

Maraca

Materials:

Several bottle caps
Construction paper, colorful contact paper, tin foil, or paint
6 to 10 pieces of 12" ribbon or paper (1/2" wide)
Paper towel roll
Piece of lightweight cardboard
Tape

Directions:

Decorate the paper towel roll with colorful paper, contact paper, tin foil, or paint. Put several bottle caps inside the roll. Cut out two small cardboard circles to fit the ends of the roll and tape them securely. Tape several colorful streamers, ribbons, or paper on one end of the roll.

Tambourine

Materials:

2 paper plates
Yarn and needle
Bottle caps
Magic markers

Directions:

Punch holes along the edges of both plates. Sew the plates together with yarn and a plastic needle. Place the bottle caps between the two plates before finishing. Decorate with magic markers.

Sand Blocks

Materials:

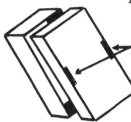

2 small boxes with tops (about 2" by 2" by 4")	Ruler
	Measuring tape or string
2 pieces of elastic (6" long and 1/2" wide)	Tape
	Scissors
Paint, construction paper, tin foil, or colorful contact paper	Thread and needle
	Paste or household cement
6" by 6" piece of sandpaper	

Directions:

Make two slits slightly larger than the width of the elastic where indicated on the top of the box.

Measure across the widest part of the child's hand. Measure across the box from one slit to the other.

Add these two measurements together, adding 1". Cut a piece of elastic this length for each box. Thread the elastic through the slits in the tops and sew the ends together. Tape tops on the boxes. Cover the boxes with paper, tin foil, colorful contact paper, or paint.

Cut a piece of sandpaper to fit the opposite side of the box. Glue the sandpaper to the box using paste or household cement. (White glue will melt the sandpaper.) Allow to dry.

Shaker

Materials:

Empty oatmeal box	Glue or paste (nontoxic)
Clothespin (nonclipping type)	Tape
Small plastic medicine bottle cap (1" to 2" in diameter)	12" by 12" piece of construction paper,
Bells or buttons	colorful cloth, or
Scissors	contact paper
Paintbrush	Paint (nontoxic)

Directions:

Cover an oatmeal or salt box with material, construction paper, or contact paper. Cut a hole in one end of the box, large enough to fit a clothespin.

Put several buttons or bells inside the box. Cut a hole the same size as the clothespin in the plastic bottle cap. Glue the plastic cap over the hole in the box, making sure the holes line up. Allow to dry. Paint the clothespin. Insert the clothespin through the holes in the cap and the box. Leave enough of the clothespin sticking out of the box for a handle (about 2"). Glue the clothespin in place and allow to dry. Tape around the bottom of the clothespin and plastic cap for more support.

Creating Space

In setting up space in your home for music and movement, most providers find it helpful to think about the ways in which children will be playing with materials. In general, three types of activities take place:

- Listening to music (playing tapes and records or discs).

- Moving freely to music (tapping, galloping, gliding, slithering, and running in response to music).

- Exploring sound (discovering the sounds different musical instruments make).

Nearly any room in your home can be used for conducting these activities. The key, however, is to select a room in which the furniture can be readily pushed aside, since you want to be able to create a space where children will be free to march, gallop, or exercise to music.

In addition to providing space for active movement activities, you'll want to choose a spot for quiet listening times. Soft furnishings such as pillows on the floor, a fluffy sofa or chair, or a beanbag chair will allow children to listen to music in a comfortable atmosphere. Like reading books, listening to music is most enjoyable when the setting is relaxed and removed from busy activities. If you have a pair of earphones that can be plugged into a turntable or cassette player, you might consider doubling up your reading and music listening areas.

Storing Materials

Because it requires small muscle skills to operate a record, cassette, or disc player without damaging the equipment, most providers find it wise to store these items out of the reach of infants and toddlers. Older preschoolers and school-age children who are able to responsibly use these materials can have access to the equipment if it is not easily damaged.

Musical instruments and props for dancing, such as scarves, streamers, or hats, should be made available (in net bags on hooks, or on low shelves) to all the children. Allowing children to get at these materials whenever they want encourages creativity and an appreciation for music. (Note: children should be well-supervised when playing with scarves and streamers to make sure that these materials don't get caught around their necks.)

Assembling and arranging materials and space for music and movement activities can be as creative for you as it is for the children. In the next section we'll focus on how you can work with children to encourage their growth and learning through music.

III. Helping Children Learn Through Music and Movement

Children respond to music and movement in different ways, based on their ages, skill levels, and preferences. An important goal in planning music experiences is to understand what activities appeal to different age groups. By carefully observing each child at play, you can tell whether the activities you have planned are age-appropriate and what additional props or materials might stimulate new music and movement experiences. You will notice the many ways in which each child differs in responding to music and to creative expression. Children will exhibit preferences for types of music and times of day when they most enjoy these activities.

Here are some activities you can do to enhance music and movement experiences for children of varying ages.

Infants

Infants are very aware of sounds around them. From early infancy they respond to the singing of lullabies with their own cooing sounds. Quiet, soothing music is most appropriate for young infants. Older infants will enjoy listening to music with rhythm, especially if adults dance with them and also seem to enjoy the music.

Music and Movement Activities That Help Infants Develop	Why These Activities Are Important
Emotionally...	
Try singing or humming while changing infants' diapers, rocking them to sleep, or burping them after feeding.	The melodious sound of your voice calms children and strengthens the bond between you.
Respond to the infant's moods with songs that reflect their feelings. For example, when an infant is quiet or uncomfortable, sing lullabies and folk songs. During active moods, play "Itsy Bitsy Spider" on the child's body.	Children will appreciate having their moods respected. They will also learn to associate music with comfort.
Socially...	
Play records or tapes about children and families. Sing songs that tell of babies and parents, such as "Shortnin' Bread."	Songs about families make infants feel secure in their family child care home.

Encourage children of all ages to form an impromptu marching band. Even a crawling infant can hold onto a band of bells or bang a pot-lid to music.

Babies love the company of older children. An activity like this lets them be part of the group music experience.

Cognitively...

Point out familiar sounds to infants: "Do you hear the clock ticking?" or "Let's listen to the bird singing."

Listening and hearing are critical components of musical learning for infants.

Give infants wooden spoons and pot lids to bang or beanbags to shake. Let the children discover what happens when they bang and shake these objects.

Children learn best when they are in charge of their own learning. They'll discover cause and effect on their own if you give them tools for experimentation.

Respond to infants' cooing sounds with songlike conversation.

Language stems from infants' coos and babbles.

Physically...

Encourage infants to dance with you to music. If they can stand, hold their hands and sway together.

Children will discover more about music when they respond to it physically.

Give infants a homemade maraca or drum to experiment with.

When children hit a drum or shake a maraca, they not only make music but also stimulate their own physical development.

Toddlers

Toddlers are very interested in singing and enjoy songs and nursery rhymes. They like to "make music" and may sing spontaneously during play. They tend to move their entire bodies when listening to music and are constantly developing many new large and small muscle skills. They sway, clap, and march and may join in when others sing and dance.

Music and Movement Activities That Help Toddlers Develop

Why These Activities Are Important

Emotionally...

Have toddlers take out and put away musical equipment on their own during free play.

Giving toddlers this responsibility encourages independence.

Encourage toddlers to become proficient with simple rhythm instruments such as maracas before introducing them to more complicated ones such as triangles.

Because toddlers frustrate easily, you don't want to overwhelm them with instruments that are complex to play. They'll enjoy music more when they can master what's required.

Teach older toddlers finger plays that focus on families. For example, "These are Grandmother's glasses/This is Grandmother's cap/This is the way she folds her hands/And lays them in her lap."

Finger plays are fun and serve the purpose of keeping families in mind during family child care.

Socially...

Have children form a mariachi band in which every member of the band can play whatever he or she likes.

By doing their own thing, children can be together without getting into fights over instruments.

During movement activities, have children pretend to be a ballet dancer, a tightrope walker, a rodeo rider, etc.

Children love to imitate adults and adultlike actions.

Cognitively...

Provide children with time to practice playing a favorite instrument.

As toddlers gain skills and begin to make music, their creative play is reinforced.

Label feelings and movements for toddlers so they can learn to put words to what they are experiencing: "You look happy" or "Mary is swinging her arms."

Describing what they are doing strengthens toddlers' language and thinking skills.

Have a variety of instruments and music on hand to tap toddlers' varying interests.

Toddlers have short attention spans and need a variety of appropriate materials to turn to during music time.

Physically...

Take music and movement activities outside when the weather permits. Play background music that reflects the mood of the day's weather, and encourage children to dance or run to this music.

Outdoor movement activities are a great way of helping children burn off energy, learn to appreciate music, gain a sense of their bodies, and develop large muscle skills.

Encourage older toddlers to do finger plays on their own. "Open Shut Them" or "This Is the Way We Wash Our Clothes" are good choices.

Finger plays help toddlers develop eye-hand coordination in a fun context.

Preschool Children

Older children enjoy listening to music. They are more aware of rhythm and enjoy moving, walking, or jumping when someone claps rhythmically or plays an instrument. They are interested in using musical instruments and like to repeat favorite songs over and over. They move their bodies creatively and enjoy props such as scarves, streamers, and hoops.

Music and Movement Activities That Help Preschoolers Develop

Why These Activities Are Important

Emotionally...

Teach preschoolers movement activities that will improve their coordination and balance, such as walking backward on a line, racing while carrying a hard-boiled egg on a spoon, etc.

By mastering control of their bodies, preschoolers strengthen their self-images as well as their physical abilities.

Choose background music that fits the children's moods. Some classical music, for example, can be comforting to a child who is unable to sleep at nap-time.

Children will feel that you respect them when you respond to them as individuals. They'll also start associating music with comfort.

Socially...

Play musical games such as "The Farmer in the Dell" or "Go In and Out the Windows" that bring children together for a group experience.

Children learn to cooperate by playing games such as these.

Encourage preschoolers to make up their own songs or to change the lyrics to songs they enjoy singing.

Preschoolers love to make up silly songs and to personalize music to describe what they are feeling and doing.

Thank preschoolers for their enthusiasm and participation and praise their talent.

By doing this, you help children feel good about themselves and about their musical efforts.

Cognitively...

Encourage the children's participation in music: "What instruments should we use in the band to-day?"

By talking with children about music you encourage them to reflect on what they are doing and describe these thoughts for you.

Give preschoolers unfamiliar musical instruments (an autoharp or Jew's harp, for example) to examine. Let them decide how these instruments should be played and try out their ideas before explaining their customary use.

Preschoolers love to experiment with materials on their own. They have no preconceived notions and may surprise you with their responses.

Encourage the children to clap for themselves when they feel they've sung a song particularly well.

Encouragement of this sort promotes pride and self-esteem.

Provide raw materials such as beans, jars, wires, or tin boxes and invite the children to create their own musical instruments.

Preschoolers learn best whey they interact directly with real-life materials. This activity will challenge their creativity and problem-solving capabilities.

Physically...

Encourage preschoolers to try all the instruments used in a marching band, such as bells, tambourines, maracas, and triangles.

Hand-held instruments provide learning experiences as they enhance small muscle control.

Try doing movement exercises outside where the children can blow like the wind, roll like a barrel, or gallop like an antelope.

Outdoor movement activities permit children to refine their balance and coordination in a fun setting.

Ask preschoolers to help you make a drum from an oatmeal box and canvas.

This activity allows children to assist you—something they value highly. At the same time it strengthens their eye and hand control.

School-Age Children

In general, school-age children are very interested in popular music and in doing the latest dances or exercises. Most will welcome an opportunity to listen to music alone or with their friends. Music and movement activities provide school-age children with important opportunities to relax, unwind, and develop their personal music tastes.

Music and Movement Activities That Help School-Age Children Develop

Why These Activities Are Important

Emotionally...

Allow school-age children to take out and put away records and tapes on their own.

Most children of this age love music. By giving them permission to do music-related activities on their own, you encourage independence.

Suggest calisthenics or aerobic dancing activities to promote a good body image.

Fitness activities are both popular and healthful. Children who participate in these activities gain both peer approval and self-assurance.

Socially...

Encourage school-age children to practice the latest dance steps.

When you do this, you let older children know that you respect them and their need to be "in tune" with their peers.

Respect the children's taste in music even if it's not your own. (This is why headphones were invented.)

Older children are working on developing an aesthetic sense and need to feel free to experiment.

Ask the children to lead the younger children in musical games such as "Hokey Pokey."

Many older children enjoy the leadership role and will delight in exaggerating their actions for the younger children.

Cognitively...

Suggest that school-age children help you make some homemade instruments that the younger children can use—kazoos, drums, and tambourines, for example.

Older children can find satisfaction in seeing a project through from beginning to end. In this case they have the added benefit of seeing their efforts used musically.

Ask the children to invent some ways of making instruments using objects and materials you have at home.

This request demands that children think abstractly and solve problems. Most children love a challenge of this sort.

Encourage the children to make up a musical game they could play with friends, such as a variation on "Name That Tune."

Because children love playing games and following rules, you can enrich their musical play by combining the two.

Suggest to the children that they write their own lyrics to popular songs.

Coming up with lyrics that rhyme with the original ones is a challenge but all the more fun for creative children.

Physically...

Encourage school-age children to develop an interest in musical instruments they could play in their school's band or orchestra.

By so doing you accomplish several things: you increase the children's appreciation for music, you assist them in gaining peer acceptance (especially if being in the school band is desirable), and you encourage the development of physical skills as the children practice playing their instruments.

Encourage children who show ability and interest in dancing or gymnastics to pursue these activities.

Most older children like to develop special talents. Movement-related specialties have the added advantages of promoting physical abilities and improving body images.

Special Activities

To support children's growth and development in the ways just described, you need only give children different types of music to listen to and different types of instruments and props to experiment with. Here are some further thoughts on helping children learn through music and movement.

Listening to Music

Music can be played as part of other learning experiences. For example, try playing music during an art activity. Ask the children who are painting or drawing to create artwork to the music: "What does the music make you think of?" "What kinds of colors does this music make you think about?" "Does this music make you feel like painting quickly or slowly?" The children may not seem to respond at first, or they may be unable to answer the questions. Keep asking them and talking to them, and bear in mind that the music may be influencing them even if they are not aware of it.

Free play is an especially good time to expose toddlers to various types of music. They usually don't have the attention span or the ability to sit still and listen to music, but they may enjoy hearing it while they do something else. Sometimes they stop what they are doing to listen to a favorite song or a melody that particularly appeals to them.

Young children are also fascinated by the sounds in their environment, such as those that animals make. Beginning with infants as young as seven months, you can start to identify and imitate animal sounds when you are reading a book or listening to a record or to various animals outdoors. For example, when reading to young infants, you might ask, "What does the cat say, Sheila? It says 'meow,' doesn't it?" For infants 15 to 18 months old, you can point to and name an animal and ask the children to tell you what sound it makes. At about this age, children will enjoy hearing songs that include animal sounds, such as "Old MacDonald." When reading, you can also point out sounds that other objects make, such as the telephone (ring, ring), the train (choo, choo), and the bell (ding, ding). Older children will enjoy guessing games in which you or the voice on a record makes sounds that they can identify.

Finger Plays

Infants and toddlers enjoy watching and imitating adults doing finger plays. Some well-known finger plays are "Itsy-Bitsy Spider," "Where Is Thumbkin?" and "Open/Shut Them." Children enjoy the combination of song and movement, but most infants and young toddlers can manage only one at a time—either singing or moving their hands. They don't yet have the coordination needed to do both. As they get older (around three or four), they are better able to do finger plays with you.

There are many books available on finger plays; the Appendix to this chapter offers some recommendations.

Singing

As an activity, singing can include many things: learning a song, making and imitating sounds, creating rhythms and chants, and making up words to a familiar tune. Here are some suggestions:

- Act out story songs such as "The Old Woman Who Swallowed a Fly." You may want to make props for the children to use.

- Reinforce the fun of singing by making a tape of the children singing. They love to listen to their own voices. They can sing individually, all together, or with you.

- Sing the same song in different ways: loudly, softly, in a whisper, quickly, slowly, sitting, standing, marching, hopping, or with and without instruments.

- Try singing or chanting directions to the children: "It's time to clean up, clean up, clean up."

Here are some tips to remember about singing with young children:

- They like singing quick, lively songs more often than slow ones.

- They enjoy funny songs and nonsense songs.

- Their ability to carry a tune improves with practice and good listening habits.

- They do not always understand what songs are appropriate to a time or situation. If they want to sing "Jingle Bells" in May or "Good Morning" before going home, that's OK.

Infants are a great audience for providers who like to sing. They are responsive, clap their hands, and don't care if you can't carry a tune. Singing to and with infants can start in the first months of life. Infants enjoy hearing their own names. Try making up rhymes or songs to a familiar tune and include the child's name. Singing can ease difficult situations for both infants and young children. For example, try singing "This is the way we wash our hands" with a child who finds this an unpleasant or fearful activity.

Toddlers' attempts at singing can be enjoyable for caregivers and toddlers alike. Their songs may consist of a sound repeated over and over, such as "B B B B B" or "DADADADADADA." Gradually they can sing the words to a song, or half-babble, half-talk through a song such as "Happy Birthday" ("Happy, happy, happy, BBBBBBBB"). Toddlers enjoy hearing caregivers sing and may hum along or just move their bodies to a song. In either case, they are practicing their skills while being creative in their own ways.

Creative Dance and Movement

Dancing and movement can be included in music experiences for even the youngest children. Try dancing with the babies by holding them in your arms and moving to a song. When infants begin to stand and walk, you can hold their hands and move to the music. Some begin to move up and down as soon as the music begins. When they are able to walk well, you can play "Ring Around the Rosy." Some infants enjoy sitting in your lap, facing you, and playing musical games such as "Row, row, row your boat" while holding hands and rocking back and forth.

As toddlers become steady on their feet and their balance improves, they often become very creative in their movement. They enjoy holding your hands and moving to the music, but they will also enjoy experimenting with what their bodies can do. You might make suggestions such as these:

- "Let's wiggle our fingers silently."
- "Let's stamp our feet really loudly."
- "Let's clap our hands softly."

Playing different types of music encourages children to move the way the music makes them feel. Use music that is fast and slow, loud and soft, happy and sad. Once the children feel comfortable moving to music, you can add props to further stimulate their imaginations: streamers, lightweight fabric, sheets, scarves, feathers, balloons, capes, and ribbons. Preschool and school-age children especially enjoy using props to move creatively to music. Ask the children to make up their own ways of moving across the room or from the room to the outdoors.

Have the children imitate the various ways that animals walk and move. They can creep like a cat, waddle like a duck, kick like a mule, slither like a snake, or jump like a kangaroo. This can be done with or without music. Have the children pretend to be the wind, rain, snow, or thunder. How do they think a car moves, or a truck, a rocking chair, or a weather vane? Some children enjoy using props such as hats when they are dancing. Have the children suggest other props to use.

Musical Games

Children of all ages enjoy games that are set to music, such as "The Farmer in the Dell," "Bluebird," and "Fly Through My Window." These games combine music, movement, and group cooperation and are generally appropriate for 3- to 5-year-olds. Younger ones will enjoy "Pat-a-Cake" and other similar games. Young school-age children enjoy musi-

cal games such as the "Hokey Pokey," the "Mexican Hat Dance," or the "Bunny Hop" that involve more complicated movement to a beat. Older school-age children enjoy these same types of games, especially when they're sung fast so that movements must be quickly made or chaos will result.

With experience, children can begin to make up their own musical games. Try setting up a series of hula hoops or tires on the floor or ground; ask each child to move through the hoops or tires in a different way. The children can create a chant to describe what they are doing; for example, "Kim is a hopping, hopping, hopping," "Jamie is a leap frog, leap frog, leap frog."

Maggie (3-1/2 years)
Micky (4 years)
Marie (2 years)
Matt (4-1/2 years)

Involving Children of All Ages

Involving children of different ages is easy to do with music and movement activities because many of the activities allow each child to participate at his or her own level—at the same time. For example, when singing together, an infant may just listen and enjoy the music of others; a toddler may hum a lot and use few words; a preschooler may get more of the words and be better at following the melody; and a school-age child may not only know the entire song but may also add dance movements or gestures. Here is an example of what can happen when children of different ages share in a music and movement experience:

"Maggie, Marie, Micky, and Matt go slowly down the stream. Merrily, merrily, merrily, merrily, life is but a dream."

The children are beaming with smiles as you sing "their" chorus of "their" favorite song. Using the fact that you have four children whose names start with M and who are all at ages that enjoy "Row, row, row your

boat," you create daily fun at your morning group time. Singing songs together formally for about eight minutes gives these energetic children a way to pace their day and their activity level.

"I love this music," says Micky, the most energetic of the four. You smile, remembering that he came to your family child care home with the label of "wild man." He would often throw his body around in uncontrolled energy spurts. After several weeks (which seemed long to everyone), Micky settled down and now flows with the day. You are convinced that the opportunities for singing and movement made the difference for him. Of course, all the kids love "Hokey Pokey" and running like unicorns with streamers in their hands, but, for Micky, movement and music seem to be what make his day.

As you and the children are clapping your hands to your knees as you sing, you think about Marie, who had trouble thinking of anything to do when she heard music. She thought music was only for listening to, and it took several suggestions to get her to loosen up. Now you smile as she leads the group through clapping their hands to their feet, their elbows, their cheeks, their ears, the floor, and more.

Matt considers himself "too old for this dumb stuff." You allow him to find his own activity as you sing with the others, believing that he really doesn't think it's dumb but that he's reluctant to give singing a try for other reasons. After your singing circle, you say to him, "Matt, I need someone to play the clean-up drum. Would you like to do it?"

"Yeah—I know just where it is," he responds and goes to retrieve the drum. His playing is quite elaborate ((he even uses the side of the drum for a different sound). You realized that Matt needed an "excuse" to explore music, and asking him to play the drum that signals clean-up time was the perfect ploy. Now, he'll even play when there are no chores to be done.

Maggie and Micky were born to sing—both are highly verbal children who use words and song with every movement they make. Whether it's dancing in the living room, coloring in the playroom, or swinging in the backyard, their voices are always in use. You think about Maggie, who joined your care as a small baby. It seemed as if even then, she wiggled her toes and kicked her feet to the beat of the music. And Micky is never without a song under his breath (or at the top of his lungs).

When offering music and movement to children, it's helpful to remember these pointers:

- Not every child comes to the experience with the same interest.
- Personalizing the music and letting children take the lead will involve them to a greater degree.
- Children's energy can be channeled positively into creative movement and into musical games that involve gestures and movements.
- Props and story lines can assist children in exploring their musical interests.

If some parents want to know more about your music and movement program, consider using the letter on the next page and sharing the list of recommended records, tapes, and songbooks that follows.

A Letter to Parents on Music and Movement

What We Do and Why

We do a lot of singing and dancing in our program. Music during the day gives us all a lift. Sometimes the children start to sing on their own; at other times I plan a special music activity. Singing and moving to music give the children a chance to move freely, practice new skills, and feel good about what their bodies can do.

Here are some of the things I do to encourage a love for music and movement:

- We listen to records and tapes during play time.

- Before the children take a nap, I sometimes play something quiet and relaxing, such as gentle classical music or lullabies.

- Sometimes we take a tape recorder outside and play jazz or folk music, and the children dance and pretend to be different animals or make-believe creatures.

- I give the children colored scarves and paper streamers to use as they dance to the music.

Sometimes we play with musical instruments. Many of these instruments are homemade. For example, I made shakers by filling yogurt containers with beans and sealing them with duct tape and glue. I bought some large bells and sewed them onto heavy ribbon. The children like to shake them and march around the living room. I use empty coffee cans with plastic tops as "drums." We have quite an impressive orchestra!

Singing and learning new songs is a good way to help children learn new words and language skills. We have a special time every day for singing together or doing finger plays. The younger children sing along or listen; they also like playing with toys that make music, such as chime bells and toy radios. The older children help teach the younger ones the words to songs.

What You Can Do At Home

You probably listen to music at home, and you may have special songs and dances that you share with your child. I would be delighted to have you and your child share your favorites with the other children.

I have a list of songbooks and records that young children enjoy which I can share with you. I also have directions for making musical instruments from household objects such as empty oatmeal containers, dowels, and paper plates. I'd be delighted to share these resources with you—just ask me!

Recommended Records And Tapes

Children's Songs and Folk Music

American Folk Songs for Children; Stories and Songs for Children; Birds, Beasts, Bugs and Little Fishes; and *Precious Friends* (Pete Seeger)

And One and Two; Ella Jenkins' Nursery Rhymes; Country Games and Rhythms for the Little Ones; I Know the Color of the Rainbow; This a Way, That a Way; and *You'll Sing a Song and I'll Sing a Song* (Ella Jenkins)

Baby Beluga; Singable Songs for the Very Young; Rise and Shine; and *One Light, One Sun* (Raffi) (song books are also available)

Children's Greatest Hits, Activity and Game Songs, and *Music for Ones and Twos* (Tom Glazer)

Comets, Cats, and Rainbows (Paul Strausman)

Family Hug, The Flyers, Step into the Light (The Flyers)

Free to Be You and Me (Marlo Thomas)

Little White Duck and Other Children's Favorites (Burl Ives)

Sesame Street: Let Your Feelings Show; Sesame Street: The Anniversary Album; and *Sesame Street Gold: The Best of Sesame Street* (Sesame Street Records)

Sing Along with Bob and *Songs and Games for Toddlers* (Bob McGrath)

Finger Play

Wee Sing Silly Songs and *Wee Sing Nursery Rhymes and Lullabies* (Wee Sing Tapes)

Exercise and Movement

Animal Walks, Bean Bag Activities, and *Folk Dance Fun* (Kimbo Records)

Creative Movement and Rhythmic Exploration; Feelin' Free; Movin'; and *Home-made Band* (Hap Palmer)

Exercise! (Sesame Street Records)

Play Your Instruments and Make a Pretty Sound (Ella Jenkins)

Music for Twos and Threes (Tom Glazer)

Quiet Music

Lullaby Magic, Morning Music (Discovery Music)

Classical recordings of Bach, Brahms, Beethoven, Chopin, and Mozart, plus traditional children's favorites:

Amahl and the Night Visitors (Menotti)

An American in Paris (Gershwin)

The Children's Prayer from *Hansel and Gretel* (Humperdinck)

Introduction to the Orchestra (Britten)

La Mer (Debussy)

Peter and the Wolf (Prokofiev)

Pictures at an Exhibition (Moussorky)

The Planets (Holst)

Toreador Song from *Carmen* (Bizet)

Songbooks/Fingerplay Books

Cole, Joanna. *Eentsy, Weentsy Spider: Fingerplays and Action Rhymes* (New York: Mulberry Books, 1991).
Here are nearly forty fingerplays and action rhymes that have been chanted, sung, and loved by generations.

Cromwell, Liz, and Dixie Hibner. *Finger Frolics: Fingerplays for Young Children, Revised Edition* (Livonia, MI: Partner Press, 1983).
A collection of 350 fingerplays under the categories of seasons, holidays and the world around us, country, nursery rhymes, and activity verses.

Cromwell, Liz, Dixie Hibner and John Faitel. *Finger Frolics 2: Fingerplays for Young Children* (Livonia, MI: Partner Press, 1996).
300 new fingerplays for the 21st century. Categories include health and fitness, life skills, ecology and recycling, American Sign Language, as well as traditional categories.

Fox, Dan, and P. Fox. *Go In and Out the Window: An Illustrated Songbook for Young People* (New York: Henry Holt & Company, 1987).
A beautiful collection of children's songs lavishly illustrated with works from the Metropolitan Museum of Art. The selections range from nursery songs and folk songs to ballads and lullabies.

Hart, Jane. *Singing Bee! A Collection of Favorite Children's Songs* (New York: Lothrop, Lee, & Shepard, 1982).
More than 125 lullabies, Mother Goose rhymes, finger plays, games, folk songs, rounds, and holiday songs with piano accompaniment and guitar chords.

Moomaw, Sally. *More Than Singing: Discovering Music in Preschool and Kindergarten* (St. Paul, MN: Redleaf Press, 1997)
"The Wheels on the Bus" and rhythm bands are not the only ways to share music with children. Here are more than 100 ideas for songs, rhythms, instrument making, music centers, with extensions into literacy, math, and science. And you don't have to read music—the accompanying cassette contains all of the songs.

Seeger, Ruth Crawford. *American Folk Songs for Children* (New York: Doubleday, 1980).
Ninety favorite folk songs, including ballads, work songs, chants, spirituals and blues. The introductory chapter explains how to sing the songs, improvise on the words, and use the songs at home and at school. Most of the songs are easily adaptable for young children and can be used for musical finger plays and game songs.

Shiller, Pam and Thomas Moore. *Where is Thumbkin? 500 Activities to Use with Songs You Already Know* (Beltsville, MD: Gryphon House, 1993).
Sing over 200 familiar songs and learn new words set to familiar tunes. This book provides easy song-related activities that span the curriculum in areas such as math, art, and language, and includes a special section just for toddlers.

Outdoor Play

I. Why Outdoor Play Is Important

In the outdoor environment, children can engage in all the activities that have been discussed so far, with more freedom and exuberance. The outdoors also offers its own wonders to young children. Outdoor space extends a child's world and provides new and different opportunities for play, growth, and exploration.

Being outdoors means more than just "running around" or "letting off steam." Outdoors, children have the opportunity to explore and observe nature firsthand. They experience the changing seasons and note different types of weather; they watch things grow and die. When children play outdoors they learn about what their bodies can do: they run, jump, climb, and move in a less confined space than indoors. They gain confidence in their abilities as they learn, practice, and refine their motor skills.

The outdoors contains many opportunities for children to be creative and to demonstrate their ideas and feelings. It provides another setting for dramatic play, as children create playhouses with two chairs and an old blanket. They play with sand and water to create castles and tunnels. They play games such as tag and hide-and-seek. They also make up new games using materials such as balls, hoops, and jump ropes.

Being outdoors is also important for children's health. Fresh air, sunshine, and the chance to move their bodies freely all contribute to growth and development.

Here are some of the many opportunities for learning in all areas of development while outdoors:

Children develop thinking skills by:

- Using their senses to learn about the world (touching and smelling a flower).

- Experiencing cause and effect (running through a sprinkler and being surprised at getting wet).

- Developing language skills (conversing in the sand box).

- Learning to plan and to solve problems (deciding to play house and creating a space by placing an old blanket behind a large tree).

- Following through on a task (watering a garden they have planted).

- Learning about science (asking why the bird has a piece of string in its beak and finding out about how a nest is built).

Children develop socially by:

- Making friends (bringing another child a flower to look at).

- Learning to share and take turns (giving another child a chance to ride the tricycle).

- Learning to cooperate (painting the house with water as a group).

Children develop emotionally by:

- Feeling successful and competent (learning to ride a tricycle).

- Learning to be independent (going down a slide at the park unassisted).

- Expressing creativity (making up a new ball game).

Children develop physically by:

- Refining small muscle skills (poking in the sand and dirt with fingers).

- Developing large motor skills (learning to jump).

- Coordinating eye and hand movements (using colored chalk to decorate the sidewalk).

- Learning coordination and balance (jumping rope or riding a seesaw).

Once you have thought about the many opportunities for learning that exist outdoors, you can begin to create an interesting outdoor environment. The next section will help you do this.

II. Setting the Stage for Outdoor Play

Children can perform almost any indoors activity outdoors, from cooking (making up sandwiches at the park for a picnic) to art (making a footprint mural on butcher paper). You can encourage these and other activities that are more exclusive to the outdoors by setting up activity areas outside. Whether you have a house with a yard or live in an apartment and take the children to play at a nearby park or playground, you can provide interesting and stimulating outdoor experiences for the children in your family day care program.

Things You Can Do Outdoors

The outdoors has the advantage of having lots of room, with built-in interest areas such as trees, gardens, grassy play areas, and sometimes playground equipment. By adding materials and props, you can make each activity area even more interesting.

Children need only the most basic equipment to enjoy outdoor play fully. A good place to start in planning your outdoor area is to think about the different kinds of things children like to do outside. Then identify a place where you can provide these experiences. Here are some suggestions.

Digging and Pouring

Young children love to dig in sand or dirt and pour sand or water. A sandbox can be created using a tire or a wooden box that can be covered. Another option is to have a "dirt hole" where the children can dig or a "mud hole" where they can make mud pies and cakes. The sand or dirt area should be large enough so that two children can play there together without feeling crowded.

For digging and pouring, you can provide the following materials:

- Buckets and shovels
- Funnels
- Plastic bowls or containers
- Plastic scoops or spoons
- Cars, trucks, or trains
- Sifters or colanders
- Pots, pans, or molds
- Small cardboard boxes or old plastic blocks
- Natural objects such as twigs, leaves, shells, and sticks, which the children can collect on walks and then use in the sand and dirt

(For more information on this topic, see the chapter on Sand and Water.)

Planting a Garden

If you have an area that could be used for a garden, this can be an exciting outdoor activity for children. Planting and caring for a garden give children a sense of satisfaction as they see the results of their own efforts. They also learn responsibility as they weed the garden and water the plants. They learn math concepts as they measure the growth with a yardstick. It's a good idea to start with seeds that grow quickly, such as beans, peas, or grass seed, so the children don't have to wait too long for plants to emerge. Children then actively experience their accomplishments when Mung beans or alfalfa sprouts they grew themselves are served for snack or lunch.

When planning a garden area, the following materials are suggested:

- Child-sized garden tools or sturdy plastic or wooden spoons
- Seeds or plants (if you let local nurseries know your plans, many will donate seeds)
- Dirt and fertilizer (make sure it is nontoxic)
- Watering cans, plastic measuring cups, or small plastic pitchers
- Something to use to mark the plants, such as tongue depressors with the plant's name written on them or the package the seeds come in glued to a stick

Water/Snow Play

During the summer, outdoor water play is a wonderful, cooling experience. You can use wading pools, a sprinkler, garden hose, or watering cans. (Remember that children in a wading pool or near water must be supervised at all times.) Babies can splash and play with water toys. Children can blow bubbles, wash their dolls and doll clothes or dishes in plastic tubs, or "paint" the house with water and large paint brushes. In the winter, snow play is also appropriate as long as the children are dressed warmly and have boots and a

change of clothes ready. They can build with snow in some of the same ways they do with sand. Playing in the snow also lends itself to dramatic play.

Games

There are many traditional games that children enjoy outdoors, such as tag, Follow the Leader, Red Rover, leap frog, jump rope (for school-age children), hide and seek, walking like animals, beanbag tosses, and so on. Although children often play these games spontaneously, you can suggest one when the children seem bored outside or just can't decide what to do. Encourage them to make up their own games by asking: "What do you think we could do with these balls? Or hoops? Or jump ropes?"

Caring for Animals

If you are a pet lover, children can learn to help care for the family pet or a special pet, such as a rabbit, which is kept outdoors. Children learn many things about the life cycle—birth, growth, and death—when they care for an animal. If you live in an area where there are animals nearby, children can learn to put out food for them, watch them build their nests, and so forth.

Picnics

Children love to eat outdoors, whether it's snack or lunch. They can be happy eating in the yard or on the front steps. You don't always have to walk to the park to enjoy a picnic. Think ahead of what you will need for a picnic so that preparation and waiting times will be at a minimum. For example, you'll need something to sit on (an old tablecloth) and a way to transport the food (a backpack). Be sure to include clean-up supplies and some books for quiet time. Look for shady spaces so that children are not always in direct sunlight.

Art Experiences

Bringing art materials outdoors provides a whole new experience for children. In addition to letting children use colored chalk on a sidewalk, you can tape paper to the side of the house or to a large cardboard box to create an outdoor easel. Children can sit at a picnic table or child-sized table to color with crayons, glue collages, or make wood sculptures. Finger painting outdoors gives children more freedom to be messy than indoors. Children can finger paint directly on a vinyl tablecloth. If they want a picture, place a piece of paper over the painting and lift it up to make the imprint. It helps to bring out one plastic tub of soapy water and one of plain water with paper towels handy so the children can clean up themselves.

Outdoor Dramatic Play

With some very simple props, children can create imaginative outdoor dramatic play settings. They can make a playhouse from a large cardboard box. They can invent all kinds of games using a ball, piece of sturdy rope, a plastic hoop, and some old tablecloths or blankets. When wheel toys such as tricycles, wagons, wheelbarrows, or any plastic riding toys are available to scoot on, older children use them in made-up games such as "ice cream truck driver" or "gas station." They often include the younger toddlers and even the infants in their play as they take the baby to the "store" or ask the toddler what kind of ice cream he wants.

To stimulate this type of outdoor play, you can provide the following:

- Ropes, balls, and plastic hoops.
- Dress-up clothes for outdoors, including hats, suitcases, and paper bags.
- Plastic containers to store collections such as leaves, pebbles, or sticks.
- Old blankets, tablecloths, or shower curtains.
- Outdoor chairs and a small table, if available.
- Large cardboard boxes.

(For more information on this topic, see the chapter on Dramatic Play.)

Music and Movement

This experience is easy to plan either in your own outdoor area or at the playground or park. Children can pretend to move like the wind, sway like the trees, or glide like the clouds to music on a tape. A tape recorder or a radio tuned to classical music or jazz can be a great stimulus for dance and movement. If you provide some props, such as scarves, streamers, or hoops, children will create even more ways to move and enjoy music. They also enjoy exercise games outdoors.

Neighborhood Walks

Walks are a wonderful way to explore the outside environment with children. Children of all ages like to collect things along the way and put them in their pockets or in a bag attached to a stroller. They can look for changes in the seasons, including buds forming on trees, leaves falling, and birds and squirrels building nests. On their walks they encounter and enjoy the creatures around them: worms after a rain, bugs of all sorts climbing on trees, butterflies, or birds in early spring. Noticing and talking about these things enhances the walk and helps children learn to be good observers and to describe what they see.

Another idea is to have a "let's look for" walk. On these walks children look for specific things, and you can talk with them about what they see. This is also a wonderful way to promote language development. Here are some ideas of what you might have children look for:

Animals	Vegetable gardens
Flower gardens	Birds
Signs	Shapes
Colors	Rough, smooth, or soft textures
Trees	Vehicles
Stores	Trash
Water	Shadows
Seeds	

To make the walk even more exciting, you could take along the following:

Magnifying glass
Binoculars
Bags, cartons, and something to collect things in
Measuring tape or rulers
Camera

If there is a local store within walking distance of your home, this can be the focal point of a neighborhood walk. Before you go, talk about what you need to buy and why, and where in the store the items you need are located. If there is more than one way to get to the store, try varying the route you take on the way home.

A neighborhood walk to the post office or mailbox always intrigues young children, especially if they get to mail something themselves. Children also like to take a walk when the garbage collectors are on their route or the mailperson is on their street. If there is any construction going on, the purpose of a walk might be to look at the progress being made.

Children love to jump in puddles after a rain. A walk exclusively for puddle jumping can provide a needed break in an otherwise dreary day. When the children wear raincoats and boots and roll up their pants, this type of walk can be great fun. An infant or young toddler in a stroller can enjoy the sights and sounds of the older children as they splash, and can experience puddles firsthand when you stop for a break. Let even the youngest children have a chance to dip their hands and feet in puddles.

When you return from a neighborhood walk, you can use the experience to support children's learning by:

• Inviting the children to draw pictures of what they saw and did.

• Having the older children dictate stories to you about the field trip.

• Adding props for dramatic play that focus on the location (e.g., a firefighter's hat, grocery bags, empty food boxes).

• Reading stories about similar places and talking about similar trips that the children have taken with their families.

Storing Outdoor Play Equipment

The toys and materials children need for outdoor play can be stored in an outdoor shed or garage or kept indoors in individual bags or boxes, ready to be taken outdoors when needed. Here are some practical suggestions:

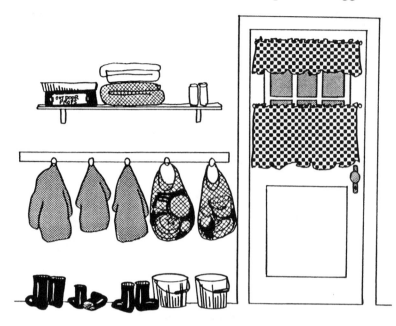

- Use a plastic bag or net grocery bag to store sand and water toys. The bag can be hung on a hook near the door, in the kitchen, or in a closet. Place a bucket or pad underneath to catch falling sand and/or dripping water.

- Use a sturdy cardboard box for balls, ropes, and hoops that can be stored in the shed, garage, or indoors in a closet or other storage area.

- Keep special activity supplies together in their own box or bag so you can get to them easily when needed.

- Collect old blankets, tablecloths, or shower curtains and keep them in a bag or box ready to go outside.

Logistics

One reason why some providers don't take children outdoors often is that "it's too much trouble." Getting a group of young children toileted, dressed, and ready to go outside can challenge even the most organized provider. Here are some suggestions to help you get children outdoors without excessive delays:

- Borrow or request that parents supply the equipment you need to transport infants and toddlers (e.g., a double stroller, backpack, or snugglie). Encourage toddlers who are walking to walk at least part of the way.

- Set some basic, simple rules for the older children to follow when you all go for a walk. For example, have children hold hands or hold on to the stroller. Give simple directions: "You can walk to the corner, but stop at the tree."

- Figure out a way to attach a bag or sack to the stroller and keep it ready with whatever you need for outdoor time. For example, include bottles or crackers for snacks, tissues, baby wipes and diapers, paper towels, something to sit on, and a book to read to the children. Check the supplies each night so you are ready for the next day and just have to add something to drink for snack.

- Let the children help carry things outside or to the park. Ask parents to provide backpacks that 2- to 5-year-olds can wear, and place a few items in each.

- Encourage the children to learn self-help skills for getting dressed, and have them help each other. For example, teach them the "family child care flip" for putting on jackets and sweaters. The flip goes like this:

Place the jacket or sweater on the floor with the inside facing up and the hood or collar at the child's feet.

Show the child how to put his/her arms in the sleeves and flip the jacket over his or her head.

- Encourage the children to put on their own hats, mittens, and scarves as soon as they show interest and an ability to do so.

- Give the children time to practice these self-help skills at other times during the day. Allow older children who know how to tie or zip to help you with the younger children. For younger children, start the zipper for them and let them pull it up themselves.

- Help the children learn that when they are outdoors, you need to supervise and help each of them and that because of this, some compromises are necessary. For example, when you are supervising an active toddler who is trying to eat the dirt, you won't be available for gardening with the preschoolers. On the other hand, if the toddler is involved with toys or books on a blanket, you will be available to help the preschoolers. When the baby wakes up and needs a bottle outdoors, the older children need to find something to do on their own that you can watch. When the baby is in her stroller or playing on the grass, you can be available to join them in a game of catch. The goal is to balance the children's interests with your need to supervise a group of children of varying ages who have different needs.

- Coordinate with another provider for neighborhood walks or extended mornings at the park. Although you will have to watch more children, the joint adult supervision will give both of you more flexibility in what you plan for the children, and you will enjoy the adult company.

- Encourage children's independence outdoors. Show them where outdoor equipment is stored so they can help carry and return things.

Maintaining Safety Outdoors

A large part of ensuring children's safety outdoors is allowing children to move at their own pace. Because you are caring for children of different ages, the younger ones will typically want to imitate the older ones. Children need to know it's OK to say that they're afraid to do something. They should be encouraged to try out new activities when they are ready. The outdoor Safety Checklist included in Setting the Stage (pages 24-25) can be used both for your own outdoor area and for public parks and playgrounds. Listed below are some specific, day-to-day outdoor safety rules that you can teach the children and help them practice:

- Never walk in front of swings.

- Take turns on the slide and don't crowd the ladder.

- Check metal slides on very hot days to be sure they aren't too hot to sit on.

- Tell your partner before you get off the seesaw.

- If you find something sharp or dangerous-looking on the ground, leave it there and tell an adult.

- Don't walk up slides—other children may be ready to slide down.

There will be times when you need to intervene in children's play because of safety. For example, if a child is standing dangerously close to a swing or if a child picks up a stick to throw at another child, you need to step in to prevent an accident from occurring. When intervening for safety reasons, be sure to give clear, specific directions. For example, if Sally is standing in front of a slide and another child is about to slide down and hit her, simply yelling her name will not prevent an accident. She is likely to stand there and look at you. She will, however, move out of the way if you say, "Move quickly, Sally! Jahmal is coming down the slide." This tells Sally what to do and why. After the incident is over, you can remind her of the rule and why it is important to follow rules.

Scheduling Outdoor Play

At this point you may be wondering how often you should take the children outside. Most experts believe that in order to provide children with the types of experiences described in this chapter, you should schedule being outdoors twice a day. Obviously, though, the weather and children's moods will affect when and how often you go outdoors. On a beautiful day you may want to go out early and stay longer, whereas on a very cold day, outdoor time might be shorter.

On a particularly nice day, providers sometimes want to take the children out for the entire morning or afternoon. Although children can enjoy an extended outdoor time, it's important to remember that they will tire easily or engage in aimless running around if there aren't enough constructive things to do. For example, if you are planning a whole morning at the local park, be sure to bring some books for a quiet break time, enough snacks and juice for hungry and thirsty children, and an idea for a game or two. Be flexible about the amount of time you stay; watch for cues that the children are getting tired, and be ready to head for home.

Children enjoy being outdoors in all types of weather as long as they are appropriately dressed. Your common sense should tell you, however, when it's not wise to go outdoors. For example, on particularly hot days, try going out early in the morning rather than in the middle of the day. Make sure shade and drinks are available. Stay indoors when dangerous conditions exist, including lightning storms, extreme cold (be sure to consider the wind-chill factor), or air-quality alerts, and learn safety rules if you are caught in a storm.

Planning ahead and having things ready will make it easier to enjoy the outdoors with children. In the next section we'll look at how you can use the time you're outdoors with children to help them grow and learn.

III. Helping Children Learn Through Outdoor Play

Getting the children to play outdoors is one of the easiest tasks you have. Almost every child loves being outside. However, focusing children's play requires that you observe and think about what the children are doing. Watching children play outdoors will give you a better idea of the many kinds of learning and exploration that occur. It will also help you decide what types of equipment or toys the children need to extend their play and to think up new ways to enjoy the outdoor environment. Your observations will also give you more information about the children's interests, abilities, and growth.

The following are some suggestions of what to look for when you observe a child outdoors:

- What does the child like to play with?

- What equipment does the child choose on the playground?

- Are there play areas or equipment that the child avoids?

- How does the child play with others? Who initiates play?

- How long does the child play in each area?

- Does the child act differently (e.g., in terms of language, social skills, physical skills) outdoors than indoors?

- Does the child seem confident or cautious when trying new things?

What children do outdoors depends a lot on their age and individual abilities. Remembering what children are like at each stage of development will help you plan successful outdoor experiences. Here are some suggestions for activities for children of varying ages and developmental stages.

Infants

To infants the outdoors feels like a new world. There are different things to see, explore, smell, and feel. There is fresh air, wind, and sunshine to feel, clouds to look at, people to watch, and different surfaces to crawl on. There are many ways in which you can provide outdoor play experiences for infants.

Outdoor Activities That Help Infants Develop	Why These Activities Are Important
Emotionally...	
For a change of scene on a nice day, feed infants outdoors or place mats for napping in the shade of a tree.	When you make these routines pleasant for both infants and yourself, children learn to associate these activities with being content and safe.

Play with infants outdoors every day, if possible. Let an active child crawl in the grass. Cuddle with a quiet child under a tree and look through a picture book together.

Responding to infants on their own terms teaches them that you respect them as individuals. This also helps strengthen the bonding process.

Socially…

Invite parents to join you on nature walks.

When parents participate in family child care activities, infants learn that parents are part of family child care, too.

Make sure infants are situated on blankets where they can watch older children at play.

Infants enjoy sharing in a group experience, even when it's from a distance.

Cognitively…

Give infants lots of experiences in touching grass, smelling flowers, listening to the wind, feeling the bark, etc.

Babies learn through all their senses. By letting them explore the outdoor world, they gain an understanding of what the outdoors is like.

When you have infants' attention, blow on a dandelion. Then give the children their own dandelion to play with. Let them try blowing on other flowers to compare what happens.

Even infants can be scientific investigators. When children try things on their own, they learn to observe, solve problems, and gain an understanding of cause and effect.

Take infants on a walk in which you discuss what you see and hear. Respond to babbling with further descriptions.

Infants gain a foundation for language by babbling and cooing.

Physically…

Give infants opportunities to crawl through grass, raise themselves up to a picnic table, or roll down a small hill.

At the same time that children are learning about the outdoors, they will be developing gross motor skills.

Give infants leaves, twigs, and flowers to play with. Encourage them to crawl or walk to touch things they show an interest in.

You can use infants' natural love of nature as an incentive for them to practice physical skills such as crawling, reaching, and grabbing.

Toddlers

Toddlers need space in which to try out and practice new skills. The outdoors becomes an ideal setting for toddlers who are eager to run, jump, hop, and climb.

Outdoor Activities That Help Toddlers Develop	**Why These Activities Are Important**

Emotionally…

Encourage toddlers to put on and take off their own jackets, hats, scarves, and gloves.

Children appreciate learning how to become more self-sufficient.

Steer toddlers to activities they can master: painting a house with water or weeding a garden.

Toddlers love being outdoors, but they sometimes gravitate to activities that are too advanced for their skills, such as carpentry, organized games, or sports played by older children. Toddlers (as well as the older children) will enjoy being outdoors more if they spend their time on appropriate activities.

Walk around the perimeter of the play area with a toddler to give the child the sense of being alone with you.

Spending time one on one will strengthen the child's attachment to you.

Socially…

Set up the sandbox so that each toddler has space to play alone but can share the others' company.

This set-up lets the socially oriented toddler enjoy "parallel" play with other children.

Play games such as "Simon Says" or "Follow the Leader," which call for toddlers to imitate your actions.

Toddlers delight in doing the same things adults do. These games, which allow them to imitate your every move, are both fun and helpful for toddlers.

Cognitively…

Play games such as "Hokey Pokey," "Ring Around the Rosy," or "Farmer in the Dell" that allow a child to repeat actions.

Repetition is not just a great source of fun for toddlers, it's also a foundation for learning. Through practice children develop their thinking and physical skills demanded by these games.

Ask lots of questions: "What do you think the birds in that tree are doing?" or "Can you think of anything we could do with these fallen leaves?"

Open-ended questions encourage toddlers to express their thoughts and feelings in words.

Let toddlers know that they are free to move from one activity to another while outdoors.

Part of the thrill of playing outside is the wealth of activities available. Giving children permission to switch activities when they desire puts them in charge of their own learning and motivates them to want to stay outside.

Physically…

Provide lots of equipment such as balls, hula hoops, and ride-on trucks for toddlers.

The outdoors provides the best place to help toddlers develop large muscle skills.

Provide props for play in the sandbox and for art, gardening, and other activities. Sifters, crayons, and trowels are all good play materials.

These props will not only enrich the play experiences but will also help toddlers work on their small motor skills.

Preschool Children

Three- to five-year-olds need lots of space, time, and practice to get better at the skills they learned when they were toddlers. They are eager to try out new and more complicated stunts outdoors and will enjoy showing off and talking about what they can do.

Outdoor Activities That Help Preschoolers Develop

Why These Activities Are Important

Emotionally…

Show preschoolers how to do stretching and fitness activities.

Children like these activities because they make them feel like the adults they see doing aerobics and working out. Fitness activities also help children develop a positive body image.

Let children select outdoor activities that match their moods. An active child might wish to play with toys or sand and water; a quiet child might wish to garden or look at a book.

Preschoolers vary widely in personality and emotional development. By responding to each child as an individual, you help each one feel respected for who he or she is.

Socially…

Set up group activities that will allow children to play together, such as playing dodge-ball or painting a mural.

Preschoolers love to play cooperatively with their age mates.

Encourage preschoolers to act out favorite stories using the outdoor area as their stage. For example, children could pretend to be Hansel and Gretel or the runaway gingerbread boy.

Children will enjoy dramatizing these stories more outdoors than if confined to an indoor stage area. The outdoor location enhances dramatic play by permitting the children to run from would-be captors.

Praise the children frequently for their efforts and contributions to maintaining the outdoor environment: "Thank you for remembering to water our tomato plants today."

Encouragement is vital to preschoolers' sense of self-esteem.

Cognitively…

Encourage children to talk about the outdoors: "Why do you think the leaves have started to fall off the trees all of a sudden?"

Open-ended questions spur conversation and encourage children to think.

Introduce gardening or woodworking tools that are new to the children. Let them experiment with the tools before showing them how they are usually used. Supervise carefully to ensure safety.

Preschoolers like to experiment, explore, and discover on their own. They might even come up with some unusual uses for these materials.

Set aside one day for beautifying the outdoor area. Assign each child a particular area to be responsible for. Post signs such as "This garden was weeded and made prettier by Sean."

Children take pride in seeing a task to completion. Giving them recognition for their contribution reinforces their pride.

Help the children conduct real-life experiments. Have them plant vegetable gardens in different areas and see which vegetables thrive best in each area.

The outdoors is a ready-made science lab. When children have the opportunity to interact with their environment firsthand, learning is guaranteed.

Physically...

Provide lots of activities that encourage the children to use their small muscles: woodworking, gardening, digging, etc.

By participating in these activities on a regular basis, preschoolers will automatically refine their physical skills.

Provide outdoor equipment and areas that promote development of large muscles: swings, climbing equipment, hoops, and unobstructed grassy areas for running.

The outdoors is probably the best and most natural site for working with preschoolers on developing large motor skills, coordination, and balance.

Keep lots of toys and props on hand for outdoor play: sieves and funnels for the sandbox, weeders for the garden, nails and hammers for woodworking, etc.

Props serve many purposes. They extend learning and enhance enjoyment while naturally improving small muscle and eye-hand coordination.

School-Age Children

Children who have been in a structured school setting all day almost always enjoy being outdoors. They like to plan their own time and activities and often want to play with a friend. Some older children may want to help you on occasion with the younger children, but this shouldn't become their only outdoor activity.

Outdoor Activities That Help School-Age Children Develop

Why These Activities Are Important

Emotionally...

Encourage school-age children to spend time outdoors on their own.

Most older children love to be outdoors. Giving them permission to do this whenever they so choose makes them feel more independent as well as happy about being in family day care.

Praise older children to build up their self-confidence in sports: "You're hitting that softball a whole lot further than you could last week."

Older children need encouragement in all areas. Being skilled physically is very important during these years; children who are less talented in sports may need confidence-building from you.

Socially...

With parental permission, encourage children to participate in after-school sports activities with their friends.

Children this age have a need to be with their peers. By recognizing this need, you make them feel more comfortable with themselves and with you.

Let school-age children be responsible for deciding which outdoor activities they want to participate in.

Respecting the children's opinions sends a double message: they are valued and that they are free to express themselves with you.

Ask older children to assist you in taking the younger children on a nature walk.

Many older children enjoy taking on leadership roles.

Cognitively...

Provide outdoor space where school-age children can do long-term activities, such as planting a garden or building a tree house.

School-age children take pride in seeing long-term projects to completion.

Present the children with mental challenges: "Where can we hang this hammock so it won't be in the sun?"

Older children love solving mysteries of all sorts. A challenge like this helps them learn to think abstractly and problem solving.

Give the children and a friend some balls, a bat, and a hoop and ask them to invent their own game.

School-age children have a fascination with rules and like challenges of this sort.

Suggest that the children plan a scavenger or treasure hunt for either their friends or the younger children. Let them write clues and post picture signs as appropriate.

Older children will like the mental challenge of this activity, pitting their wits against others.

Physically...

Provide a variety of sports equipment: soccer balls, jump ropes, basketball and hoop, etc.

Older children are eager to develop their physical prowess. By giving them access to equipment, you allow them to practice skills of their own choosing.

If a child shows particular interest in a given sport, ask a school coach to suggest some exercises you can do with the child to improve his or her skills.

By doing this, you not only help children improve their talents but also let them know that what's important to them is also important to you.

Involving Children of All Ages

When you follow safety rules and routines and are prepared, outdoor play can be an extremely relaxed time of day and can give children of many ages a chance to play well with each other. Imagine this scene in your family child care program:

Pang (3 months)
Jose (1-1/2 years)
Jacob (4 years)
Jean (4 years)
Nell (6 years)

Carrying Pang in your arms, you cross the yard to talk with your neighbor, who is outside with her two children. "Will you hold Pang while I spread out the blanket?" you ask. She is happy to do so, and you put down the blanket for the babies to sit on. They have brought dolls and stuffed animals to play with for the afternoon.

You and your neighbor sit on the blanket, too, and watch Jacob and Jose ride up and down the sidewalks on their trike and "big wheels." Jacob has already set boards across the sidewalk to mark the limits of the children's riding area.

"Who wants ice cream?" Jacob yells. He has turned over his tricycle and is cranking the pedals to churn imaginary ice cream.

"Oh, Jacob," you call, "how much is a double-scoop ice cream cone?"

"One dollar," he replies.

"Well, then, I'd like one scoop of chocolate and one of strawberry. Can you deliver it to me?"

"Coming up!"

Soon the other children are playing the same game, and they order cones with many scoops of different flavors, exchanging imaginary dollar bills.

As Jean and Nell come walking up to your house after school, the young children wave and cheer. The school children are pleased at this welcome, and they join you and the younger ones on the blanket for a few minutes to relax. Soon they have taken the chalk you brought out and have gone to color on the sidewalk leading up to your door.

The children come over to the blanket at their leisure to refresh themselves with an afternoon snack and then return to their play. Because your neighbor is teaming up with you today, you are free to leave the sleeping baby on the blanket to help Jose come down the slide. He feels very confident climbing the steps but is not sure he wants to go down without a hand to hold.

After a little over an hour, it is time to pick up the blanket, toys, and bikes and move indoors to another activity.

Here are a few things to keep in mind during outdoor play time:

- Allow different-aged children to play at different activities when outside.

- Allow dramatic play, art, and other activities to take place outdoors, blending with large muscle play.

- Ask children questions that will extend their play, and join in their play even if that means simply holding a conversation while supervising others.

- Encourage children to be quiet and relaxed outdoors. This can be a time for being peaceful as well as for rough-and-tumble play.

- Schedule outdoor play appropriately, considering not only the weather and activities but also the length of time necessary for whatever outdoor activities you are planning.

- Allow children to practice skills and to master them, and provide the support they need to move on to new challenges.

Parents should be informed about your outdoor program and whether you intend to take children on neighborhood walks. The letter that follows is one way to share such information with parents.

A Letter to Parents on Outdoor Play

What We Do and Why

Outdoor play is important for children's health and physical fitness. In addition, the outdoors gives us a rich environment in which to learn. Almost everything we do indoors we also do outside. I've set up areas for sand and water play, woodworking, and gardening. We also do art, look at books, and even cook outside.

Unless it is extremely cold, hot, or storming, we go outdoors at least once a day and sometimes twice. We don't always stay in the same place when we go outside. Sometimes we go for a neighborhood walk. As we walk, we talk a lot about what we see. Sometimes there are construction projects to look at, or a moving van, or the mailman is passing by. At other times the older children try to guess who lives in a house by looking at what is outside the house. For example, I might ask the children:

- "Do you see any signs that a baby lives in this house?"
- "Do you think the person who lives there likes flowers?"

We look for things to collect on our walks, such as leaves, rocks, or dandelions. We talk about the changes in weather and about where the birds go in the winter. We walk, jump, trot, walk backward, and hop sometimes, too. The babies enjoy listening to the different sounds outdoors and seeing what is going on. Being outdoors is a new environment for the children to explore. I point things out for them, saying things such as "there goes the mother bird" or "here comes the mail carrier."

The time we spend outdoors gives children a chance to be in a space where they can move around freely and develop their muscles. It also gives them time to learn to play together, make up their own games, try out new skills, and learn about nature and how things grow.

What You Can Do at Home

Your neighborhood offers different sights, sounds, and objects to explore. As you take a walk, sit with your child in a park, plant a garden together, or head for the store, take time to talk to your child about what you both observe around you. Giving your child words to describe what he or she is experiencing helps your child develop new vocabulary and understandings. Asking questions helps your child express ideas in words and engage in conversations.

The curriculum I'm using, *The Creative Curriculum for Family Child Care*, has a number of good ideas for using the outdoors with children. I'll be happy to share it with you.

Notes

Notes

Notes

Notes